PRIMA GAMES WE ARE STRATEGY

FREE eGUIDE!

Enter this code at primagames.com/code to unlock your FREE eGuide:

5FDE-KEEV-3R95-JPRD

CHECK OUT OUR eGUIDE STORE AT PRIMAGAMES.COM

All your strategy saved in your own personal digital library!

Mobile Friendly:
Access your eGuide on any web-enabled device.

Searchable & Sortable:
Quickly find the strategies you need.

Added Value:
Strategy where, when, and how you want it.

BECOME A FAN OF PRIMA GAMES!

Subscribe to our Twitch channel twitch.tv/primagames and join our weekly stream every Tuesday from 1-4pm EST!

*Tune in to **PRIMA 365** on our YouTube channel youtube.com/primagamesvideo f   ʰ day!*

www.primagames.com

ATARI® FLASHBACK
THE ESSENTIAL COMPANION

ATARI 2600 HISTORY

Although the Atari Video Computer System, a.k.a. VCS, or, as its now more commonly known, the Atari 2600, was released in late summer of 1977, eventually becoming the industry's first blockbuster system, the story of home videogames actually began much earlier. The industry's slow burn began in the early 1950s when an engineer by the name of Ralph Baer was trying to figure out how to take advantage of the growing number of household TVs for something other than watching standard broadcasts.

Unfortunately for Baer, despite success creating lines and checkerboard patterns on a TV screen, neither the technology nor the vision of those around him were sufficient to make additional progress on his astounding idea of playing games on a television. It would take Baer several career changes over more than a decade to finally make the breakthroughs needed in both technology and getting a corporate partner to understand the possibilities of his revolutionary concept.

There were earlier games that used video displays of some type, of course, including *OXO* (1952), *Tennis for Two* (1958), and *Spacewar!* (1962), but they were all impractical for mass market consumption for one reason or another, although no less historically important.

The EDSAC was only the second electronic, digital stored-program computer to go into regular service and was in use until July 11, 1958.

Alexander Douglas's *OXO* was a simple graphical single player versus the computer tic-tac-toe game on the Electronic Delay Storage Automatic Computer (EDSAC) mainframe at the University of Cambridge. Although more proof of concept than a compelling gameplay experience, *OXO* nevertheless set the precedent of using a computer to create an immediately accessible virtual representation of a real-world activity. *OXO*'s evolution can be seen in the Atari 2600's *3-D Tic-Tac-Toe* (1980).

For a visitors' day at the Brookhaven National Laboratory in Upton, New York, William Higinbotham and Robert Dvorak created *Tennis for Two*, a small analog computer game that used an oscilloscope for its display. *Tennis for Two* rendered a moving ball in a simplified side view of a tennis court. Each player could rotate a knob to change the angle of the ball, while the press of a button sent the ball toward the opposite side of the court. As with *OXO*, few people got to experience *Tennis for Two* but, in many ways, it can be considered the first dedicated videogame system, which—essentially—are just simplified personal computers.

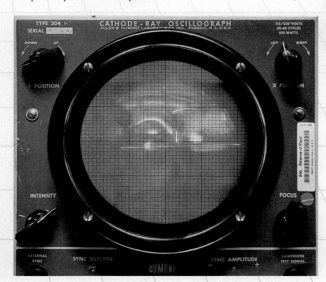

Tennis for Two running on a DuMont Lab Oscilloscope Type 304-A.

Without the benefit of hindsight, though, this milestone was even lost on the game's creators, who, after a second visitors' day one year later, disassembled the machine's components for use in other projects.

Although this was historically tragic, it was intrinsic of the hacker mindset of forward progress that would eventually guide the videogame and personal computing revolutions in the years to come. As will be shown, *Tennis for Two*'s evolution can be seen in both Baer's work and in Atari's earliest arcade and home products. Of course, the Atari 2600 itself has *Video Olympics* (1977), which contains a wide variety of paddle and ball games, including the iconic *Pong*.

Spacewar!, initially designed by Steve Russell, Martin Graetz, and Wayne Wiitanen, with later contributions from Alan Kotok, Dan Edwards, and Peter Samson, was the result of inspired engineering and hundreds of hours of hard work. Developed on the DEC PDP-1 mainframe at MIT, *Spacewar!*'s gameplay was surprisingly sophisticated and ambitious, pitting two spaceships against each other in an armed duel around a star that created gravitational effects on the two craft.

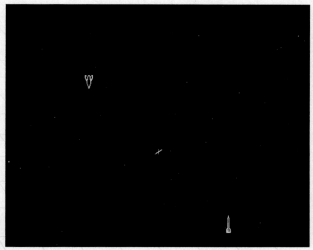

Original 1962 Spacewar! game code running on a PDP-1 emulator in JavaScript.

Each player controlled a ship via the mainframe's front-panel test switches or optional external control boxes, adjusting each respective craft's rotation, thrust, fire, and hyperspace, which was a random, evasive screen jump that may cause the user's ship to explode. Over the years, the game was improved and inspired many clones and spiritual successors, including the first commercially sold arcade videogame in 1971, *Computer Space*, which was designed by Nolan Bushnell and Ted Dabney, who would go on to found Atari just one year later. Other notable clones and games that made use of key *Spacewar!* elements include the Atari 2600's own *Space War* (1977) and the arcade and Atari 2600 smash hit, *Asteroids* (1979).

It was this ability to inspire and influence that was perhaps *Spacewar!*'s greatest contribution to the future of computing and videogames. Even with still privileged access to the host computing hardware limiting the game's wider exposure, enough of the industry's key future movers and shakers got to see first-hand that these machines could be used for something more than serving the often sober computational needs of businesses, universities, and the government. In short, they could also delight and entertain anyone lucky enough to try. This concept of entertainment for everyone brings us back to Baer.

His first true attempt at building a home videogame console in the mid-1960s was a simple game of tag featuring two squares ("Chase"), which soon morphed into his legendary "Brown Box" prototype. The prototype included several additional diversions, including paddle and ball and target shooting games. After getting rejected by several TV manufacturers, Baer finally signed an agreement in 1971 with Magnavox, who released a refined version of the prototype the following year, renaming it the Odyssey Home Entertainment System.

Although relatively limited in its capabilities, requiring considerable setup and imagination from its players, the Odyssey nevertheless boasted several features that became industry standards. These features included detachable controllers, additional controller options (a light rifle/gun), and interchangeable game cartridges. These cartridges appeared to offer players an assortment of different games to play, but were really just plug-in cards that turned the console's

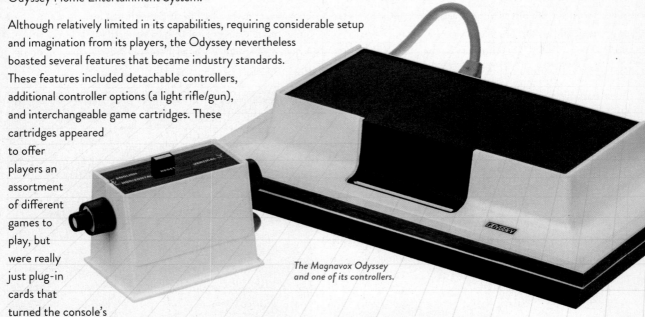

The Magnavox Odyssey and one of its controllers.

built-in features on or off like a streamlined selector switch. Twelve games were included with the system, with an additional 10 eventually released separately. The Odyssey could display only white squares and lines on a black background, so two different sizes of color overlays were provided to enhance game play and accommodate different televisions. Many games also included external enhancements such as playing cards, maps, dice, and game boards.

The Magnavox Odyssey used television overlays like the ones shown here, along with traditional board game playing pieces, to enhance immersion.

Much of the system's playability came from these accessories, since the on-screen interaction was so limited. The system only registered object collisions, and there was no sound or score tracking.

Perhaps the Odyssey's most enduring legacy was inspiring Nolan Bushnell at a Magnavox product demonstration in 1972. Later that same year, Bushnell founded Atari and, with the help of engineer Al Alcorn, developed *Pong* for the arcade. *Pong* had simple instructions, "Avoid missing ball for high score." A smash hit was born.

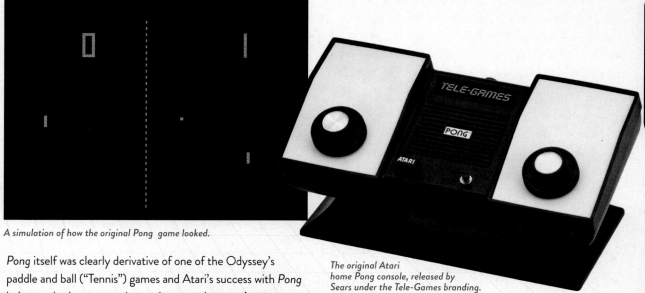

A simulation of how the original Pong game looked.

The original Atari home Pong console, released by Sears under the Tele-Games branding.

Pong itself was clearly derivative of one of the Odyssey's paddle and ball ("Tennis") games and Atari's success with *Pong* led several other companies to also copy the game's concept. Magnavox eventually filed a successful lawsuit against Atari for copyright infringement, forcing the fledgling company to settle for a lump sum and other manufacturers to pay hefty licensing fees.

Pong's simple but compelling game play was in stark contrast to Bushnell's and Dabney's earlier *Computer Space* for Nutting Associates.

Despite its striking cabinet design, relatively large and inviting screen, and four straightforward action buttons (Fire Missile, Thrust, Rotate Left, and Rotate Right), *Computer Space* was too complex for the general public's first exposure to videogames. Bushnell later admitted that the game appealed mostly to his engineering friends who had enjoyed its inspiration, *Spacewar!*. Although less impressive in nearly every way than *Computer Space*, it was *Pong*'s emphasis on approachability and fast-paced fun that would first define and then later establish an entire industry. This lesson would come to serve the Atari 2600 well.

Although the Odyssey received a small sales boost from the popularity of *Pong* and the various clones that sprung up in the arcade, the console never achieved critical mass success in American homes, selling a few hundred thousand units before it was discontinued in 1975. Instead, that success occurred when Atari created a home version of *Pong* that same year, complete with automatic scoring and sound. Then-dominant retailer Sears agreed to distribute *Pong* under their own brand name, Tele-Games, to great success, legitimizing the viability of Baer's plan to market videogame systems for home use. Atari released its own branded version of the console starting in 1976, just as an explosion of *Pong* clones saturated the home videogame market.

Although these machines were extremely popular for a time, and offered increasingly sophisticated feature-sets, there were simply too many systems for the market to sustain them all for long. This was particularly the case in light of the rise of fully programmable consoles that used interchangeable cartridges for more diverse gameplay possibilities, starting with Fairchild's Video Entertainment System (VES) in 1976. This home videogame breakthrough was followed one year later on the home computer side with the release of the preassembled and relatively user-friendly Apple II, Commodore PET, and Tandy TRS-80 systems, each of which featured its own interchangeable software, first on cassette tapes and, later on, disks.

Although the Fairchild Channel F's use of interchangeable, programmable cartridges meant that new types of games could be developed and released on a regular basis, including games that weren't simple paddle and ball variations, its technology was a still a bit limited and none of its games particularly inspiring. After the release in 1977 of RCA's primitive black-and-white, cartridge-based console, Studio II, the third offering from Atari—now effectively an industry veteran at five years old—proved the charm. Of course, the release of the Atari 2600 was not an immediate success, selling only a few hundred thousand units in its early months. Instead, it built momentum slowly through to the end of the decade when its fortune's finally exploded.

All three of the early cartridge-based consoles suffered from competition from bargain bins full of *Pong* clones, which had oversaturated the market after the introduction of General Instruments' AY-3-8500 "Pong-on-a-chip."

These systems often advertised four to six games that were usually just subtle variations of the same basic ball and paddle game — all for $100 or less. The VCS's initial price of $199 (around $800 in today's dollars) was a substantial investment and the modest library of game cartridges certainly didn't distinguish the launch. However, an influx of funds from parent company Warner Communications supported Atari during these years and a growing supply of quality game cartridges, advertisements, and positive press helped Atari sell millions of VCS consoles by 1980.

The first system, known today as the "heavy sixer," featured dense internal RF shielding (giving it its considerable weight) and six chrome selector switches for power on/off, color/black-and-white, player A difficulty, player B difficulty, select, and reset. The design featured sharp angles with black plastic and wood-grain styling that gives it a distinctive—and now iconic—1970s aesthetic.

The first revision of the Atari 2600 from 1978, known as the "light sixer." Atari would come to continually revise the design of their legendary console.

With miniscule system memory of 128 bytes of RAM (literally 128 characters of text) and Motorola's 8-bit 6507 microprocessor running just over 1 MHz, the Atari 2600 seems at first glance anything but a powerhouse. Sound is limited to two channels, but, if thoughtfully programmed, could support decent sound effects and music. Graphics, while displayed at a fairly low resolution and with limitations on the number of flicker-free objects per line, could draw from an impressive 128-color palette. In fact, the platform's use of colors and color cycling became the Atari 2600's signature feature, enabling interesting effects that helped extend the effective life of the console far beyond what could have ever been imagined during its development.

The iconic Atari CX-40 joystick.

The first Atari 2600 units shipped with two joysticks, a single pair of paddles, and the two-player *Combat* cartridge, which contained several tank and plane action games inspired by individual Atari arcade games. The eight other launch titles, several of which were also interpretations of popular Atari arcade games, were *Air-Sea Battle*, *Basic Math*, *Blackjack*, *Indy 500*, *Star Ship*, *Street Racer*, *Surround*, and *Video Olympics* (each of these are, of course, found on the Atari Flashback hardware). Although these games were relatively simplistic and not much better than games for rival systems, their variety hinted at what was to come. As an increasing number of competing manufacturers would come to tout their systems' technological superiority, Atari could boast of a substantially larger variety of games and ways to play them.

As celebrated Atari designer Howard Scott Warshaw and others have pointed out, despite the massive research and development budget in comparison to its peers, the VCS was primarily built to play two games—*Pong* and *Tank* (a popular Atari arcade game that was incorporated into *Combat*): "That was it. You had two players, two missiles, one ball, and a playfield." It definitely didn't seem like a huge leap from the aforementioned *Pong* consoles. All this started to change in 1980, but it wasn't one of Atari's own games that made the initial difference.

*Sears sold their version of the Atari 2600 under
their own Tele-Games branding. Several variations were released
between 1977 and 1983. Sears also re-branded and re-named several games,
including a handful of exclusives.*

Instead, it was a licensed conversion of a game that had swept across Japan and was now taking over America: Taito's arcade blockbuster, *Space Invaders*, which has a unique port on the two Atari Flashback consoles (the Atari Flashback Portable does not feature this port, but can play the original Atari 2600 version via its SD card slot!). Designed by Tomohiro Nishikado and adapted for the Atari 2600 by ex-Fairchild employee Rick Mauer, *Space Invaders* was the first non-Atari licensed game. The game grossed over $100 million and caused a tremendous surge in system sales that left the competition in the dust.

Mauer wasn't the only programmer at Atari gifted at adapting high-end arcade games to the relatively limited capabilities of the 2600. *Asteroids*, ported to the VCS by Brad Stewart, introduced bank-switching, a technique invented by Carl Nielsen that allowed access to cartridge memory beyond the prior 4KB limit. Although the earliest VCS cartridges were generally 2KB - 4KB in size, greater memory sizes (including modern homebrew creations at 32KB and beyond) allowed for increased depth and complexity, contributing to the system's impressive longevity. *Asteroids* was another big hit for the VCS.

*The front of the box for the Atari
2600 version of Space Invaders.*

Another blockbuster early title was Warren Robinett's *Adventure* (1979), a pioneering graphical action adventure game. It was also among the first games with a notable "Easter Egg." Gamers who found or knew the secret could find the name of the game's programmer.

*The front cover of a 1981 Atari
catalog describing 43 first-party game cartridges.*

Robinett included the Easter Egg to protest Atari's then policy of keeping a game's programmer anonymous. The policy might have made sense to Atari's management at the time, but it ultimately led to an exodus of top star talent and subsequent rise of third-party software houses whose often excellent products would compete directly with Atari's own lineup.

It all began with the departure of four prolific and talented programmers—David Crane, Larry Kaplan, Alan Miller, and Bob Whitehead. They later founded Activision in 1979, one of the earliest and often considered best of the platform's third-party software developers. Activision raised the bar on Atari 2600 game quality. Their landmark titles included *Pitfall!* (1982), one of the first running and jumping multi-screen games, *Space Shuttle - A Journey into Space* (1983), a surprisingly sophisticated flight and mission simulator, and *Private Eye* (1984), a multi-screen action adventure game. Grossing over $70 million in their first year, the founders of Activision were the first outsiders to benefit from—and directly influence—the Atari 2600's growing popularity.

The front of the box for the Atari 2600 version of Pitfall!. Pitfall! is one of several Activision games included on the Atari Flashback systems.

Atari was no stranger to litigation, though courts seldom ruled in its favor. They did score a minor victory in 1972, however, by settling a dispute with Magnavox over arcade *Pong* by paying a small, one-time licensing fee. This arrangement was much more favorable than those Magnavox reached with Atari's rivals. Magnavox, with the engineering expertise of Baer, won videogame patent court cases for many years to come. However, when Atari tried to shut down Activision, their complaint was eventually thrown out. This did lead, however, to a licensing arrangement in which Atari would receive a royalty for each VCS cartridge sold. Other companies took Activision's lead, which eventually brought us to the industry-standard licensing model between console maker and software houses still in use today.

The success of third-party software companies, especially those composed of their own ex-employees, was bittersweet for Atari. While companies like Imagic made small fortunes with well-crafted games like *Demon Attack* (1982) and *Cosmic Ark* (1982)—fortunes that former would have flowed directly to Atari and Warner —there's no denying that they also contributed to greater system sales and market penetration, keeping the VCS dominant even in the face of technologically superior competition.

Of course, not every third-party game maker was an Activision or Imagic. There were also companies like Ultravision, whose clunky one-on-one fighting game *Karate* (1983) and copycat shooter *Condor Attack* (1983) are rightfully forgotten. Interestingly, *Condor Attack* was a clone of *Demon Attack*, which itself was inspired by yet another game, Centuri's 1980 arcade game *Phoenix*. Atari officially converted that game in 1982 and tried to force Imagic to remove their version from the shelf. Atari lost yet again. Eventually, their inability to prevent third-party companies from saturating the market with cheaply-made "shovelware" (low-budget and poorly made games) would damage not just Atari's reputation, but also that of stellar publishers like Activision and Imagic.

Of course, rival system manufacturers went to great lengths to knock Atari off its throne. Competing systems such as Coleco's ColecoVision and Mattel's Intellivision II offered external expansion modules that allowed their systems to play Atari 2600 cartridges. Naturally, Atari sued, but Coleco countered that they were protected by antitrust laws. Again, Atari settled out of court, getting instead a royalty for each adapter unit and clone console sold.

A later four-switch model of the Atari 2600.

In 1978, Atari released a revised console model with lighter RF shielding and a slightly streamlined case. The last Atari 2600 revision with VCS branding, released in 1980, moved two of the six switches to the top of the unit.

In 1982, Atari released the Atari 5200 SuperSystem. To standardize the product line, the VCS officially became the Atari 2600 Video Computer System, or simply Atari 2600. This design was streamlined like the previous revision, but with an entirely black exterior.

Interestingly, when Atari released the 5200, no backward compatibility option was offered, confusing some consumers and hurting system sales. Atari tried making amends with a smaller 5200 system redesign and an awkward, outsized add-on module that enabled the backwards-compatibility gamers demanded.

Packaging for the original Atari 2600 version of Pac-Man.

Unfortunately, this add-on was incompatible with the earlier, larger 5200 consoles without modification at a service center.

Atari's console sales peaked in 1982, after which a glut of poor third-party game titles and bad licensing decisions caused heavy losses throughout the industry. Product dumping, with high volumes of poor-quality games sold at or below cost, caused full-priced, high-quality game sales to suffer. However, two games in particular released that year are always brought up when discussing the fall of the Atari 2600 and videogames in general: *Pac-Man* and *E.T. The Extra-Terrestrial*.

In what should have been the deal of the year, if not the decade, Atari obtained sole rights to Namco's arcade smash-hit *Pac-Man* (1980). While Atari aggressively promoted and protected their exclusive right to produce *Pac-Man* and any derivative works, they apparently didn't bother to give programmer Todd Frye the time and resources needed to do a good job. With poor graphics, bad sound, and awkward controls, *Pac-Man* for the VCS was a devastating blow to Atari's reputation. It seemed to prove that the Atari 2600 paled in comparison to the thrills of a newer generation of arcade games.

Atari wrongly guessed that the name alone would generate enough interest to sell the dismal product.

Their hubris was so great that they actually famously produced more *Pac-Man* cartridges than there were Atari 2600 systems sold at the time! Fortunately, a newer—and superior—Atari 2600 homebrew port of the arcade game is included on the Atari Flashback Portable.

As for *E.T. The Extra-Terrestrial*, lead programmer Howard Scott Warshaw seemed like a logical choice for the project. He had impressed Steven Spielberg with his work on the translation of another popular film by the famous director, *Raiders of the Lost Ark*, which, in 1982, was successfully released as a sophisticated, two-joystick action-adventure. He was also the developer behind *Yars' Revenge* (1981), an action game widely considered among the best games on the platform, and one of Atari's best sellers.

The story goes that then Atari CEO Ray Kassar paid $20 million for the *E.T.* license, but the negotiations took so long that in order to make a holiday release, the entire game had to be programmed in six weeks, several months short of a typical development cycle at that time. Warshaw liked both the programming challenge and the money he was able to negotiate for the task, so he began the project in earnest.

Although Spielberg would have been happy with a copycat of *Pac-Man*, Warshaw insisted on something more original. Miraculously, he managed to meet the deadline and Atari rushed the cartridge into production with a blitz of advertising. Unfortunately, the end result confused and frustrated many players; guiding the slow E.T. alien through a seemingly endless series of nearly inescapable pits did not have wide appeal.

The Atari 7800 ProSystem pictured with its Proline Joystick.

Although the popularity of the license alone resulted in over one million units sold, Atari suffered another huge financial loss because of returns and millions more unsold cartridges. According to an urban legend, Atari buried most of the unsold inventory in a New Mexico landfill. A documented excavation on April 26, 2014 revealed this to be a half-truth. E.T. was one of a mix of titles among the roughly 700,000 cartridges buried.

By 1984, The Great Videogame Crash had taken a lot of companies out of business, due in no small part to Atari's own inflexible inventory requirements at retail outlets the year before. These requirements demanded that retail outlets had to stock more product than consumer demand could support. In that same year, Warner Communications sold a large portion of their interests in Atari to ex-Commodore executive and founder, Jack Tramiel, who seemed to have little desire to aggressively pursue the stagnant console market.

While trying to get a grip on the state-of-the-company, Tramiel shelved both the unreleased 2600 redesign and its backward-compatible, next-generation successor, the 7800 ProSystem, in favor of new Atari computers. While a few new 2600 cartridges were made available in 1985 by Activision and other companies, there were no new Atari systems to go with them.

Existing 2600 and 5200 inventory remained in the various sales channels and continued to sell, but almost two years passed before Atari attempted to reclaim their dominance in the home videogame market. By this time, the Nintendo Entertainment System (NES) had started to establish itself in America and Atari was left playing catch-up.

The Atari 2600 "Jr." presented a sleeker profile than its predecessors.

Ironically, in 1983 Atari had turned down a chance to distribute an early version of the NES. Once established in the United States, Nintendo would prove a masterful adversary, quickly cornering the market with a series of high high-profile, in combination with price fixing and monopolistic retail policies.

After the NES revived America's passion for videogames, Atari reestablished its presence in 1986 with the long-awaited, wide releases of a mothballed Atari 2600 redesign, which was unofficially referred to as the Jr., and 7800, which, in addition to playing its own advanced games that could utilize its extra memory, higher resolution, and greater color palette, was almost completely compatible with its older sibling's games and accessories. The Jr. was Atari's most significant design departure from the original heavy sixer, featuring a small and thin, black and silver enclosure that mimicked the styling of the larger 7800. Pushed as a budget-friendly option in comparison with other systems, the 2600 continued to sell fairly well in what had become a very different market nearly a decade after its original release. The Jr., with cosmetic revisions, continued to represent the VCS line until production was stopped completely in the early 1990s with an impressive 30 million units sold across all console variations.

Atari itself ceased to exist as a company in 1996, with the name and intellectual assets having been sold and bought countless times since. Naturally, it's been a brand worth saving. Atari was the first to revolutionize the arcade and then the home market twice. The only market that they wouldn't dominate for a time was the computer market, but it wasn't for lack of trying with an impressive line of 8- and 16-bit computers dating back to 1979 and lasting into the early 1990s. Today's version of Atari continues the fight to bring back much of the original's grand vision, including partnering with AtGames on the popular Atari Flashback systems.

The original games that first defined the company were always a unifying force. There's a timeless nature to the games and the modest technology of the Atari 2600 platform, which rather than being a limitation, has proven to be one of its strengths. These constraints helped focus developers on the essentials of simple fun, a spirit that survives today in homebrew creations for the Atari 2600.

Starting in the mid-1990s, homebrew authors emerged to produce a wide range of often high-quality hacks, conversions, and new original games. Some of these homebrew games are present on the Atari Flashback systems, including *Adventure II* (2005), *Atari Climber* (2005), *Chase It!* (2010), *Escape It!* (2010), *Miss It!* (2010), *Return to Haunted House* (2005), *Shield Shifter* (2009), *StripOff!* (2009), and *Yars' Return* (2005).

Despite its long journey of ups, downs, and ups again over the past four decades, it's clear that the Atari 2600 platform still has a lot of life left in it. Wherever and whenever there is someone looking for a fun way to play, the Atari 2600—and now the Atari Flashbacks—will be there to deliver.

ATGAMES ATARI FLASHBACK SERIES

Founded in 2001, AtGames entered the industry as a pioneer of plug-and-play interactive entertainment. In 2005, AtGames received an exclusive 10-year distribution agreement to make Sega-licensed products. In 2011, Atari officially chose AtGames to lead their Flashback console concept. Every year since establishing their respective partnerships, AtGames has produced popular new products based on classic Sega and Atari properties.

Even in the modern gaming era, the desire for the simple joys of classic gaming remains high—and AtGames has met this demand. Since the fall of 2012 and their release of the Atari Flashback 3, AtGames has been a standard bearer for the Atari 2600 platform. Their latest Atari 2600-centric console and portable releases, the Atari Flashback 8 Gold, Atari Flashback 8 Gold Activision Edition, Atari Flashback Classic Game Console, and Atari Flashback Portable Game Player demonstrate that their support is stronger than ever. What follows are overviews of these consoles and portable releases, including how they function in comparison to the original console.

ATARI FLASHBACK 8 GOLD

For the first time ever, AtGames released a high-definition Atari Flashback that outputs at a resolution of 720p or 1280x720 via its HDMI port. It is optimized for today's high-definition TVs. The 2.4 Ghz wireless controllers allow for gameplay from up to 30 feet away from the console.

Two legacy controller ports on the front of the console allow newly manufactured AtGames-branded, or original Atari wired joysticks, and paddle controllers to be plugged in.

The player one wireless joystick replicates several of the original console's switches.

HOW IT COMPARES TO THE ORIGINAL CONSOLE

The original Atari 2600 console featured six switches: Power (on/off), TV Type (color/b-w), Left Difficulty (A/B), Right Difficulty (A/B), Game Select (toggle), and Game Reset (toggle). The *Atari Flashback 8 Gold* replaces most of the original's switches with buttons, which are partially replicated on the wireless player one joystick.

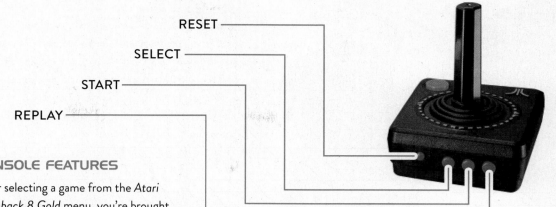

RESET

SELECT

START

REPLAY

CONSOLE FEATURES

After selecting a game from the *Atari Flashback 8 Gold* menu, you're brought to the game's summary page. This page contains a short game description and play summary. Pressing the joystick button starts the game. The Start button on the joystick is the same as pressing Start on the console. Press Reset on the joystick to return to the game's summary page.

The game page for Aquaventure.

Once inside the game, you can press Up + Select in certain games to toggle the TV type (color/b-w) or Down + Select to access the in-game menu.

The in-game menu.

From here, you can save or load games in progress or activate what's called a Scanline Filter. This latter option simulates how these games looked on a classic CRT (cathode ray tube) TV by placing subtle horizontal lines across the playfield.

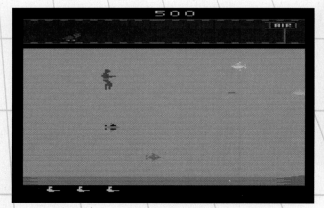

The Scanline Filter option set to "On" in Aquaventure.

You can also rewind up to seven seconds of gameplay by pressing the Replay button on player one's wireless joystick. This is a great way to overcome difficult game sections.

Rewinding after dying in Aquaventure.

Another unique feature is displaying P1-HARD or P2-HARD on-screen when you press the Left or Right Difficulty buttons, respectively. This is a great way to easily tell when you're switching between A and B difficulties.

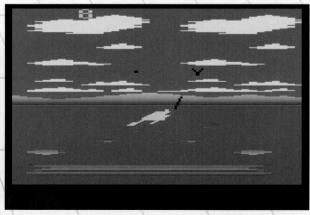

Playing on the harder difficulty in Frog Pond, where the frog has a shorter tongue.

Lastly, when playing on the original console you were limited to playing games that required a paddle controller only with paddles. On the *Atari Flashback 8 Gold*, though, you can also use joysticks. The only restriction is that player one and player two joysticks can only replicate the functionality of the player one and player two paddle controller pair. Paddle games that support a third and fourth player will require a set of paddles plugged into each controller port.

AtGames makes their own paddle controllers (pictured), or you can use the originals. Each pair of paddles plugs into one controller port.

GAME LIST

There are 120 games on the *Atari Flashback 8 Gold*:

- 3D Tic-Tac-Toe
- Adventure
- Adventure II
- Air Raiders™
- Air-Sea Battle
- Aquaventure
- Armor Ambush™
- Asteroids
- Astroblast™
- Atari Climber
- Backgammon
- Basketball
- Beamrider
- Black Jack
- Bowling
- Breakout
- Canyon Bomber
- Centipede
- Championship Soccer
- Chase It
- Chopper Command
- Circus Atari
- Combat
- Combat Two
- Cosmic Commuter
- Crackpots
- Crystal Castles
- Dark Cavern™ (Night Stalker)
- Decathlon
- Demons to Diamonds

- Desert Falcon
- Dodge 'Em
- Double Dunk
- Dragster
- Enduro
- Escape It
- Fatal Run
- Fishing Derby
- Flag Capture
- Football
- Frog Pond
- Frogger
- Frogs and Flies
- Front Line
- Frostbite
- Fun with Numbers
- Golf
- Gravitar
- H.E.R.O.
- Hangman
- Haunted House
- Home Run
- Human Cannonball
- Indy 500
- International Soccer™
- Jungle Hunt
- Kaboom!
- Keystone Kapers
- Maze Craze
- Megamania
- Millipede

- Miniature Golf
- Miss It
- Missile Command
- MotoRodeo
- Night Driver
- Off-the-Wall
- Oink!
- Outlaw
- Pitfall!
- Polaris
- Pong (Video Olympics)
- Pressure Cooker
- Radar Lock
- RealSports Baseball
- RealSports Basketball
- RealSports Soccer
- RealSports Volleyball
- Return to Haunted House
- River Raid
- Saboteur
- Save Mary
- Sea Battle™
- Seaquest
- Secret Quest
- Shield Shifter
- Sky Diver
- Slot Machine
- Slot Racers
- Solaris
- Space Attack™

- Space Invaders
- Space War
- Sprintmaster
- Stampede
- Star Ship
- Star Strike™
- Starmaster
- Steeplechase
- Stellar Track
- Street Racer
- Submarine Commander
- Super Baseball
- Super Breakout
- Super Challenge™ Baseball (Major League Baseball)
- Super Challenge™ Football (NFL Football)
- Super Football
- Surround
- Sword Fight™
- Swordquest: EarthWorld
- Swordquest: FireWorld
- Swordquest: WaterWorld
- Tempest
- Video Checkers
- Video Chess
- Video Pinball
- Warlords
- Wizard
- Yars' Return
- Yars' Revenge

ATARI FLASHBACK 8 GOLD ACTIVISION EDITION

The Atari *Flashback 8 Gold Activision Edition* takes everything already great about the *Atari Flashback 8 Gold* and remixes the game list, adding in additional classic Activision games.

GAME LIST

There are 130 games on the Atari Flashback 8 Gold Activision Edition:

- 3D Tic-Tac-Toe
- Adventure
- Adventure II
- Air Raiders™
- Air-Sea Battle
- Aquaventure
- Armor Ambush™
- Asteroids
- Astroblast™
- Atari Climber
- Atlantis
- Backgammon
- Basketball
- Beamrider
- Black Jack
- Bowling
- Boxing
- Breakout
- Bridge
- Canyon Bomber
- Centipede
- Championship Soccer
- Checkers
- Chopper Command
- Circus Atari
- Combat
- Combat Two
- Cosmic Commuter
- Crackpots
- Crystal Castles
- Dark Cavern™ (Night Stalker)
- Decathlon
- Demon Attack

- Demons to Diamonds
- Desert Falcon
- Dodge 'Em
- Dolphin
- Double Dunk
- DragonFire
- Dragster
- Enduro
- Fatal Run
- Fishing Derby
- Flag Capture
- Football
- Freeway
- Frog Pond
- Frogs and Flies
- Frostbite
- Fun with Numbers
- Golf
- Grand Prix
- Gravitar
- H.E.R.O.
- Hangman
- Haunted House
- Home Run
- Human Cannonball
- Ice Hockey
- Indy 500
- International Soccer™
- Kaboom!
- Keystone Kapers
- Laser Blast
- Maze Craze
- Megamania
- Millipede

- Miniature Golf
- Missile Command
- MotoRodeo
- Night Driver
- Off-the-Wall
- Oink!
- Outlaw
- Pitfall!
- Plaque Attack
- Pong (Video Olympics)
- Pressure Cooker
- Private Eye
- Radar Lock
- RealSports Baseball
- RealSports Basketball
- RealSports Soccer
- RealSports Volleyball
- Return to Haunted House
- River Raid
- River Raid II
- Saboteur
- Save Mary
- Sea Battle™
- Seaquest
- Secret Quest
- Skiing
- Sky Diver
- Sky Jinks
- Slot Machine
- Slot Racers
- Solaris
- Space Attack™
- Space Shuttle

- Space War
- Spider Fighter
- Sprintmaster
- Stampede
- Star Ship
- Star Strike™
- Starmaster
- Steeplechase
- Stellar Track
- Street Racer
- Submarine Commander
- Super Baseball
- Super Breakout
- Super Challenge™
- Baseball (Major League Baseball)
- Super Challenge™ Football (NFL Football)
- Super Football
- Surround
- Sword Fight™
- SwordQuest: EarthWorld
- SwordQuest: FireWorld
- SwordQuest: WaterWorld
- Tempest
- Tennis
- Video Checkers
- Video Chess
- Video Pinball
- Warlords
- Wizard
- Yars' Return
- Yars' Revenge

ATARI FLASHBACK CLASSIC GAME CONSOLE

This is the latest in the AtGames value-priced series of Atari Flashback consoles. Instead of HDMI, it features a composite connection (yellow cable for video, white for audio) and standard definition output best suited for classic CRT (cathode ray tube) TVs.

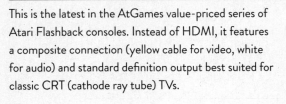

The included wired joysticks also work on the original Atari 2600 console.

HOW IT COMPARES TO THE ORIGINAL CONSOLE

Like the *Atari Flashback 8 Gold*, the *Atari Flashback Classic Game Console* replaces most of the original console's switches with buttons. There's one switch left off the Flashback console—TV Type. To change the TV Type while playing *Secret Quest*, press Select on the console and up on the joystick.

CONSOLE FEATURES

Just like its premium brethren, you're also not limited to playing games that required a paddle controller only with paddles on the *Atari Flashback 8 Gold*; you can also use joysticks. The same restriction applies in that player one and player two joysticks can only replicate the functionality of the player one and player two paddle controller pair. Paddle games that support a third and fourth player will require a set of paddles plugged into each controller port.

GAME LIST

There are 105 games on the Atari Flashback Classic Game Console:

- 3D Tic-Tac-Toe
- Adventure
- Adventure II
- Air Raiders™
- Air-Sea Battle
- Aquaventure
- Armor Ambush™
- Asteroids
- Astroblast™
- Atari Climber
- Backgammon
- Basketball
- Black Jack
- Bowling
- Breakout
- Canyon Bomber
- Centipede
- Championship Soccer
- Chase It
- Circus Atari
- Combat
- Combat Two
- Crystal Castles
- Dark Cavern™ (Night Stalker)
- Demons to Diamonds
- Desert Falcon
- Dodge 'Em
- Double Dunk
- Escape It
- Fatal Run
- Flag Capture
- Football
- Frog Pond

- Frogger
- Frogs and Flies
- Front Line
- Fun with Numbers
- Golf
- Gravitar
- H.E.R.O
- Hangman
- Haunted House
- Home Run
- Human Cannonball
- Indy 500
- International Soccer™
- Jungle Hunt
- Kaboom!
- Maze Craze
- Millipede
- Miniature Golf
- Miss It
- Missile Command
- MotoRodeo
- Night Driver
- Off-the-Wall
- Outlaw
- Pitfall!
- Polaris
- Pong (Video Olympics)
- Pressure Cooker
- Radar Lock
- RealSports Baseball
- RealSports Basketball
- RealSports Soccer
- RealSports Volleyball

- Return to Haunted House
- River Raid
- Saboteur
- Save Mary
- Sea Battle™
- Secret Quest
- Shield Shifter
- Sky Diver
- Slot Machine
- Slot Racers
- Solaris
- Space Attack™
- Space Invaders
- Space War
- Sprintmaster
- Star Ship
- Star Strike™
- Steeplechase
- Stellar Track
- Street Racer
- Submarine Commander
- Super Baseball
- Super Breakout
- Super Challenge™ Baseball (Major League Baseball)
- Super Challenge™ Football (NFL Football)
- Super Football
- Surround
- Sword Fight™
- SwordQuest: EarthWorld
- SwordQuest: FireWorld
- SwordQuest: WaterWorld
- Tempest

- Video Checkers
- Video Chess
- Video Pinball
- Warlords
- Wizard
- Yars' Return
- Yars' Revenge

ATARI FLASHBACK PORTABLE GAME PLAYER

First introduced in 2016, the *Atari Flashback Portable Game Player* was embraced by fans searching for an easy way to play Atari 2600 games on the go. This latest version tweaked the previous model's design and revamped the game list.

HOW IT COMPARES TO THE ORIGINAL CONSOLE

Unlike the AtGames Atari consoles, the *Atari Flashback Portable Game Player* replicates all of the original Atari 2600 console's six switches, and even adds some features of its own.

The Atari Flashback Portable Game Player can even be played on a TV using an optional cable.

Here's the breakdown:

ORIGINAL ATARI 2600 CONSOLE	ATARI FLASHBACK PORTABLE GAME PLAYER
Power	Power
TV Type	T
Left Difficulty	L
Right Difficulty	R
Game Select	S
Game Reset	Start
No function	Reset (returns to menu)
No function	P (Pause)

PORTABLE FEATURES

The *Atari Flashback Portable Game Player* has dedicated TV Type (T) and Pause (P) buttons. The former button works the same as the original console. When pressed, it can display some games in black-and-white or activate features in games like *Secret Quest*. The latter button pauses any game in progress.

Whenever the T, P, or Left (L) or Right (R) Difficulty buttons are pressed, a handy on-screen pop-up indicates the state. T = Mono; P = PAUSED; L = P1-HARD or P1-EASY; R = P2-HARD or P2-EASY.

Like its console brethren, players can use the directional pad to play paddle games on the *Atari Flashback Portable Game Player*. The only limitation is that, since there's only one set of controls, only one-player games are supported, regardless of whether or not they originally used joysticks or paddles.

With an optional TV cable, you can play games on a big screen. The composite cable type and display properties are similar to what you get from the *Atari Flashback Classic Console*.

Finally, perhaps the best unique feature of the *Atari Flashback Portable Game Player* is its SD card slot. With an optional SD card, you can download and play many other Atari 2600 games, including some of the great new homebrew creations.

GAME LIST

There are 70 games on the Atari Flashback Portable Game Player:

- Adventure
- Adventure II
- Air Raiders™
- Aquaventure
- Asteroids
- Astroblast™
- Atari Climber
- Black Jack
- Bowling
- Breakout
- Centipede
- Chase It
- Circus Atari
- Crystal Castles
- Dark Cavern™ (Night Stalker)
- Demons to Diamonds
- Desert Falcon

- Dig Dug
- Dodge 'Em
- Double Dunk
- Fatal Run
- Frog Pond
- Frogger
- Frogs and Flies
- Fun with Numbers
- Galaxian
- Golf
- Gravitar
- Hangman
- Haunted House
- Human Cannonball
- Kaboom!
- Millipede
- Miniature Golf
- Miss It

- Missile Command
- Night Driver
- Pac-Man (4K homebrew version)
- Pitfall!
- Pong (Video Olympics)
- Pressure Cooker
- Radar Lock
- RealSports Baseball
- Return to Haunted House
- River Raid
- Saboteur
- Save Mary
- Secret Quest
- Shield Shifter
- Slot Machine
- Solaris
- Space Attack™

- Stampede
- Star Ship
- Star Strike™
- Stellar Track
- Strip Off
- Submarine Commander
- Super Breakout
- SwordQuest: EarthWorld
- SwordQuest: FireWorld
- SwordQuest: WaterWorld
- Tempest
- Video Checkers
- Video Chess
- Video Pinball
- Wizard
- Xevious
- Yars' Return
- Yars' Revenge

AIR-SEA BATTLE

Here's your chance to become an artillery commander, a submarine captain, or an aircraft bombardier. Just hit the fire button and shoot your way through 27 different shooting games and variations. Planes, boats, and other targets appear on-screen from different directions at different speeds. Shoot 'em off your TV screen with guided missiles, torpedoes, and anti-aircraft guns.

ABOUT THE GAME

Air-Sea Battle is a great example of how diverse an Atari 2600 game can be, making it an ideal launch title. It's also the ultimate game for people who enjoy blowing things up. Having a mode for all types of terrain for a target-worthy vehicle to travel on, in addition to a thorough versus modes, made *Air-Sea Battle* quickly become a favorite on the Atari console.

If there was an issue with the game, it was the fact that the computer had an inability to handle the guided missile option during single-player games. The Torpedo game (Game 11) was a far better mode that was quite similar to guided missiles. Although one variation may not have been up to snuff, there were more than enough that would fit any play style. In fact, the number of game variations was a large selling point for the game.

On the other hand, the vast number of options may have also been a reason that people didn't play it. Sometimes, too many options can be overwhelming. Nonetheless, the cartridge was well received by the majority of Atari console owners. Despite a bit of a learning curve, the game kept players entertained for hours at a time.

OBJECT OF THE GAME

Score more points than your opponent by hitting moving objects.

HOW TO PLAY

All games end after 2 minutes and 16 seconds of play, or when either player scores 99 points. During the last 16 seconds, the score will flash to show that the game is nearing its conclusion.

ANTI-AIRCRAFT GAMES

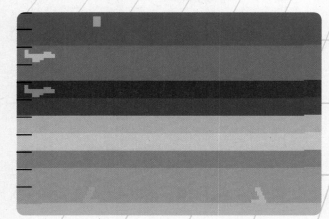

The joystick controller changes the angle of your "Anti-Aircraft Gun" and also the angle of missile flight in Guided Missile Games.

Forward = 30 degrees; center or rest = 60 degrees; back = 90 degrees (straight up).

During the Anti-Aircraft games, anywhere from one to six flying objects will move together across the playfield in a set. All objects in the set must be hit before a new set will appear. Each object hit results in one point.

Games 4 through 6 add a challenge to your marksmanship. There are various flying objects on the playfield travelling at different speeds and directions. Each object has a different score value.

GAME I

This is the Anti-Aircraft game described previously. Your missile travels at the same angle as your "Anti-Aircraft gun" at the time it is fired.

GAME 2

In this game, you and an opponent have "guided" missiles. After firing, you control the angle of flight of your missile by moving your joystick controller from front to back.

GAME 3

Using the right joystick controller, try to outscore the computer. Note that the computer continuously fires the left gun.

GAME 4

In this game, your missile travels at the same angle as your gun was in at the time it is fired.

GAME 5

Using guided missiles, try to outscore your opponent. After firing, you control the angle of flight of your missile by moving the joystick controller from front to back.

GAME 6

Here's another chance to defeat the computer. The right joystick controller serves as your gun, while the computer continuously fires the left gun.

TORPEDO GAMES

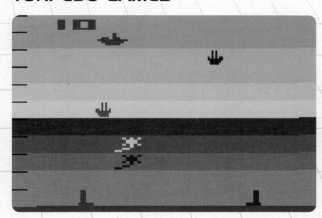

You are a submarine captain firing torpedoes at ships moving above you. Push the joystick controller to the left to move your submarine to the left; push it to the right to move your submarine to the right.

You control half the playfield while your opponent controls the other half. During Torpedo Games, one to six ships move across the playfield in a set. When one set disappears from the playfield, a new set appears. Each ship scores one point.

In Torpedo games 10 through 12, mines travel randomly across the bottom of the playfield, acting as obstructions to your line of fire. The ships move at different speeds and directions. Each ship has a different point value.

GAME 7

After firing, your torpedo travels straight up from where it was fired.

GAME 8

In this game, you can guide your torpedo after firing. By pushing the joystick controller to the left, you guide the torpedo to the left. Moving the joystick to the right moves the torpedo to the right.

GAME 9

Using non-guided torpedoes, the object is to try to sink more ships than the computer. You control the right submarine; the computer will fire continuously from the left.

GAME 10

As in Game 7, your torpedo travels straight up from where it was fired.

GAME 11

In this game, you can guide the torpedo after firing. By pushing the joystick controller to the left, you guide the torpedo to the left. Moving the joystick to the right guides the torpedo to the right.

GAME 12

You control the right submarine with the right joystick controller and, using non-guided torpedoes, try to defeat the computer-controlled left submarine.

SHOOTING GALLERY GAMES

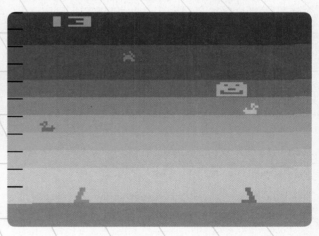

The joystick controller changes the angle of fire: forward = 30 degrees; center or rest = 60 degrees; back = 90 degrees (straight up). In addition, you can move your gun across your half of the playfield by moving the joystick controller left or right.

The targets will change direction at any time and all targets in a set must be hit before new targets are displayed. Each target has a different point value.

GAME 13

This is the Shooting Gallery Game described previously. After firing, your joystick controller has no effect on the line of fire.

GAME 14

After firing, guide your projectile into the targets by moving the joystick controller forward or backward. Moving the joystick right or left has no effect on the projectile once it is fired.

GAME 15

You control the right gun and try to beat the computer-controlled left gun which fires continuously.

POLARIS GAMES

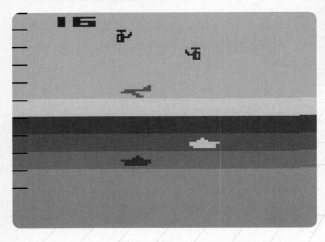

In the following games (Polaris, Bomber, Polaris vs. Bomber), you control the speed by moving the joystick controller back for slow, center (or rest position) for normal speed, and forward for fast.

You captain a ship traveling across the bottom of the playfield. The bottommost ship is the right player. The ships will occasionally change direction.

Anywhere from one to four planes fly over in a set. All planes in a set must be hit before new planes are displayed. Each plane has a different point value.

GAME 16

This is the Polaris game described previously. Your missile travels at the same speed as your ship when the missile was fired. After firing, your ship speed cannot change while the missile is in flight.

GAME 17

In this game, when you change the speed of your ship, you also change the speed of the missile while it is in flight. In effect, you can guide the missile into the planes.

GAME 18

Using the right joystick controller, you control the bottom ship. Using non-guided missiles, try to beat the computer-controlled top ship. The computer ship will move at a steady speed and continuously fire its missiles.

BOMBER GAMES

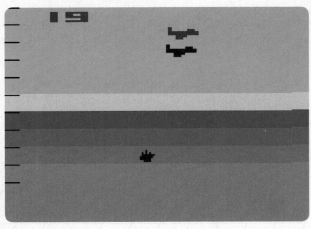

You are the pilot of a plane flying across the top of the playfield. The right player controls the bottommost plane. Planes will occasionally change direction from right to left.

From one to four ships will pass underneath the planes. When a ship is hit, a new ship will replace it from the edge of the playfield. Ships travel at various speeds and each ship has a different point value.

GAME 19

When your bomber drops the bomb, it will move across the playfield at the same speed as your plane at the time it was dropped. After firing, your plane cannot change speed while the bomb is dropping.

GAME 20

Changing the speed of your plane after dropping a bomb will change the speed at which the bomb travels across the playfield as it drops. This allows you to guide the bomb into the passing ships.

GAME 21

Using non-guided bombs, try to hit more ships than the computer. The computer plane is on top and flies at a constant speed across the playfield, dropping bombs continuously. You control the bottom plane using the right joystick controller.

* Unlike most games released on the Atari 2600, player one is controlled with the right controller rather than the left controller.

* The Tele-Games version of *Air-Sea Battle* was called *Target Fun*.

POLARIS VS BOMBER GAMES

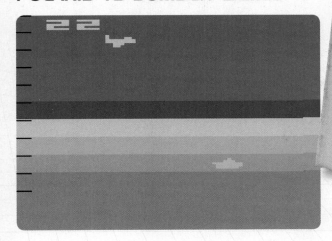

One point is scored for each hit. The ship or plane getting hit will disappear from the playfield and reappear at the edge. Both the plane and ship will occasionally change direction.

The left player flies the plane across the top of the playfield and the right player controls the ship at the bottom of the playfield. The plane drops bombs on the ship, while the ship shoots missiles at the plane.

During the game, mines will randomly travel across the middle of the playfield. In order to hit your opponent, you must avoid the mines which act as obstructions to your line of fire.

GAME 22

This is the Polaris vs Bomber game described previously.

GAME 23

Both the ship and the plane can guide their missiles or bombs. By changing the speed of your ship or plane after firing, the missile or bomb will change speed as it travels across the playfield.

GAME 24

The computer controls the plane, flying at a constant speed across the playfield, dropping bombs continuously. The right joystick controller controls the ship.

GAME 25

This version plays the same as Game 22, except that mines are added to the playfield.

GAME 26

By changing the speed of your ship or plane after firing, the missile or bomb will change speed as it travels across the playfield, allowing you to guide them around the mines and into your opponent.

GAME 27

Once again, the computer controls the plane. You control the ship using the right joystick controller.

GAME DIFFICULTY

The Difficulty buttons on the console control the size of the missile. In Position A, the missile is one-fourth the size compared to the size of the missile while in position B.

GAME OPTIONS

BATTLE TYPE	GAME #	# PLAYERS	FEATURES
Anti-Aircraft	1	2	
	2	2	GM
	3	1	
	4	2	WO
	5	2	GM & WO
Torpedo	6	1	WO
	7	2	
	8	2	GM
	9	1	
	10	2	WO
	11	2	GM & WO
	12	1	WO
Shooting Gallery	13	2	
	14	2	GM
	15	1	
Polaris	16	2	
	17	2	GM
	18	1	
Bomber	19	2	
	20	2	GM
	21	1	
Polaris vs. Bomber	22	2	
	23	2	GM
	24	1	
	25	2	WO
	26	2	GM & WO
	27	1	WO

NUMBER OF PLAYERS

In 2-player games, you and an opponent face off against each other. In 1-player games, the computer is your opponent. In Anti-Aircraft, Torpedo, and Shooting Gallery, the computer always controls the left side. For Bomber, the computer controls the higher plane. In Polaris vs. Bomber, the computer controls the Bomber in game 24 and the Polaris in game 27.

FEATURES

GUIDED MISSILE (GM)

Guided Missiles allow you to control the angle of flight of your missile by moving the joystick controller in different directions, depending on the game type.

WITH OBSTACLES (WO)

Obstacles appear in only two of the five game types. In Anti-Aircraft, observation blimps float across the lowest level of the playing field. They are worth no points when shot down. Mines float through the middle of the playfield in Polaris vs. Bomber. Mines block your shots and are worth no points.

SCORING

ANTI-AIRCRAFT (GAMES 4-6)

	Small Jet	4 points
	Large Jet	3 points
	Helicopter	2 points
	747	1 point

The "Observation Blimps" flying randomly across the bottom of the playfield are not worth any points. They only serve as an obstruction to your line of fire.

TORPEDO (GAMES 10-12)

	PT Boat	4 points
	Aircraft Carrier	3 points
	Pirate Ship	2 points
	Freighter	1 point

Hitting the mines results in no points.

SHOOTING GALLERY GAMES

	Rabbit	3 points
	Duck	2 points
	Clown	1 point

POLARIS GAMES

	Small Jet	4 points
	Large Jet	3 points
	Helicopter	2 points
	747	1 point

BOMBER GAMES

	PT Boat	4 points
	Aircraft Carrier	3 points
	Pirate Ship	2 points
	Freighter	1 point

Tips & Tricks

◆ Each target travels at its own speed, but that speed is consistent so counting the seconds at which your missiles will hit each target will always stay the same.

◆ Master the direction of your gun's angle at the resting position before changing the angle too sporadically. This should definitely help your aim.

◆ There are 27 different games. Find the ones that you enjoy most and practice at them before moving on to the games that are a little more difficult.

BLACK JACK

● Place your bets, casino gamblers! It's time to play Black Jack. One, two, or three players compete against the computer dealer. The computer deals each player two cards face up. The computer also deals two cards to itself—one face up and the other facedown. After that, Lady Luck and your sharp skill determines the winner.

ABOUT THE GAME

Based on the wildly popular card game, Black Jack features a more basic ruleset than its casino counterpart. The ability to split pairs, where the player can separate a pair of cards at equal value into two individual hands, is omitted from the Atari version.

OBJECT OF THE GAME

The object of the game is to get 21 points, or as close to 21 points, without "busting" (exceeding 21 points). You automatically score a Black Jack when your first two cards equal 21 points.

If you are satisfied with the total points of your first two cards, "stay" on that hand. If you want to add more points to your hand, request a "hit" and the dealer will give you another card. You can continue to hit until you are satisfied with your hand, or until you exceed 21 points ("bust").

When all players have played their hands, the dealer reveals the face-down card. Like the players, the dealer hits or stays to get as close as possible to 21 points without busting.

You win the game when:

◆ **Your card hand is equal to more points than the dealer's hand without exceeding 21 points.**

◆ **The dealer busts and exceeds 21 points.**

◆ **You score a Black Jack (an Ace and a face card or a 10).**

PUSH!
A tie game (push) occurs when the dealer's card points equal your card points.

HOW TO PLAY

Use the joystick and red button on your hand-held controller to:

◆ **Determine and make your bet.**

◆ **Determine and indicate whether you want to stay, double, or hit.**

A question mark underneath your total number of chips indicates it's time to place your bet for the next game.

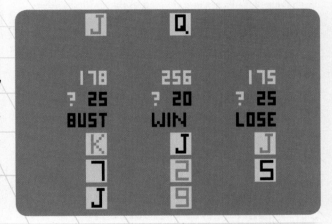

◆ **Use the joystick to change your bet from 1 to 25 chips, displayed to the right of the question mark.**

◆ **Press the red controller button to make your bet with the dealer.**

If there is more than one player, the last player to make a bet and press the controller button erases the previous game's card hands from the screen. After the computer deals two cards, players must decide to hit, stay, or double their bets.

◆ **Select HIT or STAY using the joystick.**

◆ **If you select HIT, press the red controller button and another card will appear on the playfield. Continue to HIT until you are satisfied with your hand.**

◆ **When you are satisfied with your hand, select STAY. Press the red controller button to continue.**

DOUBLE DOWN!

If game rules allow, double your bet before the first hit. (After you double the bet, you must take one hit; only one hit is allowed.) Just select DBLE using the joystick, then press the red controller button for the hit that could win the game!

GAME OPTIONS

Use the Game Select Switch for the following:

◆ **Number of Players:** Press the Game Select button to cycle through all the positions of game setups for one, two, or three players. Release the switch when the number of setups you want appears on-screen.

◆ **Leaving the Game:** A player can leave the game at any time. To do so, push the Game Select Switch until your setup disappears. (The other players' setup will remain.)

◆ **Returning to the Game:** Stop the game action by pressing the Game Select until your setup reappears on-screen along with any other setups of players who had been playing.

◆ **Going Broke:** When you "Go Broke" (lose all your chips), you can still play by asking the bank for another setup. Stop the play action and push the Game Select Switch to cycle through all the setups. When a new one appears along with the other players' previous ones, release the switch. Now place your bets and continue play.

◆ **Breaking the Bank:** When you have 1000 chips, you "Break the Bank"! Now you must start play again with 200 chips. To produce another setup, follow the directions for Going Broke. Your 1000 chip score will remain on the screen until you press the Game Select Switch.

GAME RESET

Press the reset button to reset your score to 200. You will also hear the computer shuffle the cards.

LEFT DIFFICULTY SWITCH

Push the left Skill button to B position and the computer automatically shuffles the cards after every hand. Push the button to A and the computer automatically shuffles the cards after dealing two-thirds of the deck (or 34 cards).

RIGHT DIFFICULTY SWITCH

Select the A or B position to change the rules of the game:

A POSITION: CASINO BLACK JACK RULES

◆ Computer dealer must hit a soft 17 or less.

◆ Computer dealer must stay on a hard 17 (Aces = 1 point).

◆ Your score is not affected by tie games between the dealer and you.

◆ If your hand equals 10 or 11 points, you can double your bet before the first hit. You must take one hit and only one hit is allowed.

◆ A player is allowed four hits.

B POSITION: PRIVATE BLACK JACK RULES

◆ Computer dealer must stay on 17 or more points.

◆ The computer dealer wins all tie games.

◆ You can double your bet on any combination of cards before the first hit. You must take one hit and only one hit is allowed.

◆ A player automatically wins the game when he hits four times without busting.

SCORING

CARD VALUES

OBJECT	POINT VALUE
Number Cards	Face Value (i.e. 5 = 5 points)
10, Jack (J), Queen (Q), and King (K)	10 points
Ace (A)	1 or 11 points

A card hand is called "soft" when the Ace is used as 11 points. A card hand is "hard" when any combination of cards is used except an Ace worth 11 points. For example, a soft 17 is an Ace (11 points) and a 6. A hard 17 could be a 10, 6 and an Ace (1 point).

BETTING

Each player starts play with a total of 200 chips. Bet from 1 to 25 chips on each game. Your bet is added or subtracted from your total score depending on whether you win or lose. When you score a Black Jack, you win 1 1/2 times your bet. For example, you score Black Jack on a bet of 10 chips to win 15 chips! Players are automatically removed from the game when they reach 1000 chips or have no chips remaining.

ATARI NEWS
What The Critics Had to Say

"...a good game for adults with several variations for single or double players." (10/10)

-Video magazine, Winter 1979

COMBAT

Arm yourself against your opponent with tanks, planes, or fighter jets in diverse stages in this two-player game. Blast your opponent as many times as you can for the highest score.

ABOUT THE GAME

The Atari Video Computer System experience for almost everyone started with *Combat* and its promise of 27 video games that featured tanks and jets. How exciting was it to power up the system and see things weren't simply black and white rectangles? (Answer: Very!) Combat's first game involved a red tank facing a blue tank positioned across a green field from one another.

Then there was the sound. Video games played at home usually produced simple beeps and boops. In *Combat*, idling engines growled and then roared to life when a tank lurched into motion. You heard the change in speed when bi-planes and jets increased or decreased speed.

Gameplay was equal to the sights and sounds. You needed to spend time blasting immobile targets before you could consistently bend a missile around obstacles to hit opponents, or bounce them through the mazes in Tank Pong.

Of course, the sign of ultimate disrespect was offering to play as the three jets or the giant bomber facing the three bi-planes. Everyone knew that both choices made you a big, easy target! And that's what made your victory so much sweeter.

OBJECT OF THE GAME

Whether you're driving a tank, flying a bi-plane, or piloting a jet, the objective is to score more hits on your opponent than your opponent scores against you.

HOW TO PLAY

There are three primary game types in *Combat*: Tank, Bi-Plane, and Jet. Each game type includes variations but the controls are the same. As a rule of thumb, game action for Tank and Jet-Fighter games is viewed from the top. Bi-Plane game action is viewed from the side.

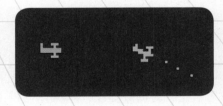

The two constants across all games are that pressing the red button fires a missile (or machine gun bullets in some Bi-Plane games) and each game runs for 2 minutes and 16 seconds.

TANK

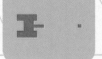

Push the joystick up to move your tank in the same direction as its gun is pointing. To spin right, push the joystick to the right. To spin left, push the joystick to the left. To turn while staying in motion, push up-right or up-left.

The main Tank variant is Tank-Pong, in which missiles bounce off walls and obstacles. Invisible Tank and Tank-Pong use the same rules as other tank games, but the tanks remain invisible until: a missile is fired; they're struck by a missile; or they collide with a barrier or wall.

BI-PLANE

Control your bi-plane's speed by moving the joystick left (slowest) or right (fastest). To dive, push up on the joystick; to climb, push down. You can play as two bi-planes flying in formation, or a trio of standard bi-planes tangling with a giant bomber.

JET

The speed of your jet is controlled by moving the joystick up (fastest) or down (slowest). Make right and left turns by moving your joystick left or right.

The two-on-two jet variation features dogfights between pairs of jets. All four jets in the three-on-one game are the same size. The trio of jets fires a wider spread of missiles, but also offers a larger target than the solo jet.

DIFFICULTY OPTIONS

Setting the difficulty to A results in a short-range missile compared to difficulty B. This holds true across all games. While playing a bi-plane or jet game, players using difficulty setting A will fly slower than those using setting B.

GAME OPTIONS

GAME TYPE	GAME #	FEATURES	TERRAIN
Tank	1	GM	OP
	2	GM	EZ
	3	SM	EZ
	4	GM	CX
	5	SM	CX
Tank Pong	6	DH & BH	EZ
	7	DH & BH	CX
	8	BH	OP
	9	BH	EZ
Invisible Tank	10	GM	OP
	11	GM	EZ
Invisible Tank Pong	12	DH & BH	EZ
	13	BH	OP
	14	BH	EZ
Bi-Plane	15	GM	CD
	16	SM	CD
	17	MG	CD
	18	MG	OP
Bi-Plane 2 vs. 2	19	GM	OP
Bi-Plane 1 vs. 3	20	SM	OP
Jet	21	GM	CD
	22	SM	CD
	23	GM	OP
	24	SM	OP
Jet 2 vs. 2	25	GM	CD
Jet 1 vs. 3	26	GM	OP
Jet 2 vs. 2	27	SM	OP

FEATURES

Your tank or aircraft employs one of three different weapons; that weapon also changes based upon the chosen game. Billiard Hit (BH) is a rule change that applies only to Tank Pong.

STRAIGHT MISSILE (SM)

Missiles travel in a straight line after being fired.

GUIDED MISSILE (GM)

Moving the joystick to the left or right after firing a missile alters the path of the missile.

MACHINE GUNS (MG)

Your aircraft fires a steady stream of missiles as long as you press the red button on the controller.

DIRECT HIT (DH)

In Tank Pong, your missiles become live as soon as they are fired.

BILLIARD HIT (BH)

In Tank Pong, your missiles won't damage your opponent until they bounce off at least one obstacle.

TERRAIN

There are two sets of terrain options in *Combat*: one for land battles and another for the sky.

OPEN AREA (OP)

There are no obstacles in the field of combat.

EASY MAZE (EZ)

The obstacles in the field of combat are large with plenty of space between them.

COMPLEX MAZE (CX)

The obstacles in the field of combat are smaller and bunched closer together.

CLOUDS (CD)

Clouds cover the field of combat, but aren't solid like the obstacles in tank games. Aircraft and missiles can move freely, but the clouds conceal anything moving inside them.

TANK GAME MAPS

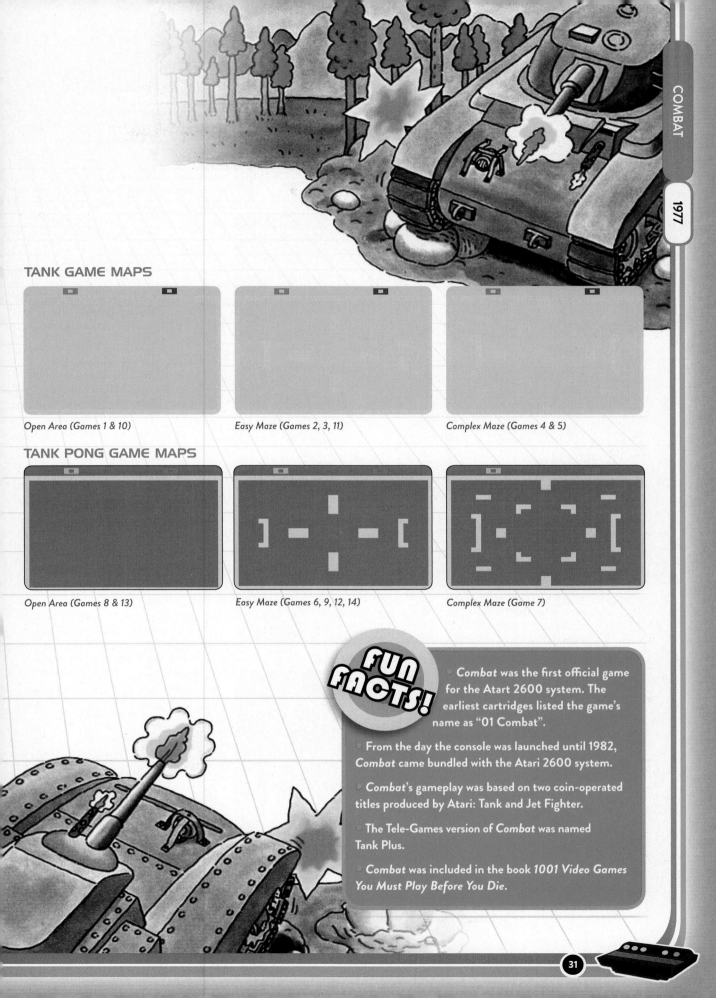

Open Area (Games 1 & 10)

Easy Maze (Games 2, 3, 11)

Complex Maze (Games 4 & 5)

TANK PONG GAME MAPS

Open Area (Games 8 & 13)

Easy Maze (Games 6, 9, 12, 14)

Complex Maze (Game 7)

FUN FACTS!

• *Combat* was the first official game for the Atart 2600 system. The earliest cartridges listed the game's name as "01 Combat".

• From the day the console was launched until 1982, *Combat* came bundled with the Atari 2600 system.

• *Combat*'s gameplay was based on two coin-operated titles produced by Atari: Tank and Jet Fighter.

• The Tele-Games version of *Combat* was named Tank Plus.

• *Combat* was included in the book *1001 Video Games You Must Play Before You Die*.

BI-PLANE GAME MAPS

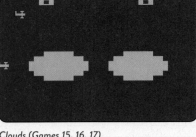

Clouds (Games 15, 16, 17)

Open Skies (Game 18)

Open Skies (Game 19)

Open Skies (Game 20)

JET GAME MAPS

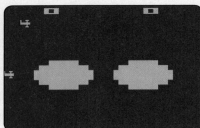

Clouds (Games 21 & 22)

Open Skies (Games 23 & 24)

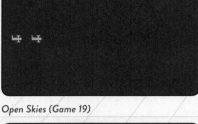

Clouds (Game 25)

Open Skies (Game 26)

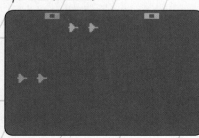

Open Skies (Game 27)

- ◆ After taking a hit, jets and bi-planes briefly spin in place. The direction they point after the spinning ends is random.

- ◆ When tanks are hit, they are knocked back slightly before spinning in place. When hit near a barrier, they are pushed through the barrier. If they're hit at the edge of the map, they'll warp to the other side of the screen.

- ◆ All controls are locked after each hit; you can neither steer nor fire. When the spinning ceases, both combatants regain full control of their vehicles.

- ◆ To string together hits, your first shot must come from near the limit of your range. If you're driving a tank, the first shot must be done while on the move (bi-planes and jets never stop moving except when they're spinning). Keep tapping the red button to fire as soon as your opponent's spin ends to earn a second hit.

- ◆ On any maze map, drive your tank into the corners of the barriers directly in front of your starting point. If you hit them just right, your tank will bounce through or around the barrier.

- ◆ Start either Game 9 (Tank Pong, Easy Maze) or Game 14 (Invisible Tank Pong, Easy Maze) and spin the red tank 180 degrees. Fire into the wall and watch the shell ricochet across the field and slam into the blue tank. The blue tank will be knocked into the red tank, sending both flying across the screen.

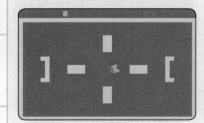

FUN WITH NUMBERS

Atari's first educational game program. Solve addition, subtraction, multiplication, and division problems on your own TV. The computer lets you know if you're right. If you're wrong, the correct answer flashes on-screen.

FUN WITH NUMBERS
VIDEO COMPUTER SYSTEM
GAME PROGRAM

8 VIDEO GAMES
• TABLE PROBLEMS
• RANDOM PROBLEMS

CX2661

ABOUT THE GAME

Fun With Numbers, or Basic Math, was one of nine launch titles for the Atari 2600 in 1977. Educationally focused, *Fun With Numbers* was an attempt to show that the Atari VCS could offer many different applications with its cartridges. Unfortunately, the low-level arithmetic and difficult controls didn't help to portray the VCS as a versatile home computer.

OBJECT OF THE GAME

Sharpen your math skills with *Fun With Numbers*. The object is to get as many points as possible in a game of 10 math problems covering addition, subtraction, multiplication, or division.

HOW TO PLAY

Use the joystick to make numbers appear on the Blackboard Screen. Push the joystick forward to cycle through numbers from 0-9. Pull it towards you to make the numbers appear in decreasing order from 9-0. The joystick is also used to move the Answer Line; move the joystick to the right and left to adjust the Answer Line accordingly.

The red controller button records your numbers with the Computer Teacher. Press the button to record your chosen problem numbers, as well as your selected answers to the math problems.

Each game features a set of 10 problems using a specific arithmetic operation (i.e., addition, subtraction, multiplication, and division). After selecting the game you want to play, a problem appears on the Blackboard Screen.

Here is an example addition problem. The top number, 7, will be underlined. Push the joystick forward until you find the number you want to work with. For example, need some practice on additions using number 8? Just follow these two steps:

1. **Press the joystick forward once until number 8 appears as the underlined top number.**
2. **Record your number 8 with the Computer Teacher by pressing the red controller button.**

REMEMBER
On occasion, there will be less than 10 problems with the top number you have selected. When this occurs, the game automatically selects problems from the next number group.

HOW TO RECORD AN ANSWER

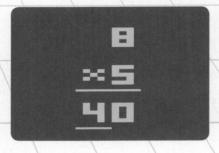

After you've selected the type of problem and number, notice the Answer Line below the math problem on the Blackboard Screen.

Use the joystick to show your answer on-screen. Push it forward to cycle through the consecutive numbers 0-9. Pull it towards you to cycle through the numbers in decreasing order, 9-0. For example, if no number is showing, you can put number 2 on the Blackboard Screen by:

- Pushing the joystick forward three times—one time for each of the numbers 0, 1, and 2

  or...

- Pressing the joystick forward as the game cycles to number 3, then release the joystick.

The line represents space for one digit of your answer. You can move the Answer Line to the right and left using your joystick. If your answer is more than one digit, you must move the Answer Line. For example, in the image shown previously, the answer is 40. To record your answer:

- Select the number 0 with your joystick; it will appear above the present Answer Line. The last digit of your answer must always appear on this line.

- Move the Answer Line one digit to the left.

- Select the number 4 with the joystick; the number 4 will appear above the Answer Line.

- Now press the red controller button to record your answer, 40.

Some division problems will have a remainder. To show the remainder, move the Answer Line two digits to the right of the quotient. Select the remainder number with the joystick. Now record your entire answer by pressing the red controller button.

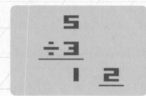

CORRECT ANSWERS

Musical tunes determine whether your answer is right or wrong. Correct answers receive a "BEEP" followed by a melodic tune. The Computer Teacher automatically presents the next problem. Wrong answers receive a "BEEP" and a melodic tune, but the wrong answer disappears as the right answer flashes on the Blackboard Screen. The Computer Teacher automatically presents the next problem.

The game ends after 10 problems. At the conclusion of the last problem, the total number of problems (10) and the number of correct answers flashes on the Blackboard Screen.

DIFFICULTY OPTIONS

Use the right Difficulty Switch to determine if each round (math problem) will be timed. In the A position, the player has a time limit to produce an answer. In the B position, there is no time limit. Use the left Difficulty Switch to determine the time limit for each round (math problem).

GAME NUMBER	LEFT DIFFICULTY SWITCH	TIME LIMIT	PROBLEM TYPE
1-4	A	12 seconds	PS
1-4	B	24 seconds	PS
5-8	A	24 seconds	CD
5-8	B	12 seconds	CS

GAMES 1-4

Games 1-4 feature single-digit problems and allow you to select the top number of each problem using your joystick.

PLAYER SELECTED SINGLE-DIGIT (PS)

If the left Difficulty Switch is set to the A position, you have 12 seconds to answer each problem. If the Difficulty Switch is in the B position, you have 24 seconds.

GAMES 5-8

In games 5-8, the computer selects the numbers in each problem. Rounds can be single-digit or double-digit math problems.

COMPUTER SELECTED DOUBLE-DIGIT (CD)

With the left Difficulty Switch in the A position, problems are double-digit. You have 24 seconds to answer each problem.

COMPUTER SELECTED SINGLE-DIGIT (CS)

With the left Difficulty Switch in the B position, problems are single-digit. You have 12 seconds to answer each problem.

GAME OPTIONS

GAME NUMBER	MATH TYPE
1, 5	Addition
2, 6	Subtraction
3, 7	Multiplication
4, 8	Division

Games 1, 2, 3, and 4 allow you to select a top number to work with for practice.

Games 5, 6, 7, and 8 are Random Problems. Follow the same rules and procedures to tackle Random Problems as you did to solve Table Problems. Random Problems feature addition, subtraction, multiplication, and division. The only difference between these games and Games 1 through 4 is the absence of a top number selection. You have no control over the numbers in these problems. For example, after you select a subtraction game, the game presents subtraction problems at random. You begin your answer immediately.

SCORING

Each game has 10 math problems with one point awarded for each correct answer. At the end of each game, two numbers flash on-screen: the number of total problems (10) on the right side and your score on the left side.

INDY 500

Fourteen one- and two-player racing games and variations. Steer your car around one of the many tracks, racing around hairpin turns to get to the finish line before your opponent.

INDY 500
VIDEO COMPUTER SYSTEM™
GAME PROGRAM™
14 VIDEO GAMES
RACE CARS • CRASH N'
SCORE • TAG • ICE RACE
ONE PLAYER • TWO PLAYERS

ABOUT THE GAME

Taking a lot of inspiration from *Sprint* and *Sprint 2, Indy 500* premiered on the Atari 2600 in 1977. Instead of ranking you by your skill, however, this game took fun to a different level. *Indy 500* had some differences from its arcade counterpart, which made it even more valuable as far as gameplay goes.

With 14 one- and two-player games, *Indy 500* brought a lot of life to this age of Atari consoles. Steering around hairpin turns and competing against both friends and time, the game served up a degree of difficulty and challenge that resulted in playing the game repeatedly.

The game shipped in a large box in order to accommodate the specialized racing controllers that allowed for a more remote control-like experience with precise steering. Whether you were battling against your friends or the clock, *Indy 500* was a game that kept many fans entertained for hours on end.

OBJECT OF THE GAME

In 1-player time trial games, you race against the clock to see how many laps you can make around the track in 60 seconds. During 2-player games, you race against another player to be the first one to complete 25 laps.

In 1-player games, a player has 60 seconds to make as many hits as possible. In 2-player games, the first player to score 50 points wins.

HOW TO PLAY

RACE CAR

Whether you compete against the clock or another player, your racecar tackles the curves of some dangerous tracks. During one-player games, you can race against the clock using the left controller to move the car. The top-left number on the playfield indicates the number of laps, while the top-right number shows the time.

In two-player games, players race against each other. The top two numbers represent the number of laps each player completes. The right score refers to the right controller player; the left number shows the left controller player's score.

You'll hear the engines when they accelerate, and the CRASH when your car crashes into the opponent's car or playfield boundaries.

Car races begin at the starting line. Then, get ready, get set... GO!

GAME 1: GRAND PRIX TRACK

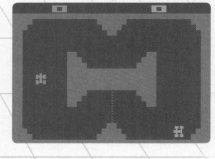

Hang onto your hats as you round the turns on this track. You're racing against an opponent who's out to complete 25 laps first to be the winner. Give him a run for his money!

GAME 2: GRAND PRIX RACE TRACK (TIME TRIAL)

Race against the clock on the Grand Prix track. You have 60 seconds to complete as many laps as possible. Try to beat your last record. This serves as great practice for races against opponents on this track.

GAME 3: DEVIL'S ELBOW TRACK

There are some wicked turns to master in order to conquer this track. At high speed, you race against an opponent. Faster and faster you go to be the first to complete 25 laps.

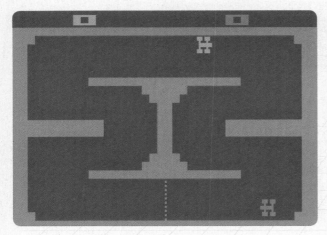

GAME 4: DEVIL'S ELBOW TRACK (TIME TRIAL)

It's a race against the devil as you practice for those competitive races. Race against the clock and try to complete as many laps as possible in 60 seconds.

CRASH N' SCORE

Score points by crashing! Each player controls one racecar using a hand-held controller. The white square is your target. When it appears on the playfield, racecars attempt to crash into it. When the crash occurs, a player scores one point and the square disappears.

The square reappears at random on another part of the playfield. Hear the engines roar and the CRASH when your car collides with the opponent's car. A "BEEP" indicates when a point is scored.

Move your car off any side of the playfield to make it reappear on the opposite side. For example, steer the car off the top of the playfield and it will reappear at the bottom of the playfield. This feature is one strategy to use to reach the square first!

Cars are color coordinated with the scores at the top of the field. The score at the right refers to the right controller player; the left number shows the left controller player's score.

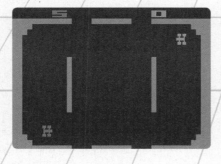

GAME 5: CRASH N' SCORE® I TRACK

In two-player games, players compete for crashes with the box. The first player to score 50 hits wins the game.

GAME 6: CRASH 'N SCORE® I TRACK (TIME TRIAL)

A single player races against the clock to score as many hits as possible in 60 seconds. The top-left number is the number of hits; the top-right number shows the time.

GAME 7: CRASH N' SCORE® II TRACK

Two players move at high speeds to be the first to score 50 hits. The playfield is more complex, as it contains six treacherous barriers!

GAME 8: CRASH N' SCORE® II (TIME TRIAL)

One player drives at high speed against the clock. The player's objective is to score as many hits as possible in 60 seconds while avoiding six treacherous barriers.

TAG

Two players take part in a regular game of tag. Each player controls one car; the car that is NOT blinking is "it."

When your car is blinking, you must avoid becoming tagged by your opponent's car. Score one point for every second you avoid being tagged.

The two numbers at the top of the playfield represent each player's score.

GAME 9: TAG – BARRIER CHASE TRACK

The first player to tally 99 points wins the game.

GAME 10: TAG – MOTOR HUNT TRACK

The first player to tally 99 points on this complicated playfield wins. The racecars move at high speed.

ICE RACE

Cars race around the icy track and compete against each other or the clock. The ice makes steering on the track difficult.

In two-player games, players race against each other. The top two numbers represent the number of laps each player has completed. The right score refers to the right controller player; the left number shows the left controller player's score.

During one-player time trial games, the player uses the left controller to race against the clock. The top left number is the number of laps, while the top-right number is the time.

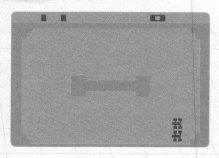

You'll hear the engines when they accelerate and the CRASH when your car collides with the opponent's car or playfield boundaries.

GAME II: ICE SPRINT RACE TRACK

Punch the engines on the straightaway and be cautious on the curves while trying to be the first one to complete 25 laps.

GAME 12: ICE SPRINT TRACK (TIME TRIAL)

Get the feel of the track while racing against the clock. Your goal? To complete as many laps as possible in 60 seconds.

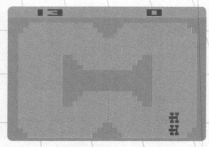

GAME 13: ICE RALLY TRACK

Your racecar is moving at high speed on an icy track as you maneuver those sharp turns to beat your opponent. The first player to complete 25 laps claims victory.

GAME 14: ICE RALLY TRACK (TIME TRIAL)

The seconds tick away as you attempt to complete as many laps as possible in 60 seconds.

CONTROLLER ACTION

In all the racing games, use the knob on the top of your controller to steer the racecar on the playfield. The red button on the side of the controller acts as the accelerator.

GAME DIFFICULTY

Slide the Difficulty Switch from the B to the A position and your racecar travels at high speed, making it more difficult to control.

GAME OPTIONS

TRACK	GAME #	# PLAYERS
Grand Prix	1	2
	2	1
Devil's Elbow	3	2
	4	1
Crash n' Score I	5	2
	6	1
Crash n' Score II	7	2
	8	1
Tag - Barrier Chase	9	2
Tag - Motor Hunt	10	2
Ice Sprint	11	2
	12	1
Ice Rally	13	2
	14	1

NUMBER OF PLAYERS

During 1-player games, you race against a 60-second clock. Depending on the Time Trial, you must complete as many laps—or score as many points—as possible. In 2-player games (except Tag), you and an opponent race to complete a set number of laps. During games of Tag, the goal is to score 99 points.

SCORING

In games of Crash n' Score, a player scores one point each time his racecar crashes into a white square.

During two-player Tag games, you score one point for each second you avoid being tagged by your opponent.

During all game types, you only lose time—not points—when you crash into any playfield boundary or barrier.

◆ Don't push too hard on the throttle for an extended period of time. The speed can really reach the high end of the spectrum by doing this, thus making it extremely difficult to maneuver.

◆ While driving controllers are not supported on the Atari Flashback system, this game works great with the console joystick or portable directional pad.

PONG (VIDEO OLYMPICS)

Don't wait four years for the Olympics. They can happen every day, right at home. With the Video Olympics Game Program, you compete in 50 games and variations in eight main events. From Soccer to Volleyball to Basketball. Play against the computer or against up to three of your toughest opponents.

ABOUT THE GAME

With the twin 1976 successes of the Winter Olympics in Innsbruck, Austria, and the Summer Olympics in Montreal, Canada, it seemed like a natural for Atari to leverage some of that interest with one of their Atari 2600 launch titles. Similar to many of the Pong clone systems from the mid-1970s that the Atari 2600 helped to drive out of the marketplace, Joe Decuir's *Video Olympics*—referred to in the AtGames Flashback products by its marquee game option, *Pong*—features practically every ball and paddle variation you can imagine. This was a great way for Atari to both put one last stamp on the Pong era that they helped bring about in the early 1970s and was eventually over-run by clones, and also end the era once and for all with a definitive cartridge compilation on a system that could play an infinite number of other games.

HOW TO PLAY

Turn the knob to move the paddles. Press the red controller button to speed hit, whammy, catch the ball, or jump the paddle depending on the game variation. Some games have a particular game feature to use in competition. Activate the following game features with the red controller button:

◆ **SPEED:** To add some speed to the return ball, press the red controller button as the ball makes contact with your paddle.

◆ **WHAMMY:** Put sharper angles on your return hits. Press the red controller button as the ball makes contact with the paddle. The angle will continue on your return hit as long as you press the red controller button, or until your opponent returns the ball.

◆ **CATCH:** Press the red controller button as the ball hits the paddle and the ball sticks to the paddle. Use this time to plan strategy, aim a shot, or pass to a team paddle. Move slowly and carefully, though, as the ball will fly off the paddle if you make fast or sudden movements.

◆ **JUMP:** Make the paddle "jump up" to hit or spike the ball during certain games. Press the red controller button and the paddle will "jump" from the bottom of the playfield to the playfield center. Make sure to activate the jump before the ball passes through the playfield center or the ball will travel through the paddle instead of bouncing off the paddle.

PONG

Pong is played much like tennis. Using a controller, each player rallies the ball by moving the paddles on the playfield. The paddles only move vertically on the playfield. When one player controls more than one paddle, all the paddles move together in unison. If there are two players on one team, the second player's paddle will be striped. Each team's paddles are color coordinated with the scores at the top of the screen. The right-hand score refers to the right controller player or team; the left number shows the left controller player or team score.

A player or team scores one point when the opponent hits the ball out of bounds or misses a hit. The first player or team to score 21 points wins the game.

The last player (or team) to score always serves the ball. Serve by pressing the red controller button after waiting at least one second after the point is made. If there are two players on one team, either player can serve. In Robot Pong, the computer always serves the ball to the player who lost the point.

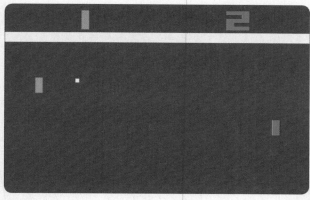

Robot Pong.

ROBOT PONG (ONE PLAYER GAME)

One player controls the right paddle and competes against the left paddle controlled by the computer.

PONG (TWO-PLAYER GAME)

Two opposing players each control one paddle.

PONG 4 (FOUR-PLAYER GAME)

It's a double game of Pong with two players on each team! Each player controls one paddle. Try playing zones with your partner; you cover the upper half of the playfield, while your partner plays the bottom playfield half.

PONG 4-I (FOUR-PLAYER GAME)

Four players can play this game variation. It's as simple as a doubles game of tennis. Two players are on each team. One team player controls the paddle at the net; the other team player covers the back court.

SUPER PONG (TWO-PLAYER GAME)

It's a doubles game of Super Pong! With two players on each team, each player controls two paddles.

SOCCER

Get ready to kick that ball into the goal! Each player uses a controller to move the kickers on the playfield. By turning the controller knob, your kickers move together in unison.

A player (or team) scores one point when the ball is kicked into the goal. The first player (or team) to score 21 points wins the game.

Each team's soccer kickers are color coordinated with the score at the top of the screen. The right-hand score refers to the right controller team or player; the left score shows the left controller player or team score. If there are two players on one team, the second player's kicker will be striped.

SOCCER (TWO-PLAYER GAME)

Two opposing players each control two kickers.

SOCCER 4-I (FOUR-PLAYER GAME)

Double your soccer fun with a soccer doubles game. Two players are on each team; each player controls one kicker.

SOCCER 4-II (FOUR-PLAYER GAME)

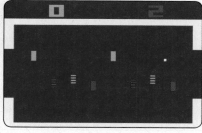

Two players are on each team; each player controls two kickers.

Soccer 4-II.

FOOZPONG

Each player or team controls two vertical rows of paddles that move simultaneously. The object? To knock the ball into the goal. A player or team scores one point for every goal. The first player or team to score 21 points wins the game.

If there are two players on one team, the second player's paddle is striped. Each team's paddles are color coordinated with the score that appears at the top of the screen. The right-hand score refers to the right controller player; the left number shows the left controller player's score.

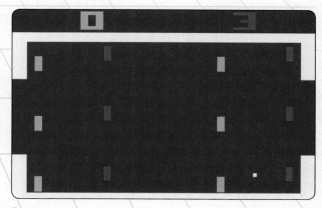

Foozpong.

Note that the vertical movement of each row is restricted; each paddle can move across only half the playfield. There are four paddles per row, but only three paddles on the row appear on the playfield at one time.

FOOZPONG (TWO-PLAYER GAME)

Two opposing players each control two rows of paddles.

FOOZPONG (FOUR-PLAYER GAME)

A doubles game of Foozpong! Two players are on each team and each player controls two rows of paddles.

HOCKEY

You're scrambling to hit the hockey puck into the goal. Hockey games include variations on the number of hockey sticks you control, the playfield, and the game features such as Speed, Whammy, or Catch.

A player or team scores one point when a goal is made. The first team or player to score 21 points wins the game.

Hockey sticks move only vertically on the playfield. When one player controls more than one stick, all the sticks move together in unison. Each player or team's hockey sticks are color coordinated with the score at the top of the screen. The right-hand score refers to the right controller player; the left score shows the left controller player's score. If there are two players on one team, the second player's stick will be striped.

HOCKEY I
(TWO-PLAYER GAME)

Each player controls one stick and tries to hit the puck into the goal.

Hockey I.

HOCKEY II
(TWO-PLAYER GAME)

Two opposing players each control two hockey sticks; shoot with the forward stick and defend the goal with the second stick.

HOCKEY III
(TWO-PLAYER GAME)

Each player controls three paddles in this game variation. Two opposing players attempt to score with one paddle that guards the goal and two paddles that cover the playfield.

HOCKEY 4-I
(FOUR-PLAYER GAME)

Four players scramble on the icy playfield to make goals. Each player controls one paddle and there are two players on each team: one forward and one goalie.

HOCKEY 4-II
(FOUR-PLAYER GAME)

Double your hockey fun with two players on each team. Each player controls a row of hockey sticks with the controller. Any one stick can move across half the playfield. There are four paddles per row, but only three paddles appear on the playfield at one time.

QUADRAPONG

The king of Pong games! Four players play this Pong game. Two players are on each team and each player controls one paddle.

Team paddles are color coordinated with the score at the top of the playfield. The right-hand score refers to the right controller player; the left score shows the left controller player's score.

The movement of each player's paddle is restricted to one side of the rectangular playfield. Each side of the rectangle has a goal. Each paddle guards a goal.

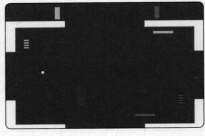

Quadrapong.

To score one point, a player must hit the ball into either goal guarded by the opposing players. (Don't score against your teammate!) The first team to score 21 points wins the game.

QUADRAPONG
(FOUR-PLAYER GAME)

Each player controls his paddle with a controller and attempts to make goals. The first team to score 21 goals wins the game.

HANDBALL

Play Handball just as you would a regular game of handball. Two or four players each control one paddle. Paddles are located on the same side of the playfield and are color coordinated with the score at the top of the screen. The right-hand scores refer to the right controller player or team; the left number shows the left controller player or team score.

When your paddle is solid, it is your turn to hit the ball. After doing so, your paddle will start to blink. If you hit the ball out of turn (when your paddle is blinking), your opponent scores one point.

You score one point when your opponent misses the ball or hits it out of turn. The first player to reach 21 points wins the game.

The second player on a two-player team will have a striped paddle and play forward.

HANDBALL (TWO-PLAYER GAME)

Each player controls one paddle and competes for points.

HANDBALL II (FOUR-PLAYER GAME)

It's a doubles game of handball! Two players are on one team. Each player controls one paddle. Either player on one team can hit the ball.

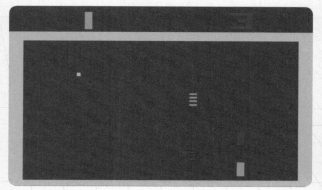

Handball II.

VOLLEYBALL

Two or four players can play volleyball. The object? To successfully return
the ball over the net in the center of the playfield.

Each player controls one paddle that moves in a horizontal line at the bottom of the screen. Paddles are color coordinated with the score at the top of the playfield. The right-hand score refers to the right controller player or team; the left number shows the left controller player or team score.

A player or team scores one point when the opponent misses the ball or hits it into the net. The first player (or team) to score 21 points wins the game.

Volleyball.

During doubles games, the second player on each team will cover the upper portion of the playfield with a smaller paddle.

VOLLEYBALL (TWO-PLAYER GAME)

Two competing players each control one paddle and volley for points.

VOLLEYBALL 4 (FOUR-PLAYER GAME)

With two players on each team, you can set up and spike the ball.

BASKETBALL

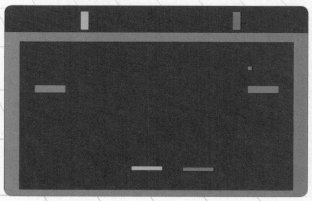

Basketball.

Get ready to shoot some hoops! Two or four players can play basketball. Each player controls one paddle that moves in a horizontal line across one half of the bottom playfield. Each player or team has a basket. The player on the left side of the playfield must shoot at the basket on the right side of the playfield. The player on the right shoots at the left basket.

Paddles are color coordinated with the score at the top of the playfield.

A player or team scores one point when the ball goes through the basket. The first player to score 21 points wins the game.

The team who scores the last point inbounds the ball onto the court by pressing the red controller button after waiting at least one second after the last point is made. Either player on a two-player team can put the ball into play.

Where you dribble the ball on your paddle determines the direction the ball will travel. For example, dribble the ball off the right side of your paddle and the ball will shoot to the right. The second player on a two player team will control a small paddle located higher on the playfield.

BASKETBALL (TWO-PLAYER GAME)

Using the paddles, each player tries to make shots and score. The first player to score 21 points wins the game.

BASKETBALL (FOUR-PLAYER GAME)

Two players are on each team. Each team tries to make shots and score. The first team to reach 21 points wins the game.

DIFFICULTY OPTIONS

Slide the difficulty switch from the B to A position to reduce the paddle size by half.

GAME OPTIONS

To select a Video Olympics game, press down the game select switch. There are 50 game variations for one to four players.

GAME TYPE	GAME #	# PLAYERS	FEATURES
Pong	1	1	SP
	2	1	WH
	3	2	SP
	4	2	WH
Pong 4	5	4	SP
	6	4	WH
Pong 4-I	7	4	SP
	8	4	WH
Super Pong	9	2	SP
	10	2	WH
Super Pong 4	11	4	SP
	12	4	WH
Soccer	13	2	SP
	14	2	WH
Soccer 4-I	15	4	SP
	16	4	WH
Soccer 4-II	17	4	SP
	18	4	CT
Foozpong	19	2	SP
	20	2	CT
Foozpong 4	21	4	SP
	22	4	CT

GAME TYPE	GAME #	# PLAYERS	FEATURES
Hockey I	23	2	SP
	20	2	WH
Hockey II	25	2	SP
	20	2	WH
Hockey III	27	2	SP
	28	2	CT
Hockey 4-I	29	4	SP
	30	4	WH
Hockey 4-II	31	4	SP
	32	4	CT
Quadrapong	33	4	SP
	34	4	CT
Handball	35	2	SP
	36	2	WH
Handball II	37	4	SP
	38	4	WH
Volleyball	39	2	JM
	40	2	
Volleyball 4	41	4	JM
	42	4	
Basketball	43	2	
	44	2	WH
	45	2	JM
	46	2	CT
Basketball 4	47	4	
	48	4	WH
	49	4	JM
	50	4	CT

FEATURES

SPEED (SP)

Press the red controller button when the ball makes contact with your paddle to add speed to a return hit.

WHAMMY (WH)

Press the red controller button when the ball makes contact with your paddle to put a sharper angle on return hits. The angle will continue as you press the button.

CATCH (CT)

Press the red controller button when the ball makes contact with your paddle to catch and hold it, even while your paddle is moving. Release the button to release the ball.

JUMP (JM)

Press the red controller button to make your paddle jump from the bottom of the playfield to the playfield center. Activate jump before the ball passes through the playfield center, otherwise the ball will travel through the paddle instead of bouncing off of it.

Tips & Tricks

◆ The angle of the ball deflection is determined by hitting one of four equal segments on a paddle. The most extreme deflections are caused by hitting the corner of your paddle.

STAR SHIP

You're sitting in your Star Ship cockpit. And your television screen is suddenly transformed into the window of your Star Ship. A constant barrage of meteors whiz toward your window. Eerie enemy space objects float from the darkest parts of space.

ABOUT THE GAME

Star Ship was the first space-themed video game released for Atari's home console. Despite lukewarm critical reception, this type of game was a necessity for a home console. After *Star Wars* released in May 1977 and became a cultural phenomenon, the demand for anything space-related skyrocketed. Everyone wanted to pilot a ship between the stars, blasting enemies, and warping at high speeds.

OBJECT OF THE GAME

Your mission in the first nine games is to score points by destroying enemy space objects, but colliding with them deducts a point. Warp Drive measures distance covered. Hitting an asteroid reduces your total points, so steer carefully. Lunar Lander tracks successful landings on the lunar surface, awarding one point per accurate touch down. All one-player games last 2 minutes and 16 seconds. Two-player games are twice as long, but you trade roles halfway through the game. Your score begins to flash when the timer hits 16 seconds remaining.

HOW TO PLAY

The flight controls change between game types, but you're usually in command of a star ship. In the two-player games of Star Ship and Lunar Lander, you take turns piloting a star ship and keeping the other player away from their objective: a command module in Star Ship and moon in Lunar Lander.

STAR SHIP

In one-player games, you guide your ship using the joystick and fire missiles by pressing the red button. The joystick acts like a flight stick (i.e., left and right move your ship left and right). Pushing up guides your ship toward the bottom of the screen, while pushing down causes your ship to climb toward the top of the screen.

In two-player games, the second player steers a Space Module, which moves in the same direction as the direction of the joystick. Avoid collisions and incoming missiles from the star ship. This time, though, the red button activates invisibility. The Space Module commander doesn't score points, but halfway through the game the players switch roles.

The window turns from blue to orange and the second player has a fresh 2:16 to beat the first player's score.

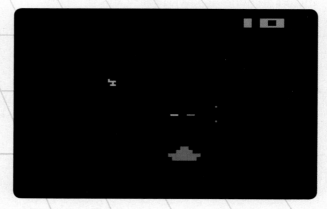

WARP DRIVE

Your space meter ticks away each parsec (a measure of space distance equal to 19.2 trillion miles) in the upper-right corner of the Space Window. You lose one parsec each time you collide with an asteroid.

LUNAR LANDER

You control the movement of the Lunar Lander with the joystick and fire retro rockets to land by pressing the red controller button. You score a point for each successful touch down on the surface of the moon. You lose a point if you collide with a meteor.

In two-player games, the second player controls the moon, which moves in the same direction as the joystick. Keep away from the Lunar Lander, but don't worry about meteors since you can't score when playing as the moon. Halfway through the game the players switch roles. The window turns from blue to orange and the second player has a fresh 2:16 to beat the first player's score.

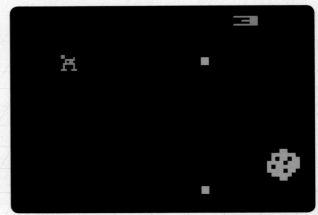

If the Lunar Lander or the Moon moves off the top, bottom, or sides of the Space Window, it will reappear at the opposite side. For example, should the Moon disappear from the top of the Space Window, it will reappear at the bottom.

DIFFICULTY OPTIONS

For Star Ship games, the difficulty switch in the A position decreases the power of your laser missiles. If you set the difficulty to the A position during Lunar Lander games, you must be right on target to score points. The difficulty switch has no effect in Warp Drive games.

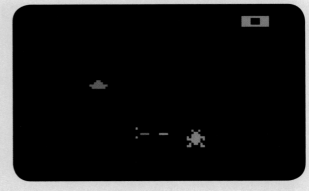

- ◆ In Star Ship and Warp Drive, the stars and your target reticle change color to indicate which enemies are approaching. In games with two enemies appearing at a time, the colors of both enemies will appear.

- ◆ When piloting the Space Module, only use invisibility when your opponent is about to fire at your module. If you can't see the Space Module, it's difficult to avoid nearby ships and asteroids.

- ◆ To get the best score in Warp Drive, keep the red button pressed for your entire run. You can't shoot anything (no weapons), so you must steer away from enemies and asteroids alike.

- ◆ In Lunar Lander, firing the retro rockets is essential for scoring. You can fly over the moon all day, but you won't earn a point until you touch down with a burst from the rockets.

"Has 17 games that look nice but are hard to get a handle on... Rated 4 [out of 10]"

-Video Magazine (Winter 1979)

GAME OPTIONS

GAME TYPE	GAME #	# PLAYERS	FEATURES
Star Ship	1	1	2X & AM
	2	1	AM
	3	1	FF & AM
	4	1	FF & 2X & AM
	5	2	
	6	2	AM
	7	2	FF & 2X & AM
	8	2	AM
	9	2	FF & AM
Warp Drive	10	1	AM
	11	1	2X & AM
Lunar Lander	12	1	
	13	1	AM
	14	1	FF & AM
	15	2	
	16	2	AM
	17	2	FF & AM

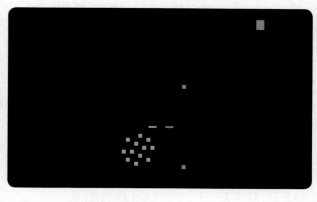

SCORING: STAR SHIP

OBJECT		POINT VALUE
Star Fighter		1
Flying Saucer		2
Space Robot		3
Space Module		2

FEATURES

The number and speed of space objects varies between games.
The other variable is the appearance of asteroids and meteors
that must be avoided, since your weapons are
ineffective against them.

DOUBLE OBJECTS (2X)
Enemy space objects appear two at a time.

FAST MOVING OBJECTS (FF)
Enemy objects move faster than normal.

ASTEROIDS/METEORS (AM)
Avoid the indestructible asteroids or meteors in the area.

- *Star Ship* was based on Atari's arcade game Starship 1.

- *Star Ship* was one of nine titles available when the Atari Video Computer System launched. The earliest cartridges listed a name and number: 03 Star Ship. It was also among the first titles dropped from Atari catalogs, vanishing partway through 1980.

- The Tele-Games version of *Star Ship* was named *Outer Space*.

- Before Atari settled on the name *Star Ship*, the game was titled "Space Mission". The change came after the initial promotional images were released, which caused some confusion for people looking to buy Space Mission!

STREET RACER

Race on a city street, or down a ski slope. Dodge oncoming cars, or fire at flying objects. "Crunch" numbers on a track or play a new game of catch called Scoop Ball. Variety is the name of this game!

ABOUT THE GAME

Street Racer was one of the launch titles for the Atari VCS/2600. Its multiple game modes (and those of its other launch titles) were routinely pushed as a value proposition for the console.

OBJECT OF EACH GAME

In one-player games, you race against the clock in an attempt to score as many points as possible within 2 minutes and 16 seconds.

During two, three and four player games, you compete against opponents to score the most points within 2 minutes and 16 seconds. Your score flashes on-screen during the final 16 seconds of game time.

Street Racer (Games 1 to 6): You're racing down the strip, avoiding other cars as they whip toward you.

Slalom (Games 7 to 12): Now you're on skis, swooshing through the downhill slalom gates.

Dodgem (Games 13 to 16): Steer cars and avoid oncoming objects.

Jet Shooter (Games 17 to 20): Pilot a plane, shooting down objects as they approach from above. If you miss, there's just a split second to avoid a crash.

Number Cruncher (Games 21 to 24): Steer motorcycles and run over numbers as they flash on-screen.

Scoop Ball (Games 25 to 27): Catch the object coming at you and then relay it to the next object.

HOW TO PLAY

As is the case in all the racing games, use the knob on the top of the controller to steer the vehicle on the playfield. The red button serves as the accelerator in Street Racer Slalom, Scoop Ball, and Number Cruncher. Use the red button as a forward thrust in Dodgem and to fire bullets in Jet Shooter.

STREET RACER

Avoid collisions and score points! One, two, three or four players each control one car on the track playfield. In one and two-player games, each player uses a separate vertical track. In three and four-player games, two players share one track.

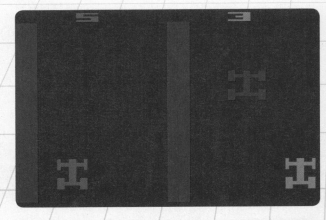

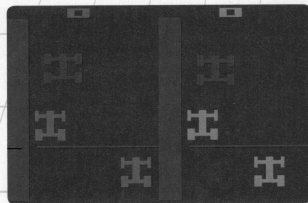

The Game Program that'll tell if you really should be out in the street driving. Controlling the action with your remote controller, steer your way through 27 different games and variations. Race against the clock or race against a friend. (Additional paddle controllers needed for 3 and 4 player games.)
Street Racer™ (game selections 1 to 6) You're racing down the strip, avoiding other cars as they who toward you.
Slalom (game selections 7 to 12) Now you're on skis, swooshing through the downhill slalom gates.
Dodgem™ (game selections 13 to 16) Steer cars to avoid oncoming objects.
Jet Shooter™ (game selections 17 to 20) Pilot a plane, shooting down objects as they come at you from above. If you miss, you only have a split second to get out of the way before they crash into you.
Number Cruncher™ (game selections 21 to 24) Steer motorcycles to run over numbers as they flash down the screen. Score the number hit.
Scoop Ball™ (game selections 25 to 27) First you catch the object coming at you. Then relay it to the next object.

STREET RACER™ GAME PROGRAM™

Each player tests his skill against computer-controlled cars. Use the knob on the controller to steer your vehicle around the oncoming cars heading straight for you! Press the red controller button to increase your speed.

Score one point for every car you pass. Your score, which appears at the top of the playfield, matches your car's color. Each game ends after 2 minutes and 16 seconds, or when a player or team scores 99 points. Your score will flash on-screen during the final 16 seconds of game time. Also, you'll hear the hum of the motors, crashes, and beeps when you score.

GAME 1

One player steers a car on a moving vertical track avoiding collisions and racing against a computer-controlled car.

GAME 2

Two players each steer a car on separate moving tracks avoiding collisions with computer-controlled cars that appear on the track one at a time.

GAME 3

Three players control one car and avoid collisions with computer-controlled cars that appear on the track one at a time. Two players share the right track and compete against one player on the left track.

GAME 4

Four players compete to avoid collisions with cars that appear one at a time. There are two players on a driving team, each sharing one track.

GAME 5

Two players each steer a car down separate tracks while avoiding computer-controlled cars that appear on the track two at a time.

GAME 6

In this game variation, four players compete to avoid collisions. Two computer cars head down the track at one time. There are two players on a driving team, each sharing one track.

SLALOM

Put on your skis and get ready for the treacherous slopes! One to four players control one set of skis. In one and two-player games, each player skis on his own private ski run. In three and four-player games, two players share a ski run.

Use the knob on the controller to steer through various gates. Press the red controller button to increase your speed down the slope. A player scores one point for every gate that is passed. If a player crashes into a gate, you only lose time—not points.

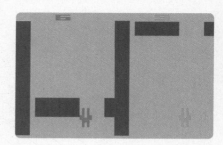

INCREASED DIFFICULTY
Slide the difficulty switch to the A position and you lose one point for every collision. In addition, the gates become narrower.

The color of your skis matches the score that appears at the top of the playfield. The game ends when one player scores 99 points, or after 2 minutes and 16 seconds. The scores will flash on-screen during the last 16 seconds of the game. You'll hear the swish and the beeps when passing through a gate. You'll also hear a sound when crashing.

GAME 7

One player skis down the right slope and passes through gates that appear one at a time on-screen. The left skier is your computer-controlled opponent.

GAME 8

Two players each have separate but identical runs down the slope. The gates appear on-screen one at a time.

GAME 9

The ski gates appear one at a time for three players who compete for points. Two players share the right side of the screen and compete against one player on the left side.

GAME 10

Four players race down the slope and through the gates to score points. Gates appear on-screen one at a time. Two players are on each ski team and share a run.

GAME 11

Two players compete for points by passing through gates that appear two at a time on the ski run.

GAME 12

Four players compete for points by passing through gates that appear two at a time on-screen. Two players are on each ski team and share a run.

DODGEM

Sharpen your driving reflexes and score points by avoiding oncoming obstacles.

Use the controller knob to steer your vehicle. Press the red controller button to accelerate; release the button and the car gradually slides toward the bottom of the track.

The goal is to move the car from the bottom of the track to the top while dodging oncoming obstacles. Score one point each time you complete the straightaway. Your car automatically returns to the bottom starting line after completing the track.

The score at the top of the playfield matches the color of your vehicle. The game ends when one player scores 99 points, or after 2 minutes and 16 seconds. The score will flash on-screen during the last 16 seconds of the game. You'll hear the motors hum, cars crash, and scores "beep."

GAME 13

One player races against the clock and tries to complete the track as many times as possible within 2 minutes and 16 seconds.

GAME 14

Two opposing players compete for points on separate vertical tracks while avoiding oncoming obstacles that appear on the track one at a time.

GAME 15

One player races against the clock and attempts to complete the track as many times as possible. Oncoming obstacles appear on the track two at a time.

GAME 16

Two opposing players compete for points on separate vertical tracks while avoiding oncoming obstacles that appear on the track two at a time.

JET SHOOTER

In this game variation, you're a fighter pilot. One or two players each control one fighter jet equipped with missiles. Each player has his or her own separate air space.

Use the controller knob to steer through the sky. Press the red controller button to fire missiles and destroy enemy aircraft approaching from the opposite direction.

Score one point for each enemy aircraft you destroy. With the difficulty switch set in the B position, you only lose time (not points) when you collide with an enemy jet. When set in the A position, you lose one point for each collision.

A game ends when one pilot scores 99 points, or after 2 minutes and 16 seconds.

The score will flash on-screen during the final 16 seconds of game time. You'll hear the missiles fire, crashes, and the hum of the engines.

GAME 17

One player guides the right jet through the skies while attempting to shoot down enemy jets that appear on-screen one at a time. The left jet is your computer-controlled opponent.

GAME 18

Two players each steer a jet in a private sky. Oncoming enemy jets appear one at a time.

GAME 19

One player steers a jet through the sky as enemy jets appear two at a time.

GAME 20

Two players each steer a jet as enemy jets appear in the sky two at a time.

NUMBER CRUNCHER

Got an appetite for numbers? One to four players each control one motorcycle that "crunches" numbers on the track.

In one and two-player games, each player drives up a vertical track. In three and four-player games, two players make up a motorcycle team and share the right track. During four-player games, two players use one track. Use the controller knob to steer your chopper down the track. Press the red controller button to accelerate.

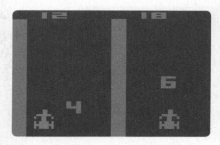

The goal is to run over the numbers (2, 4, 6) that appear on the track. A player scores the face value for each number hit. A player must run directly over the numbers with the nose of the chopper to score the points. An improperly aimed attempt will result in number collisions.

The color of the motorcycle matches the color of the score at the top of the track. Number Cruncher games end when a player scores 99 points, or after 2 minutes and 16 seconds. During the final 16 seconds, your score will flash on-screen. You'll hear the whine of the chopper engines and the crunch and crash of the numbers.

GAME 21

One player steers his motorcycle to "crunch" numbers that appear on the track one at a time.

GAME 22

Two players rumble down the tracks looking for numbers that appear two at a time.

GAME 23

Three players take a thrilling ride on the track, as numbers appear two at a time on-screen. Two players are on one motorcycle team and oppose one player.

GAME 24

Four players become a Number Cruncher motorcycle gang looking for numbers to squash on the track. Two players are on each motorcycle team and share one track. Numbers appear on-screen two at a time.

SCOOP BALL

The goal in Scoop Ball is to catch balls and deposit them into a computer scooper. A player uses a giant moving scooper to catch the balls. Two, three or four players each control one scooper. In two-player games, each player moves along a private track. Two players share the right track in three-player games; during four-player games, two players are on each track.

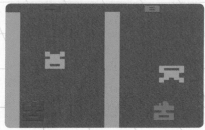

Use the controller knob to steer the scooper on the track. Press the red controller button to accelerate the scooper.

You score one point each time you catch a ball. Continue to catch balls until a computer-controlled scooper appears on-screen.

When you steer your scooper into the computer-controlled scooper, you score three points and deposit the ball (or balls) collected. If you crash before depositing your balls, you lose your chance to score.

THE SCOOPER
The scooper changes shape after you catch the first ball. After you deposit the balls, the scooper returns to its original shape.

Your scooper is color coordinated with the score at the top of the track. A game ends when a player scores 99 points, or after 2 minutes and 16 seconds. During the final 16 game seconds, your score flashes on the scoreboard. You'll hear crashes, the scooper motors, the scoop, and the deposit of the balls.

GAME 25

Two opposing players compete for balls and computer-controlled scoopers that appear on the track two at a time.

GAME 26

Three players compete for points. Two players are on one scooper team and share the right track.

GAME 27

Four players compete for points. Two players are on each scooper team, as balls and computer-controlled scoopers appear two at a time.

DIFFICULTY OPTIONS

Slide the difficulty switch from B to A and you lose one point for each collision that occurs during the game.

FUN FACTS!

As the quoted review suggests, *Street Racer* has encountered trouble standing the test of time in the eyes of some. Even its programmer, Larry Kaplan, has expressed a desire to give the game a smoother scrolling playfield to enhance gameplay.

SURROUND

Trap your opponent before he traps you!

You control a moving wall, strategically forcing your opponent's moving wall into a position where it can't move in any direction. It's a game full of quickness, skill, and smarts.

ABOUT THE GAME

Surround's concept has been around seemingly forever; it would eventually be remade time and again in future games. However, *Surround* itself is also based on multiple 1970s games, such as Atari's *Dominos*, Gremlin's *Blockade*, and Meadow's *Bigfoot*.

OBJECT OF THE GAME

The basic objective is to surround your opponent, causing him to run out of space in which to move. At the same time, you must avoid running into anything. You can set up a blockade, force your opponent into a corner, or wander off and hope that your opponent runs into something on his own.

In the game variation Video Graffiti, it's more about having fun without the competitive edge. Video Graffiti actually allows you to draw on the screen!

HOW TO PLAY

Use the joystick controller to leave tracks on the playfield. The game automatically moves the blocks. You control the horizontal and vertical movement of the tracks with the joystick.

For example, move the joystick to the left to move the tracks to the left; move the joystick forward to continue the tracks of blocks up the field; move the joystick toward you to steer the tracks down the screen.

SCORING

You score one point when your opponent steers his leader block into another part of his track or your track. If you are playing a game that does not offer Wrap-Around, you can also score a point when your opponent collides with a playfield boundary. All games have a playfield boundary except games with the feature Wrap-Around.

SURROUNDED!
The most effective strategy is to surround your opponent's tracks with your own tracks.

The first player to score 10 points wins the games. The leader block of your track is color coordinated with the score at the top of the playfield. You'll hear the tracks zip across the playfield, collide with other tracks and "beep" when a player scores one point.

VIDEO GRAFFITI

Write a word. Draw a picture. One or two players use the joystick to control the movement and directions of the track. Push the joystick forward to create a vertical line from the bottom. Push the joystick to the right and the track moves horizontally to the right.

The track will move in the direction you move the joystick. If you don't move the joystick, no line will appear.

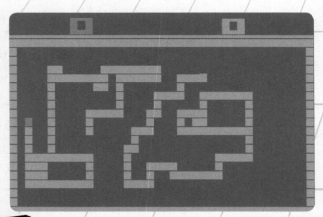

GAME OPTIONS

GAME SELECT BUTTON

Press the game select button to choose the game you wish to play. There are 14 games in total. The game number changes at the top-left corner of the screen when you press down the game select switch.

GAME RESET BUTTON

After choosing a game to play, press the game select button to start the game. Use the game reset switch to start a new game or reset a game in progress at any time.

GAME TYPE	GAME #	# PLAYERS	FEATURES
Surround	1	2	
	2	1	
	3	2	SU
	4	1	SU
	5	2	DM
	6	2	SU & DM
	7	2	SU & DM & ER
	8	2	WA
	9	2	SU & WA
	10	2	SU & DM & WA
	11	2	SU & DM & WA
	12	2	SU & DM & ER & WA
Video Graffiti	13	1-2	ER & WA
	14	1-2	DM & ER & WA

FEATURES

SPEED UP (SU)

Tracks increase in speed over time (listen for the gear shifts).

DIAGONAL MOVEMENT (DM)

Diagonal movement allowed in addition to vertical and horizontal movement.

ERASE (ER)

Pressing the red controller button interrupts laying tracks. Your leader block continues to move, but will not leave behind tracks while the button is pressed.

WRAP-AROUND (WA)

Moving off the edge of the screen moves your leader block to the opposite side of the screen.

DIFFICULTY OPTIONS

In all game variations of *Surround*, beginner players should slide the switch to the B position. This position prevents players from backing onto their previous track block.

During one-player games against the computer, slide the left difficulty switch to the B position to make playing against the computer much easier; slide it to the A position to play against a tougher computer competitor. There is no difficulty factor in Video Graffiti games.

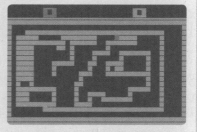

- Players can overlap each other; they just can't hit each other's tracks. Use this to your advantage!

- Look for ways to close your opponent into your track or theirs even if you're far away.

- Games with Diagonal Movement, Erase and Wrap-Around are powerful tools. Use them to your advantage to catch the opponent off guard.

FUN FACTS!

Five years after the game's release, the movie *Tron* would feature this game's very concept using breathtaking special effects courtesy of light-bearing motorcycles.

BASKETBALL

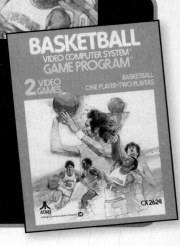

Visualize that you are sitting at center court about six rows back. The bottom of the playfield is the near side of the court. The goals are in the center of the two end lines, while the top of the court is the side farthest away.

So you press him hard. Force a wild shot. Leap high for the rebound. Then make a spectacular break for the winning baskets.

Use the difficulty switches to arrange great matches between pros and double dribblers.

Don't let those tall skinny people have all the fun!

ABOUT THE GAME

As one of the first sports games to release on the Atari, it was an extremely momentous time for gaming. Although the game is somewhat simple in its gameplay, having a video game that allowed you to play something that you only knew as a physical sport was mind-boggling at the time.

What made *Basketball* stand apart from other similar games was the way that the player shot the ball. Even to this day, there are games with even less complex controls. Your success at making a shot depended on how long you held the fire button in relation to your player's distance from the basket

Although not readily apparent on the surface, there is a lot of strategy involved in playing *Basketball* on the Atari 2600. Playing defense against your opponent is much more important than being the best shot on the court. Obviously, being a good shot is important but it's also crucial to keep the ball out of your opponent's hands by either stealing the ball or blocking a shot.

OBJECT OF THE GAME

Score more points than your opponent during one four-minute period.

GAME OPTIONS

GAME 1 (2-PLAYER GAME)

In this version, you play against an opponent. To make your game more interesting, try playing two four-minutes halves and change joystick controllers at halftime!

The closer the score, the better the computer's defense gets, plus the computer will unleash more offensive moves. Don't let the computer get more than an 8-point lead; once the score gets closer, the computer's defense will get stronger.

GAME 2 (1-PLAYER GAME)

Using the right joystick controller, it's you against the computer. Note that the computer is programmed to play tougher as the game progresses.

FUN FACTS!

• When playing against the computer, hold the right controller joystick's Fire button to freeze the computer player in its tracks and steal the ball! It's also possible to control the computer using the second joystick controller.

• *Basketball* won the 1980 "Most Innovative Game" Arcade Award from Electronic Games.

HOW TO PLAY

CONTROLLER ACTION

Moving your joystick controller in various directions moves your player around the court.

The player with the ball will dribble automatically, always facing in the direction of the goal. The defending player, on the other hand, will always face the player dribbling the ball.

To shoot, press the red controller button. This causes your player to stop dribbling and hold the ball over his head. When the controller button is released, the player will shoot. When a shot is taken as the ball is over a player's head, it results in a long, high-arching shot. When a shot is taken when the ball is held low in front of the player, it results in a short, easy shot. Every shot will always go toward the correct player's goal.

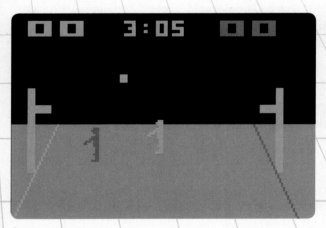

To defend against an opponent's shot, place a player between the ball and the basket. When the shooter releases the ball, depress your red controller button to make your player jump in an attempt to block the shot and recover the ball. You can only block a shot when the ball is in its upward arc. Note there is no "goaltending" in this game.

To steal the ball, put your player's feet even with your opponent's feet while he's dribbling the ball. When the ball leaves your opponent's hand while dribbling, take the ball and race toward your own basket. Stealing the ball gets much easier with practice and becomes an integral part of any defensive strategy.

GAME DIFFICULTY

When the difficulty is set in the B position, your player moves quicker from one basket to the other compared to the A position. That said, a beginning player playing the game with the difficulty set to the B position will be able to better defend and will be outrun his opponent.

NUMBER OF PLAYERS

There are two options and the difference lies between the two game variants. Choosing to either play against the computer or another player.

SCORING

In both 1-player and 2-player games, the scoring works exactly the same. During each of the four-minute halves, the goal it to score more points than your opponent. Each made basket results in two points.

Tips & Tricks

◆ The most important strategy is always staying in front of your opponent in order to disrupt a potential shot or steal the ball.

BREAKOUT

Smash your way through a multi-layer wall of bricks. The first few bricks are easy. But the closer you come to breaking out, the tougher it gets.

BREAKOUT™
VIDEO COMPUTER SYSTEM
GAME PROGRAM™
12 VIDEO GAMES BREAKOUT • BREAKTHRU ONE PLAYER TO FOUR PLAYERS

CX 2622

ABOUT THE GAME

Steve Jobs of Apple fame became Atari's 40th employee in 1974, working at the fledgling company as an hourly technician. He left Atari for a yearlong hiatus to India, returning to work with a shaved head and traditional Indian attire. Atari had already scored big with its arcade version of *Pong* and was about to repeat its success with the home version through a lucrative deal with Sears. Jobs, now a night-shift engineer thanks in part to his eccentricities and inability to relate to many of his co-workers, was asked to create a prototype for a single-player, vertical *Pong* variant called *Breakout*.

Unfortunately, the technology required to create a *Breakout* machine would tear into Atari's profits, so the company wanted a design that used as few chips as possible. Faced with such a difficult engineering challenge, Jobs sought the help of his old friend, Steve Wozniak. Then head of Atari, Nolan Bushnell, claims company management was hoping for this anyway.

Previously, Atari had witnessed Wozniak's impressive, self-built home *Pong* clone, but failed to woo him away from his position at technology giant Hewlett-Packard. Nevertheless, Wozniak, a fan of both Atari arcade games and engineering challenges, came to his friend's rescue. He completed the bulk of the work in only four days with an efficient design that used far fewer chips than any other Atari arcade game at the time. Atari's engineers were impressed and Jobs received a nice payout and bonus—most of which he famously kept for himself. Unfortunately, Wozniak's design was so efficient that it proved difficult to manufacture, so Atari went with an alternate design that replicated the experience, but used more than double the number of chips. Despite its somewhat tortured development, the game still proved irresistibly fun upon its spring 1976 release and was another big hit for Atari.

While the original arcade machine utilized a black-and-white monitor with strips of colored cellophane covering where the bricks were displayed, Brad Stewart's port for the Atari 2600 made excellent use of the platform's superior color hardware. Combined with the Atari 2600's excellent paddle controllers (which matched the arcade's controls), the cartridge version of *Breakout* proved to be a superior conversion.

OBJECT OF THE GAME

The first player (or team) to completely destroy both walls or score the most points after playing five balls wins the game. To score the maximum number of points, 864, you must destroy both walls.

At the end of two-team games, the playfield of both teams (or players) will flash on and off the screen. That way, players can compare scores. Begin a new game and create a new brick wall by pressing the reset button.

In other games, you must rely on the speed of your game skill. A timer records the cumulative minutes and seconds of each turn during a game. The team or player who destroys both walls with five balls in the least amount of time wins the game.

HOW TO PLAY

Use the controller to move the paddle across the bottom of the screen. Using the paddle, hit the ball into the wall. Each time the ball hits a brick, the brick disappears and you score points.

A player or team receives five balls per game. When you miss a ball with your paddle, the ball disappears from the screen. Press the red controller button to serve another ball until all five balls have been played.

When a team or player destroys the first brick wall, a second brick wall automatically appears on-screen. Continue to hit the bricks and score more points.

ONE-PLAYER GAMES

Using the controller, one player attempts to destroy both walls using five balls. Or, a player can win by scoring the maximum number of points, 864.

TWO-PLAYER GAMES

Two players take turns hitting the wall. Each player receives five balls and a brick wall that appears during a player's turn. One player continues to hit a ball into the wall until he misses the ball. When that happens, the opponent's wall appears on-screen. The opponent then takes his turn hitting the ball into the wall. The first player to destroy two walls, or score the most points after playing five balls, wins the game.

THREE-PLAYER GAMES

Two players act as a team and play against a one-player team. Just as in two-player games, the two teams take turns hitting the ball. Each team receives five balls and a separate brick wall. When one team misses the ball, the opposing team's wall appears and play begins. The first team to destroy a wall, or score the most points after playing five balls, wins the game.

FOUR-PLAYER GAMES

With two players on each team, these games are played just like two- and three-player games. The first team to destroy a wall, or score the most points after playing five balls, wins the game.

When a team or player destroys the brick wall, a new brick wall automatically appears on-screen. If any bricks still remain on-screen after five balls are played, begin a new game and create a new brick wall by pressing the reset button.

> In games with two-players on each team, each player controls a paddle that only moves across half the playfield.

TIMED GAMES

Some games rely on speed scores instead of point scores to win. For these game variations, a timer replaces the scoreboard in the upper-left corner. The objective is to destroy the wall as quickly as possible. The timer counts the seconds as you attempt to break your own record in one-player games. In two-, three-, and four-player games, the mission is to destroy the wall with five balls in less time than your opponent.

INVISIBLE GAMES

It's the same *Breakout* action, except this time it's in the dark! The wall is invisible until you hit a brick with the ball. When this occurs, you score points and the entire wall lights up.

PADDLE

Each player uses a standard paddle controller to move the paddle horizontally across the bottom of the play field. With the paddle, a player hits the ball into the wall.

SCOREBOARD/TIMER

Depending on the game variation, a scoreboard or timer will appear in the left corner.

Scoreboard: Some games determine winners using only point scores. During these game variations, each player's score appears in this position. Scores are determined by the bricks hit during a game.

Timer: Instead of determining the winner using the point value of bricks, some games feature a timer in the upper-left corner.

Your mission during these games is to destroy the walls in as little time as possible. The timer tracks the cumulative minutes and seconds of each turn.

THE GREAT ESCAPE

Smash your way through a multi-layer wall of bricks. The first few bricks are easy. But the closer you come to breaking out, the tougher it gets. Maybe the ball will speed up suddenly. Or take off at an insane angle.

Breakout™ may be the most addictive video game ever invented. The more you play, the more you love it. And the better you get. So when you have mastered one variation, you can try one of the 47 others. And start all over again.

Breakout™ (game variations 1 to 36) One to four players bust bricks under varied conditions. Challenge gravity, time, funny paddles, and invisible bricks.

Breakthru (game variations 37 to 48) Knock a hole through the wall in one shot. Fast, exciting variations for one to four players.

BREAKOUT™ GAME PROGRAM™

NUMBER OF PLAYERS/ TEAM NUMBERS

In this playfield position, two numbers will appear at different times during the game.

Number of Players: After selecting the game variation, you must indicate the number of players. Press Select until the number of players appears. For example, when the number 3 appears, the computer is set for a three-player game.

Team Number: The team that is currently hitting the ball is designated by a Team Number. In one-player games, the number 1 will always appear in this position. In two-player games, each player is designated by the numbers 1 or 2. In three- or four-player games, the teams are referred to as teams 1 or 2. When your team number appears, it's your turn to score.

BALLS/GAME NUMBERS

In this position, two numbers will appear at different times during the game.

GAME NUMBER

Before play begins, select the game variation you want to play by using the Select button. The number that appears refers to the game you will play.

The cartridge box art for the original release of Breakout. Later releases featured the same image as found on the front of the box.

BALLS

After pressing Reset, play action can begin. The number 5 appears in this playfield position and refers to the five balls you or your team can serve. Throughout the game, the number will reflect the number of balls that remain.

SCORING

BRICK WALL

COLOR	POINTS
Red	7 points
Orange	7 points
Yellow	4 points
Green	4 points
Aqua	1 point
Blue	1 point

There are six rows of bricks. The brick's color determines the number of points.

CONTROLLER ACTION

ACTION	PERFORM
To serve the ball	Press the red controller button to make the ball appear.
To move the paddles	To move the paddles across the playfield, turn the controller knob. Turn it clockwise to move the paddle to the right; turn it counterclockwise to move the paddle to the left.
To steer the balls	Some Breakout and Breakthru games feature steerable balls. In these games, turn the control knob clockwise to move the ball to the right; turn it counterclockwise to move the ball to the left.
To catch the ball	Some Breakout and Breakthru games feature catch. When the ball makes contact with your paddle, press the red controller button. Continue to press the button and the ball will remain on the paddle, allowing you more time to carefully aim your shots. To release the ball, release the red controller button.

DIFFICULTY OPTIONS

Change the difficulty from B to A and your paddle is reduced to half size.

FUN FACTS!

• Apple co-founder Steve Wozniak has stated that his work on the arcade version of *Breakout* was influential in his design of the legendary Apple II computer, including its color graphics commands, circuitry for paddle controllers, and speaker for sound. He even made one of the countless *Breakout* clones, *Little Brick Out*, for the Apple II.

• Atari released *Video Pinball* in 1977, a standalone console with *Pinball*, *Basketball*, and *Breakout* games built-in. The console was based on Atari's single chip 011500-11/C011512-05 "Pong-on-a-chip" hardware, which allowed for a relatively impressive ball-and-paddle game feature-set, including color.

• For its Sears Tele-Games release, *Breakout* was known as *Breakaway IV*.

GAME OPTIONS

BREAKOUT GAMES

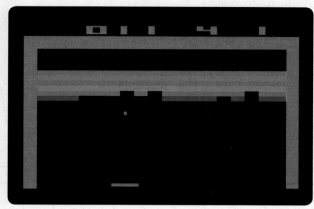

Breakout game 1.

GAME NUMBER	DESCRIPTION
1	Using a controller, players attempt to smash their way through the wall and score points.
2	This game features steerable balls so you can make every hit count.
3	Take a breather. This game features catch, which gives you time to use strategy.
4	Don't blink. The only time you'll see your Breakout wall is when the ball hits a brick. The rest of the time you're playing in the dark!
5	The pressure is on! The time at the top of the playfield will record the time it takes to complete a Breakout.
6	The timer provides the suspense. The steerable balls provide some of the strategy moves you'll make during this game.
7	How long does it take? The time in this game will tick away the seconds as you aim your balls with catch.
8	The wall lights up only when you hit a brick. Then you're playing in the dark again as the timer records your game time.

BREAKTHRU GAMES

Breakthru is played the same way as Breakout games. The only difference is the ball action. Once the ball hits a brick, the ball continues to penetrate the wall, hitting more bricks and scoring more points.

Breakthru game 9.

GAME NUMBER	DESCRIPTION
9	POW! POW! POW! Make a direct hit on a brick and the ball continues to travel through the wall in this basic Breakthru.
10	Steerable missiles increase your control over the ball during this fast game.
11	Slow down the action with catch in this game variation.
20	The Breakthru wall only appears when you hit a brick. Any other time and it's invisible.

GAME TYPE	GAME #	FEATURES
Breakout	1	
	2	ST
	3	CA
	4	IN
Timed Breakout	5	
	6	ST
	7	CA
	8	IN
Breakthru	9	
	10	ST
	11	CA
	12	IN

FEATURES

STEERABLE (ST)

You have limited control over the ball. Turn the control knob clockwise to move the ball to the right. Turn the control knob counterclockwise to move the ball to the left.

CATCH (CA)

To catch the ball, press the red button on your controller when the ball touches your paddle. As long as you keep the button pressed, the ball sticks to your paddle. This allows you to position the ball for more accurate shots at the bricks.

INVISIBLE (IN)

The wall of bricks remains invisible until the ball touches a brick.

- Be proactive! Follow the path of the ball with your paddle to have the best chance at returning it.

- Where the ball hits your paddle in one of its five sections determines the angle of return. Use this to your advantage when targeting those last few bricks.

- When the ball makes contact with the center section of the paddle, the ball will jump.

- The ball bounces off each paddle section at progressively smaller angles after the third, seventh, and eleventh hit. After the twelfth hit, the angle returns to its original size.

- The ball will speed up after the twelfth consecutive hit or when the ball hits any brick in the top three rows.

- For a great way to practice, choose any of the catch (CA) games and begin play. After catching your last ball, push the Select button and then release the ball. The game should continue in its demonstration mode with no points scored, but with unlimited balls.

FLAG CAPTURE

The computer has hidden a flag in some obscure sector of the map. It's up to you, or your opponent, to capture it first.

Strategy is the key.

You'll send out explorers to gather clues. Sometimes they'll unearth numbers or arrows. Then you'll know how far away or in which direction the flag is buried. Or, sometimes, your explorers may dig up bombs and get blown off the map!

FLAG CAPTURE
VIDEO COMPUTER SYSTEM™
GAME PROGRAM™
10 VIDEO GAMES
FLAG CAPTURE™
ONE PLAYER·TWO PLAYERS

CX 2644

ABOUT THE GAME

Published in 1978, *Flag Capture* was part of the second round of 11 games for the Atari VCS and developed by Atari's Jim Huether. Flag Capture was loosely based on capture-the-flag and, according to Huether, received a mixed reaction from players. The relatively simple graphics along with more complicated levels kept some players from enjoying it. On the other hand, Huether says, the game developed a cult following of gamers who loved the competitive aspect of the two-player games.

OBJECT OF THE GAME

Each player controls an explorer. The object of the game is to find the flag using your explorer. The first player's explorer starts in the upper-left corner square; the second player's explorer starts in the lower-right corner square.

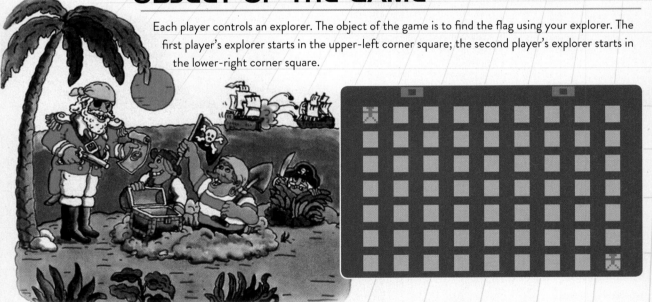

HOW TO PLAY

Explorers can move from square to square. During your turn, you can move your explorer to any square position by using the joystick to move the explorer up, down, left, right, or in any diagonal direction.

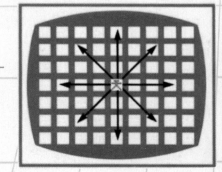

> Your explorer cannot move to a square occupied by an opponent's explorer.

When you are satisfied with the position of your explorer, press the red controller button. After doing so, one of the following objects will appear on the square.

A DIRECTION CLUE

An arrow may appear that will point to the direction of the flag. The following images show examples of Direction Arrows. The shaded area refers to the location of the flag.

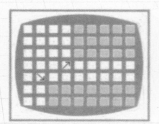 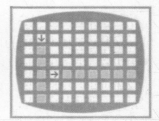

A NUMBER CLUE

A number may appear that will refer to the distance between your explorer and the flag. For example, if the number 2 appears, the flag will be somewhere on the perimeter of a two-square radius. The following image shows an example of a Number Clue. The shaded area refers to the possible location of the flag.

A BOMB

A trap has been set and you fall for it. A bomb explodes under your explorer. It's time to begin again at your starting square.

THE FLAG

Congratulations! You've found the flag.

DIFFICULTY OPTIONS

In Two-Player Solo games (games in which players attempt to score the lowest number of points), you get one point for each flag when the difficulty button is in the B position. In the A position, you score two points for each flag.

In Two-Player Free-For-All games, the moving action of your explorer is slowed down when the difficulty button is in the A position.

GAME OPTIONS

GAME TYPE	GAME #	# PLAYERS	FEATURES
Free for All	1	2	SF
	2	2	SF
Double Two-Player	3	2	MF
	4	2	WR
	5	2	SF
Solo Two-Player	6	2	MF
	7	2	WR
	8	1	SF
Timed (75 sec.)	9	1	MF
	10	1	WR

FEATURES

From a wandering flag to timed rounds, Flag Capture offers a variety of game options to keep things interesting.

FREE-FOR-ALL

Both players start moving their explorers across the maze simultaneously. There is no need to take turns. Pay attention to your opponent's clues if at all possible. The first player to find the flag scores a point.

DOUBLE TWO-PLAYER

You and your opponent take turns moving your explorers to uncover clues. The first player to find the flag scores one point.

SOLO TWO-PLAYER

In this variation, you continue to take turns until the flag is found. Next, it's your opponent's turn to find the flag. The object is to score the lowest number of points. You score one point each time you press the red controller button and receive a clue.

STATIONARY FLAG (SF)

The location of the flag remains the same throughout the game.

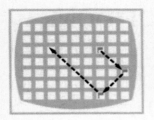

MOVING FLAG - WALL (MF)

Each time you take a turn without finding the flag, the flag moves one square and it continues to move in the same direction until it is found. When the flag encounters the edge of the playing field, it will bounce off the wall in relation to the direction it was traveling.

MOVING FLAG - WRAPAROUND (WR)

Each time you take a turn without finding the flag, the flag moves one square. The flag continues to move in the same direction until it is found. When the flag encounters the edge of the playing field, it will move to the opposite side in relation to the direction it has been traveling.

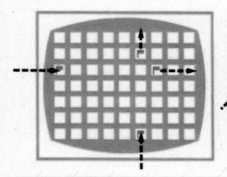
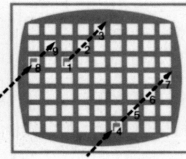

Moves 1-3:

The flag moves vertically off the top side and reappears at position 4 on the bottom side. The flag has theoretically traveled one square up and over.

Moves 4-7:

The flag moves horizontally off the right side and reappears at position 8 on the left side. The flag has theoretically traveled one square up and over.

SCORING

You score one point for each flag you find during Free-For-All and Double Two-Player games. The first player to score 15 points wins the game.

During Two-Player Solo games, you score the number of turns it takes to find the flag. For example, if you need six clues or turns to find the flag, your score is six. The first player to score 75 points loses the game. In timed one-player games, you score one point for each time you find the flag. You race against the clock to score as many points as possible in 75 seconds.

In two-player games, the second player's score appears in the upper-right playfield corner, while the first player's score appears in the upper-left corner.

In one-player games, the time appears in the upper-right corner of the playfield. In addition, you use the left controller and the score appears in the upper-left playfield corner.

FOOTBALL

This four-on-four football game focuses on high scoring touchdowns and defensive safeties. Field goals are not included, so go for the big score in this two-player game!

ABOUT THE GAME

The game's packaging featured football players in helmets and pads, but the appeal of Atari's *Football* is that it resembles the sort of pick up football game played in sandlots and backyards: four-on-four games played on a field nowhere near 100 yards long. What qualifies someone as an eligible receiver on offense? Does it matter? Everyone go deep!

The games may not have been pretty (the resemblance to football at times was superficial at best), but nothing matched the excitement from those plays where everything went exactly as planned. What greater joy was there than watching the shocked expression on an opponent's face after you scored the go-ahead touchdown or picked off their last-ditch pass and sealed your victory? That feeling wasn't diminished because it happened in in front of the television set.

OBJECT OF THE GAME

Score more points than your opponent.

HOW TO PLAY

The game clock at the top-center of the playfield begins counting down from 5:00. The clock counts down while the ball is live and stops between plays. The number at top-left is the orange player's score, while the number at top-right is the white player's score.

The small arrow under the game clock points to the team with possession of the ball. The number to the left of the white player's score is the down indicator. The question mark (?) beneath each score is a reminder to program your play; it disappears after doing so. The play automatically begins seconds after both players have entered a play formation.

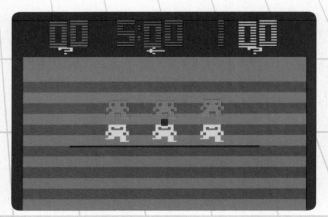

The left player's orange team begins on offense and drives toward the goal line at the bottom of the screen. The right player's white team begins on defense. On offense, the white team drives toward the goal line at the top of the screen.

The offensive player has four downs to get the ball past the first down marker, which appears as a dark blue line on-screen. When the offense moves the ball past the first down marker, they receive another four downs. After scoring or punting, your opponent receives the ball and becomes the offensive team.

To tackle an opposing player, move one of your players into the opponent's ball carrier. If your opponent attempts a pass, you can intercept it by moving one of your players into the ball's path.

The offensive team scores a touchdown (seven points) by moving the ball past the opponent's goal line. The defensive team can score a touchdown by intercepting an offensive team's pass and moving the ball past the offensive team's goal line. If a player gets tackled behind his own goal line, the result is a safety (two points). After a safety, the team that scored the safety is awarded possession of the ball near midfield.

CALLING PLAYS

There are five offensive plays and five defensive plays.

The offensive plays are:

◆ Split Left

◆ Tight Right

◆ Split Right

◆ Tight Left

◆ Punt

The defensive plays are:

◆ Wide Left

◆ Tight Right

◆ Wide Right

◆ Tight Left

◆ Deep

Left and right refer to the side of the television screen as you face it, so the orange team will move to its right despite the play stating it goes left.

The first word in each play (Tight and Split/Wide) indicates how your linemen set up. Tight means your players are essentially shoulder to shoulder. Split and Wide mean there's a gap between the center and the linemen on both sides.

The second word in each play (Left and Right) provides two pieces of information. First, it indicates which side of the formation your quarterback or defensive back lines up before the snap. Second, your blockers will push in that direction.

Push up on the joystick to call Split Left (offense) or Wide Left (defense). Push right on the joystick to call Tight Right. Push down on the joystick to call Split Right (offense) or Wide Right (defense). Push left on the joystick to call Tight Left. Press the red button to call Punt (offense) or Deep (defense).

DEFENSIVE PLAYS

Right and left refers to how the teams are viewed on the playfield.

1 WIDE LEFT
2 TIGHT RIGHT
3 WIDE RIGHT
4 TIGHT LEFT
5 DEEP

C015739-25 Rev. 1   Printed in U.S.A.

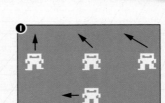

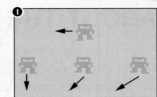

Split Left/Wide Left

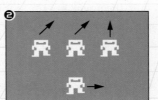

Tight Right

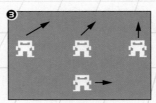

Split Right/Wide Right

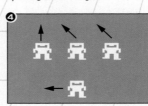

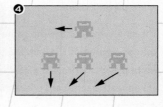

Tight Left

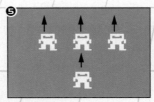

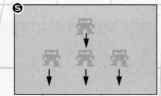

Punt/Deep

DIFFICULTY OPTIONS

When placed in the A position, your players cannot move from side to side as quickly as in the B position. This handicaps a more experienced player.

GAME OPTIONS

All three games in *Football* are designed for two players.

For Game 1, on offense you control the player possessing the ball and the flight of the ball during a pass or punt. After a completed pass, control automatically switches to the player who catches the pass. On defense, you control the defensive line as a unit unless you press the red button, which switches control to the defensive back.

In Game 2, players not under your control follow the play you selected exactly as programmed.

After you choose a play in Game 3, you have no control over the players. On offense, you only control when the ball is passed, but otherwise can't move players or influence the flight of the ball in the air.

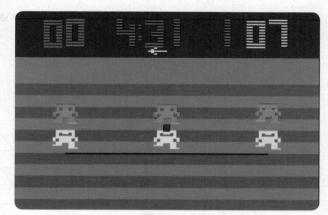

One design feature that set apart Atari's *Football* from other games of the time was setting up the field with goal lines at the top and bottom of the screen. Almost every other football game was a side-scroller.

What is the screen flicker issue mentioned in "What the Critics Had to Say"? Before play begins, the three linemen on each side were all visible. Once the play began, however, the Atari system couldn't display eight players on-screen at the same time—only four players (two from each team) appeared at the same time. The flickering was due to the players rapidly appearing and vanishing while the ball was live.

- The linemen set up (Tight or Wide) as soon as both plays are selected. The quarterback and defensive back remain invisible until the snap, which keeps your exact call a secret until the ball is in play.

- Keep things tight. Choosing a wide formation on defense gives your opponent big holes to run or pass through. Wide formations on offense leave your quarterback vulnerable to a hard charge and you can't pass the ball over the heads of approaching linemen.

- If you manage to break through the defensive line, run at an angle away from the defensive back to gain more yards before being tackled.

- Unless you play against someone unfamiliar with the game, completing a pass for more than a few yards was typically more luck than skill. You can't lob the ball over defenders and the ball doesn't travel faster than the defense can run. You can guide the ball toward the receiver, but you won't gain control over the receiver until he catches the ball. With a touch of the red button, the defender instantly switches from controlling the players rushing the quarterback to the defensive back, providing two chances for an interception.

- Only the defensive back can field a punt. If your defensive back can't get to a punt quickly enough, though, the ball will stop on its own. You take over on offense where the ball comes to rest.

HANGMAN

HANGMAN™
VIDEO COMPUTER SYSTEM
GAME PROGRAM
9 VIDEO GAMES 1ST GRADE TO HIGH SCHOOL
ONE PLAYER • TWO PLAYERS
CX 2662

You have just one guess left and one letter to go. Get it right and win. Guess wrong and the computer makes a monkey out of you.

The nine game variations help little people earn big and big people earn a little. You also get to drive one another crazy.

ABOUT THE GAME

Hangman comes from a popular word game usually played with pencil and paper. The game features a somewhat macabre depiction of a person hanging from a gallows. The game master draws the head, body, legs, and arms for incorrect guesses. The Atari version softens the concept of the traditional Hangman game by instead using a monkey hanging by its arm.

Don't let this game make a monkey out of you when you test your word skills! Line spaces appear at the bottom of the screen. One space equals one letter of the Hangman Word. If there are six spaces, for example, the Hangman Word could be LUXURY.

OBJECT OF THE GAME

The object of the game is to complete the Hangman Word within 11 incorrect letter guesses. Games 1, 2, 3, and 4 are one-player games in which you compete against the computer. During Games 5, 6, 7 and 8, two players compete to guess the Hangman Word first within 11 incorrect guesses. The first player to score five points is the winner. In Game 9, one player composes the Hangman Word for an opponent to guess.

HOW TO PLAY

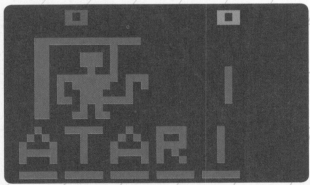

The Hangman playfield.

Use the joystick to select the alphabet letter you choose to enter into the computer. Letters of the alphabet appear one at a time on the right side of the screen.

Push the joystick forward to cycle through the alphabet letters from A to Z. Pull the joystick towards you to cycle through the letters in reverse order from Z to A. When the letter you want appears on-screen, release the joystick and press the red controller button to enter the letter.

◆ If the letter you select is in the Hangman Word, it appears in the appropriate blank (or blanks) and that letter is removed from the alphabet cycle.

◆ If the letter you select is not in the Hangman Word, a part of the monkey appears in the upper-left corner of the screen and that letter is removed from the alphabet cycle.

If you don't complete the Hangman Word after 11 incorrect selections, the Hangman Word automatically appears in the spaces and the monkey is completed in the upper-left corner.

In one-player games, the number of games you win appears in the upper-left corner; the number of games you lose appears in the upper-right corner.

In two-player games, a player scores one point for completing the Hangman Word. The first player's score appears in the upper-left corner, while the second player's score is in the upper-right corner.

DIFFICULTY OPTIONS

When the difficulty is in the A position, a player has 20 seconds to select the next letter. When the difficulty is in the B position, there is no time limit.

GAME OPTIONS

Games 1, 2, 3 and 4 are one-player games against the computer. You score one point for every Hangman Word you complete, while the computer scores one point for each Hangman Word you do not complete.

GAME 1

One player competes against the computer that uses words from a first through third grade vocabulary.

GAME 2

One player competes against the computer that uses words from a first through sixth grade vocabulary.

GAME 3

Playing with words from a first through ninth grade level, one player competes against the computer.

GAME 4

Words from a first through high school vocabulary are used for competition between one player and the computer.

Games 5, 6, 7 and 8 are two-player games against the computer. After you select the game vocabulary, you and your opponent take turns selecting alphabet letters to find the word generated by the computer. Both players together are allowed 11 incorrect selections. When you make a correct letter guess, you receive a consecutive turn. The first player to complete the Hangman Word scores one point and starts the next word. The first player to score five points wins the game.

GAME 5

Two players compete to complete the Hangman Word from a first through third grade vocabulary.

Although the name of the game is *Hangman*, the resulting image displayed when you fail to guess a word is a monkey hanging onto a bar by its hand.

GAME 6

Two players test their word skill with Hangman Words from a first through sixth grade vocabulary.

GAME 7

Words from a first through ninth grade vocabulary are used for competition between two players.

GAME 8

Two players compete using words from a first through high school vocabulary.

GAME 9

Now it's your turn to choose the Hangman Word! Instead of playing with a computer word, one player composes the Hangman Word with the joystick controller; the opposing player receives 11 guesses to complete the Hangman Word.

To enter your own Hangman Word into the computer, cycle through the alphabet letters on-screen while your opponent avoids looking at the screen. The Hangman Word may be between one and six letters.

If you want CAT to be the Hangman Word, cycle to the letter C with the joystick and enter it into the computer by pressing the red controller button. Repeat this process for the letters A and T. To enter the same letter in succession, cycle to the letter and enter it into the computer. Cycle off the letter and move back to the letter again. Now enter it into the computer and the letter appears a second time.

Two players take turns composing and completing the Hangman Word. You score one point when you complete the Hangman Word your opponent has submitted. The player who scores five points first is the winner.

◆ Start your letter guesses with vowels. These are the most commonly used letters and will usually give you a good start on guessing the word.

HOME RUN

Play a scaled-back, fast-paced version of baseball, America's pastime.

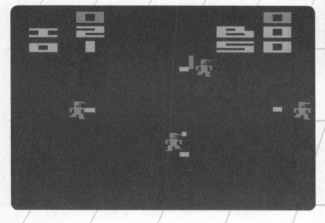

HIT AND RUN

Toss down the rosin sack and dig in at the batter's box. Thump your bat menacingly on home plate. Give the pitcher your steeliest stare. Now wait for your pitch.

Bring the crowd to its feet with a deep drive to center field. And doff your cap as you score the winning run.

Mix up your pitches. Keep the batter off balance. But be careful. Balls and strikes count. So do double plays, triple plays, force outs, tag outs, and sacrifice flies.

A flip of the difficulty switch and a bush league team can play major league ball in 8 dynamite games and variations. It's the great American video game.

HOME RUN™ GAME PROGRAM™

ABOUT THE GAME

Like many of the early Atari sports games, *Home Run* more closely resembled neighborhood games played with friends compared to organized games with nine players per side. That resemblance made *Home Run* a comforting game to play on relaxing summer days.

It can be argued that *Home Run* most resembled the always-popular wiffle ball, with pitches dancing in every direction at variable speeds. Just like wiffle ball, the primary action involves the pitcher trying to prevent the batter from making any contact with the ball.

Once you adjust to the speed of the fielders and the responsiveness of the joystick (expect to overrun everything when you start out), *Home Run* games tend to become low-scoring affairs with one team being shut out or kept to a single run. This is why *Home Run* is such an exciting game to play. One solid hit could mean the difference between winning and losing. As long as you have one out in your last at bat, you still have a chance to get that one hit.

OBJECT OF THE GAME

Score more runs than your opponent.

HOW TO PLAY

The left (blue) player is the visiting team and first to bat. In one-player games, the computer controls the blue team. The right team (red) is the home team and bats second.

The pitcher puts the ball into play after you press the red button. You control the speed (up for fast, down for slow) and direction (left and right) of the ball with the joystick.

Three strikes (either swinging or pitched) result in an out. Four balls (any pitch not struck and not thrown over the plate) result in a walk, where the batter advances to first base. A pitch that hits the batter also advances the batter to first base.

When the batter hits the ball, you take control of the outfielder(s). Balls that are hit in fair territory must be run down. A ball that goes into foul territory counts as a strike and the batter returns to home plate. Each hit ball is considered a

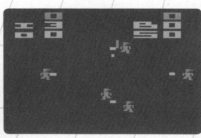

grounder, which means you must tag out base runners. You can either run into the batter, or run to the bag if a force play is in effect.

When you're up to bat, move the joystick from the neutral (center) position to any other position to swing. Running between bases is automatic. You must press the red button before reaching a base to stop the runner at that base. After three outs, the teams switch between fielding and batting. One inning consists of each team taking a turn at bat. Nine innings constitutes a complete game.

Each base runner who crosses home plate scores a run, as long as it happens before the third out of an inning. To hit a home run, the ball must cross directly over second base and reach the edge of the screen.

DIFFICULTY OPTIONS

The difficulty buttons control the speed of the outfielders and batted balls. In the A position, the outfielders and batted balls will move more slowly than in the B position.

GAME OPTIONS

1-PLAYER GAME #	2-PLAYER GAME #	# OF FIELDERS
1	5	1
2	6	2
3	7	3 (tight)
4	8	3 (wide)

Games 1 & 5

Games 2 & 6

Games 3 & 7

Games 4 & 8

FEATURES

In games with more than one fielder, only the fielder who scoops up the ball remains on-screen. The other fielders vanish instantly.

FUN FACTS!

The Tele-Games version of *Home Run* was simply named Baseball.

Home Run was one of the first sports-themed games for the Atari 2600 in which the player determined how many players were on the field. *Basketball*, *Football*, and *Championship Soccer* used fixed numbers of players and always fewer than the game they emulated.

Tips & Tricks

◆ Fielders are much faster than base runners. You have plenty of time to scoop up the ball and make an out. It's also possible to turn double plays, in which two outs are recorded on one play.

◆ A ball that reaches the edge of the screen (but doesn't cross over second base) ends the play. All runners stop at the next base they reach.

◆ Try to hit the ball down the third base line, which pulls defensive players away from your runner heading to first. When a runner advances to second, hit the ball down the first base line to protect the lead runner.

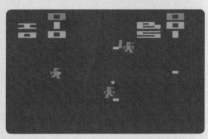

◆ Runners continue to advance until the ball is caught, even if the fielders are inches from the ball. You must press the red button before the runners reach the next base to make them stop. There's no way to return to the previous base!

◆ When playing defense, use a softly hit ball to your advantage. Let the runner try to advance a base, then pick up the ball and go for the out.

◆ The computer tends to focus on getting outs at second base. It concedes most of the others, unless there's an easy play. Once you get a runner on first, getting to second is another story. If you can move a runner to third with less than one out, though, there's a good chance to score that runner.

ATARI NEWS
What The Critics Had to Say

"*Home Run* can turn you into a regular Sandy Koufax, complete with singing curve, blazing fastball, and deceptive change-up. You can even hurl an authentic screwball if the spirit moves you."

Arcade Alley, *Video Magazine* (Summer 1979)

"Although even the most complex of the variations only puts three men on each team, the cartridge can still be enjoyed within its limitations."

- *Electronic Games* (July 1982)

MAZE CRAZE

You're a cop confronting danger and suspense as you and an opponent traverse across the city blocks. The first player to reach the exit on the right side of the maze wins the game.

Throughout the game you may encounter armed robbers, blockades, and other obstacles that prohibit you from finishing your best.

You'll hear the footsteps of cops, as well as sound effects when someone bumps into a dead end. And don't forget about the special sound effects when someone exits a maze! You'll also experience the unique sound that occurs when a robber captures a cop!

ABOUT THE GAME

More than a basic maze runner, *Maze Craze* was a successful game because Atari pushed the envelope. Incorporating an A.I. into a maze puzzle not only gives the game an interesting concept, it also gives it story and personality.

The game itself is subtitled "A Game of Cops n' Robbers," which gave gamers the opportunity to become police officers patrolling the streets for criminals up to no good. The mazes are randomly generated, so having a game you could literally get lost in gave this game an unlimited amount of replayability. Because of this, it really was like bringing the arcade back to your home.

OBJECT OF THE GAME

While playing as a cop on a beat, the objective is to exit the maze before your opponent while avoiding various obstacles and dangers in the city.

HOW TO PLAY

Each game mode offers different variations or features that can assist or hinder the player from successfully exiting the maze.

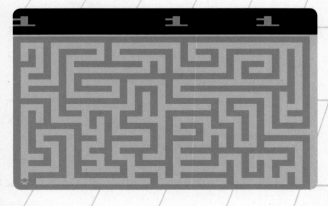

CAPTURE

You must become a hero and capture three robbers to win the game. To do so, move your cop toward a robber and make contact. During games that feature Capture, color-coded bars appear for each player at the top of the screen.

Each time you capture a robber, the appropriate bar disappears (i.e., blue bar = blue robber).

2, 3 OR 5 ROBBERS

Depending on the game type you're playing, two, three or five robbers appear on the right side of the screen. They will be lurking around corners waiting for you. If a robber touches you, it's game over!

WOUNDS

In this version, a cop gets paralyzed when touched by a robber. After a few short moments, the cop will regain strength and gradually return to normal speed.

I'M WOUNDED!
When wounded, a cop will continue to move in the same direction he was facing when the wound occurred. You can only change direction when he reaches the next intersection.

TERROR

Your cop cannot exit the maze until the robbers knock your opponent out of the maze.

BLOCKADE

Confuse your opponent by leaving a dead end (or blockade) in the maze. You opponent can go through the blockage, however, they can still serve as useful strategy. Press the red controller button to leave a blockade. When you set up a new blockade, though, the previous one will disappear.

AUTOMATIC PEEK

This is your way out of the darkness! During invisible mazes or blackouts, the computer flashes the complete maze on-screen every few seconds. Try to locate the way out before your opponent.

PLAYER PEEK

During invisible games, a player can peek at the complete maze by pressing the red controller button. The maze remains on-screen for a brief period of time.

SCOUTS

During invisible mazes, your cop has a partner (or scout) who moves ahead of him. Although the scout randomly leads the way, you are free to ignore any suggestions.

MORE OPTIONS

All 16 *Maze Craze* games have four visibility options. Games 6 and 7 feature additional game variations: Game 6 with visibility 1 is a 5 Robbers game variation, while Game 6 with all other visibilities is a Player Peek Game Variation. Game 7 with visibility 1 combines the 5 Robbers and Terror Game Variations. All other games allow you to choose your visibility options.

CONTROLLER ACTION

Each player controls a blue or red cop. Your cop's "beat" (or patrol territory) consists of a maze of city blocks. You must move your cop from the left side of the maze to the exit on the right side of the maze.

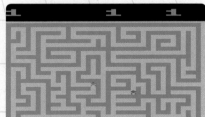

GAME DIFFICULTY

GROUP 1: NORMAL MAZE

◆ Middle third of the screen hidden from view, it flashes periodically.

◆ Middle half of the screen hidden from view, it flashes periodically.

◆ Entire screen hidden from view, it flashes periodically.

GROUP 2: TWO COPS

◆ If you get touched, you can't move until the other player gets caught or finishes the maze.

◆ The middle third of the screen is hidden from view until you press Fire.

◆ The middle half of the screen is hidden from view until you press Fire.

◆ The entire screen is hidden from view until you press Fire.

GROUP 3: THREE COPS

◆ The middle third of the screen is hidden from view until you press Fire.

◆ The middle half of the screen is hidden from view until you press Fire.

◆ The entire screen is hidden from view until you press Fire.

GROUP 4: THREE COPS

◆ You must touch all three before dashing to the exit; otherwise, you won't reach it.

◆ You must touch all three cops; the middle third of the screen is periodically hidden from view.

◆ You must touch all three cops; the middle half of the screen is periodically hidden from view.

◆ You must touch all three cops; the entire screen is periodically hidden from view.

GROUP 5: THREE COPS

◆ The middle third of the screen is constantly hidden from view.

◆ The middle half of the screen is constantly hidden from view.

◆ The entire screen is constantly hidden from view.

GROUP 6: FIVE COPS

◆ The middle third of the screen is hidden from view until you press Fire.

◆ The middle half of the screen is hidden from view until you press Fire.

◆ The entire screen is hidden from view until you press Fire.

GROUP 7: FIVE COPS

◆ The middle third of the screen is hidden from view, but you can press Fire to use tracers to exit the maze.

◆ The middle half of the screen is hidden from view, but you can press Fire to use tracers to exit the maze.

◆ The entire screen is hidden from view, but you can press Fire to use tracers to exit the maze.

GROUP 8: THREE COPS (MUST TOUCH)

◆ You can drop fake walls by pressing Fire.

◆ The middle third of the screen is hidden from view until you press Fire.

◆ The middle half of the screen is hidden from view until you press Fire.

- The entire screen is hidden from view until you press fire.

GROUP 9: TWO COPS
- The middle third of the screen is constantly hidden from view.
- The middle half of the screen is constantly hidden from view.
- The entire screen is constantly hidden from view.

GROUP 10: TWO COPS
- The middle third of the screen is constantly hidden from view.
- The middle half of the screen is constantly hidden from view.
- The entire screen is constantly hidden from view.

GROUP 11: THREE COPS
- The middle third of the screen is constantly hidden from view.
- The middle half of the screen is constantly hidden from view.
- The entire screen is constantly hidden from view.

GROUP 12: THREE COPS (MUST TOUCH)
- The middle third of the screen is periodically hidden from view.
- The middle half of the screen is periodically hidden from view.
- The entire screen is periodically hidden from view.

GROUP 13: TWO COPS
- If caught, only briefly stunned.
- The middle third of the screen is hidden from view until you press Fire.
- The middle half of the screen is hidden from view until you press Fire.
- The entire screen is hidden from view until you press Fire.

GROUP 14: THREE COPS (MUST TOUCH)
- The middle third of the screen is hidden from view until you press Fire.
- The middle half of the screen is hidden from view until you press Fire.
- The entire screen is hidden from view until you press Fire.

GROUP 15: THREE COPS
- The middle third of the screen is periodically hidden from view.

- The middle half of the screen is periodically hidden from view.
- The entire screen is periodically hidden from view.

GROUP 16: NORMAL MAZE
- Middle third of the screen is constantly hidden from view.
- Middle half of the screen is constantly hidden from view.
- Entire screen is constantly hidden from view.

NUMBER OF PLAYERS

There are two options and the difference lies between the two game variants: Choosing to either play against the computer or another player.

FEATURES

SPEED

How fast can your cop react to danger? The number at the top-left side of the playfield represents the speed at which cops and robbers travel:

- Medium; Fast; Slow; Calculatingly Slow

VISIBILITY

During some games, all or some of the city blocks may suffer blackouts. The top-right number represents the amount of the maze you can see during a blackout:

- Straightforward action with the entire maze visible throughout the game.
- A small portion of the maze is visible.
- Danger increases with a large portion of the maze invisible.
- The ultimate in suspense with the entire maze invisible.

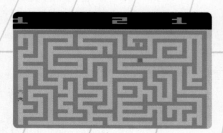

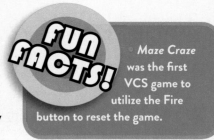

SCORING

There is no scoring in *Maze Craze*; you either beat your opponent or, like all criminals, you lose!

- The cops always stick to the same wall, which means they will always turn right or left when they reach a fork in their path, depending on the side of the closest wall.

NIGHT DRIVER

The road ahead is dark and winding. Better drive defensively. You know you're getting somewhere because the fence along the side of the road seems to keep moving. Don't get drowsy now. The longer you stay on the road, the higher your score. Watch out for those oncoming cars!

Keep your eyes peeled and fasten your seat belt. You never know what will jump out on the road at night.

ABOUT THE GAME

Night Driver is the home port of the 1976 arcade game, which in turn is cited as one of the earliest first-person racing games. It was distributed in a sit-down cabinet, complete with steering wheel! Rob Fulop did the programming for the Atari VCS/2600 version of *Night Driver*. He was also involved in other notable ports, such as *Missile Command* for the VCS and *Space Invaders* for multiple Atari systems.

OBJECT OF THE GAME

The object of the games is to obtain the high score. The computer tallies the score automatically while you drive the course.

You're in the driver's seat and the track is on the TV screen. Your vehicle is permanently fixed at the bottom of the screen. You need to accelerate and steer the car through one of the four tracks. If you veer off the track and hit a pylon or oncoming car, a simulated crash scene appears on-screen.

HOW TO PLAY

The knob on the Paddle controller serves as the steering wheel, while the red button is the accelerator. Hold the controller with the red button on the left. You must press that button to accelerate and start the action.

Turn the controller knob to the right to steer the car to the right and left to steer to the left. Try to avoid hitting the pylons on either side of the road as well as any oncoming cars. Your initial tendency will probably be to "oversteer" the car, which may result in a crash. Don't be discouraged if this happens. With time and practice, you will get the hang of it and eventually become quite skilled.

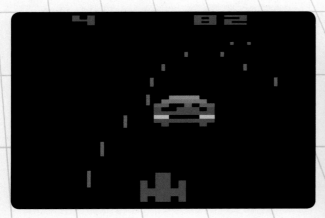

WATCH YOUR SPEED!

When first starting out, don't use maximum acceleration throughout the entire course. Instead, let off slightly or even all the way while winding through tight turns and difficult spots on the track. This should prevent any crashes and low scores.

GAME OPTIONS

TIME LIMIT	GAME #	TRACK
90 seconds	1	Novice
	2	Pro
	3	Expert
	4	Random
None	5	Novice
	6	Pro
	7	Expert
	8	Random

GAMES 1, 2, 3 AND 4

These game variations are timed. At the beginning of each game, a "clock" starts counting down from 90 seconds at the upper-right corner of the screen.

GAMES 5, 6, 7, AND 8

These game variations have no time limit. They can be played for an indefinite period of time; there isn't a clock on-screen.

Beginning players should start with Games 1 and 5, as these games have the easiest track (Novice), while Games 2 and 6 have the medium difficulty track (Pro). The Expert track in Games 3 and 7 is more difficult than the Novice or Pro tracks.

All of the tracks described thus far (Games 1, 2, 3, 5, 6, and 7) are stored in the game's program memory. So even though the Novice, Pro and Expert tracks get progressively more difficult, each track always follows a fixed course. This makes it possible for players to eventually memorize the track as their driving skill increases. The "random" track, which appears on Games 4 and 8, follows a different course each time, making it challenging for the most skilled players.

DIFFICULTY BUTTONS

The right difficulty button controls the maximum speed that your car will travel. In the A position, the car will travel the fastest; in the B position, the maximum speed will be slower. Beginners should start with the right difficulty in the B position.

The left difficulty button can act as a warning device, depending on its position. In the A position, oncoming cars *will not* honk before they appear on-screen. In the B position, however, oncoming cars will honk just before they appear.

SCORING

As you pass certain spots on the track (which are invisible to the player), the computer automatically tallies one point to your score, which is displayed in the upper-left corner of the screen. In games with no time limit (Games 5, 6, 7 and 8), a player's scoring possibilities are infinite.

NIGHT DRIVER GAME PROGRAM™

TAKE A MIDNIGHT RIDE
The road ahead is dark and winding. Better drive defensively. You know you're getting somewhere because the fence along the side of the road seems to keep moving. Don't get drowsy now. The longer you stay on the road, the higher you score. Watch out for those oncoming cars! Keep your eyes peeled and fasten your seat belt. You never know what will jump out on the road at night. **8 Games**

◆ Don't give in to the temptation to constantly accelerate! Slow down every few seconds to avoid potential crashes. Although doing so may cost a little time, an accident will cost even more time.

◆ Similarly, nudge your car rather than trying to completely steer it with the joystick. This should prevent any "oversteering" problems, thereby preventing you from driving off of the road.

FUN FACTS!

The first-person view and nighttime atmosphere of the game were actually tricks to conserve processing power. In the arcade version, the "car" was actually a plastic piece of art externally mounted to the bottom of the screen. In the 2600 version, the car is a stationary in-game figure located at the bottom center. This means that, technically, the player is controlling the road independently of the car.

OUTLAW

As a gunslinger, take aim to shoot targets or your opponent's gunslinger.

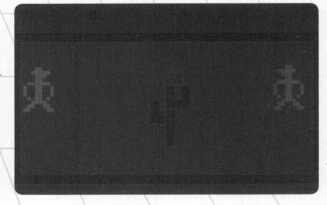

ABOUT THE GAME

At the time of *Outlaw*'s release on the Atari Video Computer System, the United States was at the tail end of a decades-long love affair with Western films and television serials. The game's design, from the package art to the bowlegged walk of the gunslinger, evoked the same feelings as the movies and shows. The children playing the game when it first hit shelves may not have spent time in front of the television wearing cowboy hats and toy gun holsters, but there was a good chance that the parents who bought the games did.

Gameplay held up its end of the bargain. The ability to crouch and aim (being limited to only three angles did nothing to diminish how cool it was), blow holes in stagecoaches and catci, and bounce shots into your target added to the fun. Of course, the biggest thrills came from the Six Shooter games. In particular, taunting foes who foolishly fired their six shots while your gun was far from empty. You also needed to master bowlegged dancing to entice poor shots when you were the one stuck with a depleted six-shooter.

The three Wall games were a test of nerves. How much of the wall can you blast away and remain safe from incoming shots? How much of a gap in the wall do you need to make accurate shots at your opponent? Game 12, featuring a moving wall and six-shooters, was the ultimate one-on-one Outlaw showdown.

OBJECT OF THE GAME

The objective in two-player (Gunslinger) games is to score 10 hits against your opponent before your opponent scores 10 hits against you. One-player (Target Shoot) games are a race against the clock. You must hit a bouncing target 10 times to stop the timer, which counts down from 99.

HOW TO PLAY

Your gunslinger moves in the direction you push the joystick. A gunslinger always faces the same direction, so pushing back on the joystick causes your gunslinger to walk backward.

To fire your six-shooter, press and release the red controller button. If you press and hold the button, your gunslinger stays in a crouched position and you can aim your gun up or down. Release the button to fire your gun. Bullets ricochet off the top or bottom boundaries of the playfield, a method you need to master for games with indestructible barriers.

GUNSLINGER

Two gunslingers face each other across the playfield with a barrier between them. Whenever a gunslinger is hit, the game pauses the action to tally the score.

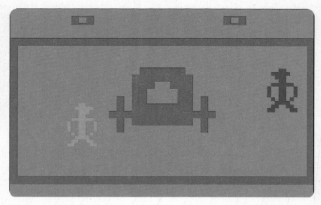

Gunslinger - Stage Coach

TARGET SHOOT

Your gunslinger starts on the left side of the screen with a bouncing target on the right side and a barrier in between. Your gunslinger remains crouched after firing a bullet until that bullet hits a barrier, the target, or the boundary beyond the target.

DIFFICULTY OPTIONS

With the difficulty set to A, your bullets disappear immediately if your gunslinger is shot. If the difficulty is set to B, your bullets continue in flight even if your gunslinger goes down.

GAME OPTIONS

GAME & BARRIER TYPE	GAME #	FEATURES
Gunslinger - Cactus	1	
	2	GT
	3	BW
	4	BW & 6S
Gunslinger - Stage Coach	5	
	6	MB
	7	BW & MB
	8	
	9	6S & MB
Gunslinger - Wall	10	BW & 6S
	11	BW & MB
	12	BW & 6S & MB
Target Shoot - Cactus	13	
	14	BW
Target Shoot - Stagecoach	15	
	16	BW

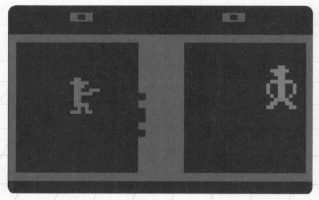

Gunslinger - Wall

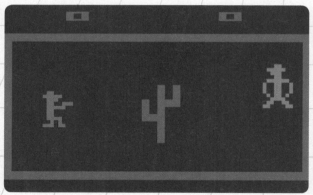

Gunslinger - Cactus

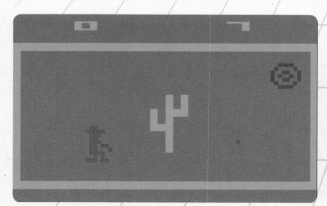

Target Shoot - Cactus

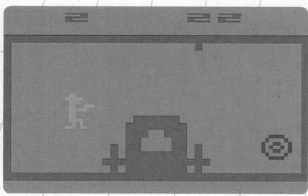

Target Shoot - Stage Coach

FEATURES

There are two features that impact your gunslinger and another two that alter the way you interact with the barrier.

GETAWAY (GT)

You can move your gunslinger immediately after firing.

SIX SHOOTER (6S)

Your gun only has six bullets in it. Guns are reloaded with an additional six shots only after both players have exhausted their six shots.

BLOWAWAY (BW)

You can shoot away pieces of the barrier until it completely disappears.

MOVING BARRIER (MV)

The barrier between gunslingers (or gunslinger and target) scrolls down continually during the duel.

Don't watch TV tonight. Play it!

THE ATARI VIDEO COMPUTER SYSTEM™

We're the games you play on your own TV set. We're the Atari Video Computer System. (Remember 'Pong'? Well, that was just the beginning.) Atari is now a sophisticated, computerized programmable unit that hooks up to your television in a matter of seconds.

Atari features a greater selection (20 different Game Program™ cartridges, over 1300 game variations and options—and with many more to come). We're sport games. We're mind games. We educate. We entertain. We can be played by one player (against the computer). Two players, three or four.

We're the system that's especially designed to change colors to protect and safeguard your TV tube from any damage. We offer crisper colors (when played, of course, on a color TV). We pride ourselves in truer-to-life sound effects, which play through your own TV's sound system.

We're Atari. And if someone in your family hasn't asked for us yet, get ready. They're going to.

ATARI.

20 cartridges now available. 1300 game variations.

FUN FACTS!

° Despite sharing the name *Outlaw* with an arcade cabinet also produced by Atari, the two versions of the game had little in common. The arcade game was strictly one-player and its controller was a plastic six-shooter.

° The Tele-Games version of *Outlaw* was named *Gunslinger*.

° The descriptive text for Games 11 and 12 in *Outlaw's* original instruction booklet incorrectly included Getaway as part of both games; however, the game option table on the back of the instruction booklet was correct. Unfortunately, the instruction booklet's game option table was not perfect. It neglected to note the Six Shooter limitation for Game 12.

Tips & Tricks

◆ Unless you're playing a game with Getaway, gunslingers are stuck in an immobile crouch while their bullets are visible. They're at their most vulnerable, making it the best time for you to score a hit.

◆ To get the fastest Target Shoot times, learn how to bank shots and time straight shots over and under the barriers without moving closer to the target. You could blast away enough of the barrier and walk to the target side of the screen, but gunslingers aren't the fastest walkers.

◆ Six-Shooter games offer the most excitement since they add an extra element of gameplay. It's important to learn how responsive your gunslinger is to joystick input so you can taunt opponents into emptying their guns with movements into their firing line while giving yourself enough time to safely move before the bullet finds its mark.

OUTLAW®

Squeeze the trigger. Your gunfighter kneels, and aims. Release the trigger. The lead starts flying. Blow away walls, stage-coaches, and cacti. Nail your opponent with a clever ricochet. Shoot it out through 16 games and variations, including three target practice games.

**16 games
One to two players
CX2605**

SLOT RACERS

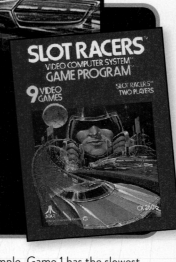

Schreech! Pow! Smash! This is the super chase scene and you're in it—right behind the wheel of a Super Chasemobile car equipped with power and incredible gadgets. Enjoy the simple pleasures of breakneck speed, killer missiles, and crazy mazes.

It's you and your favorite adversary, pursuing one another through bleak, big city streets. And blowing each other away with bazookas on your hoods.

The first to blast his opponent 25 times is the winner.

So get set for the wildest action since cops discovered robbers.

ABOUT THE GAME

Atari's *Slot Racers* is a game that isn't really about slots or racing. The object of the game is to face your opponent one-on-one and destroy the other vehicle using missiles. The battlefield is a simple maze that your car (and fired missiles) will automatically travel around.

As one of only a handful of two-player games for the Atari 2600, Slot Racers wasn't particularly sought-after by consumers. However, it was a game that would inspire future car combat games. Like most of the Atari games released around this time, the game variations were centered on speeding the game up or replacing the playfield with something slightly different.

Slot Racers may not have been the most popular game, but it was a game that influenced many others, like the developer's future ventures. The creator of *Slot Racers*, Warren Robinett, also became the developer for *Adventure*, which was actually a critically acclaimed game that was loved by a great number of gamers.

OBJECT OF THE GAME

The first player to score 25 points wins the game.

HOW TO PLAY

There are four chase mazes. Each player steers one car through the maze. Chase your opponent and attempt to hit him or her with one of the secret missiles fired from your car's headlights. You score a point each time you hit your opponent with a missile. The differences between the nine games are:

◆ **The speed of the cars.**
◆ **The speed of the missiles.**
◆ **The direction of the missile path.**

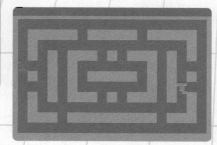

GAMES 1 - 4

Select your favorite maze pattern. These games feature missiles that travel faster than the cars. Note that the speed of both the missiles and cars increases with each game number.

For example, Game 1 has the slowest moving missiles and cars, while Game 4 features the fastest moving missiles and cars.

GAMES 5 - 7

Drive your car fast on these mazes. In these games, the cars travel faster than the missiles. Note that the speed of the cars increase with each game number. For example, Game 5 features the slowest moving cars, while Game 7 offers plenty of speed.

GAMES 8 AND 9

Missiles do not automatically turn corners during these game variations. That's why some of your missiles may become trapped in front of a wall. In Game 9 you're driving a racecar, while Game 8 features slower cars.

MAZE I

MAZE 2

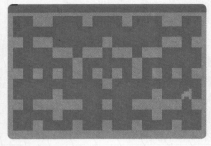

MAZE 3

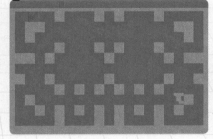

MAZE 4

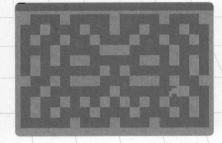

CONTROLLER ACTION

Use the joystick controller to steer the car and fire missiles.

STEERING THE CAR

Push the joystick forward to accelerate the car and pull the joystick toward you to slow down. Push the joystick to the left to turn left and push it to the right to turn right.

FIRING MISSILES

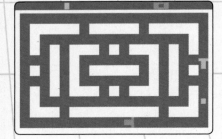

To fire a missile, press the red controller button. After doing so, there are three possible ways for the missile to travel. Use the joystick to control the direction of the missile.

To turn the missile left after firing, push the joystick to the left while pressing the red controller button.

To turn the missile right after firing, push the joystick to the right while pressing the red controller button.

Note that the missile will automatically turn at every corner (except in Game modes 8 and 9) when you press the red controller button without pushing the joystick.

DRIVING TIPS

When steering the car, you cannot turn into a wall. In fact, the car will automatically turn the corner to avoid hitting a wall.

After turning your car or missile into a street, remember to return the joystick to its center position.

For example, if you push the joystick to the left to turn the car to the left, push the joystick back to its center position; otherwise, the car will continue to make left turns.

GAME DIFFICULTY

HANDICAP (DIFFICULTY BUTTON)

When the difficulty is in the B position, you can shoot consecutive missiles. Note that if a previously fired missile is still on-screen when a new missile is launched, the old missile will disappear.

While in the A position, you cannot fire another missile if another missile is currently on-screen. Before you can fire another missile, the missile on the screen must hit your opponent's car, or you must retrieve the missile on-screen by steering your car into it.

NUMBER OF PLAYERS

Slot Racers is a two-player only game.

SCORING

You score one point each time you hit your opponent's car with a missile. The score of the left controller player appears in the upper-left corner; the right controller player's score appears in the upper-right corner.

FUN FACTS!

The developer of *Slot Racers*, Warren Robinett, later developed one of the most successful games for the Atari 2600, a game called *Adventure*.

Tips & Tricks

◆ Don't push too hard on the throttle for extended periods of time. The speed can really reach the high end of the spectrum, making it extremely difficult to maneuver.

SPACE WAR

Take the controls of a sleek starship. Trek for light years with a flick of the joystick. Penetrate the boundaries of strange galaxies. Beware the gravity of a strange sun. Drift invisibly through hyperspace.

ABOUT THE GAME

Space War has a long history behind it. It is a generational successor to the original 1962 PDP-1 game *Spacewar!*, which is one of the world's first widespread, multi-platform video games. As *Spacewar!*'s popularity grew, it spawned multiple clones, derivatives and upgrades, including Nolan Bushnell's and Ted Dabney's *Computer Space* from Nutting Associates.

Inspiration from *Spacewar!* can also be seen in other Atari games such as *Asteroids*. Meanwhile a traditional port of the 1960s classic would be released for the VCS/2600 almost two decades later. Even before the 1980s, it showed its age in terms of graphics and design, but there is no denying its impact on gaming even today.

COMPUTER SPACE

NA-2010

OBJECT OF THE GAME

Space War games last 10 minutes or until one player scores 10 points.

During Space Shuttle games, you are given 10 minutes to score a maximum of 10 points. During two-player games, each player maneuvers his own Star Ship to score points. In two-player games with two Space Modules, the target Space Module is the same color as your Star Ship. The first player to score 10 points or the most points in 10 minutes wins.

HOW TO PLAY

SPACE WAR GAMES

You and an opponent blast off into space. Each player controls one Star Ship using the joystick controller. The object is to score points by shooting your opponent's Star Ship with missiles fired by pressing the red button on the joystick controller. Aim the nose of your Star Ship in the direction you want to fire.

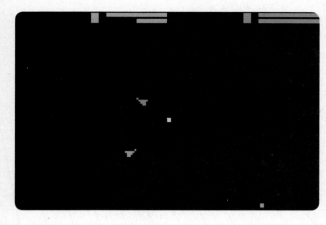

A player's score appears at the top of the playfield and is color coordinated with the Star Ships.

The two lines to the right of your score refer to fuel and missile supply. The top line is the fuel gauge; the bottom line is the number of missiles remaining. Each player begins with eight missiles. Once the arsenal is depleted, the game automatically resets each player with eight additional missiles, but only when both players run out.

In most *Space War* game variations, fuel cannot be resupplied. In games 6 and 7, though, players can refuel and resupply missiles by docking with the Starbase. Fuel is used by adding "thrust" to your Star Ship or by putting your ship into Hyperspace.

GAME 1

It's war in space, as two players attempt to score 10 points first. There are galaxy boundaries in this game variation.

GAME 2

Engage in combat in a galaxy that features galaxy boundaries and Hyperspace.

GAME 3

Battle your space opponent in a galaxy that has Warp Drive. Use Hyperspace as a defensive move.

GAME 4

The Space Sun in the center of the galaxy exerts a gravitational pull during combat. Avoid your opponent or collision with the Space Sun by utilizing Hyperspace. Galaxy boundaries also exist in this game variation.

GAME 5

The Space Sun, Warp Drive, and Hyperspace are the features in the galaxy playfield.

STARBASE GAMES

GAME 6

You can refuel and receive additional missiles at any time by steering your Star Ship to the Starbase. This galaxy also features galaxy boundaries and Hyperspace.

GAME 7

Steer your Star Ship to the Starbase at any time during the game to refuel or receive more missiles. This galaxy also features Warp Drive and Hyperspace.

SPACE SHUTTLE GAMES

The objective is to connect your Star Ship with the Space Module and score points in the process. The recommended strategy is to match your Star Ship's speed to the Space Module's speed. After doing so, slowly maneuver your Star Ship toward the Space Module. During Space Shuttle games, the Star Ships have an unlimited supply of fuel.

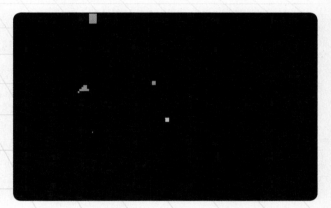

In one-player Space Shuttle games, you control one Star Ship using the left joystick controller and compete against the clock.

TWO-PLAYER GAMES

GAME 8

Two players each control one Star Ship and attempt to connect with the Module, which is color coordinated with the Ship. Warp Drive is present in this galaxy.

GAME 9

Two players each control one Star Ship and compete to connect with the same Space Module. This galaxy features Warp Drive.

ATARI NEWS
What The Critics Had to Say

"To say this ancient shooter hasn't aged well is an understatement… Its ultra-simple gameplay involves thrusting around a wide-open screen while firing at your opponent."

-Video Game Critic, 3/3/2004

GAME 10

Each player controls a Star Ship and attempts to connect with the color coordinated Space Module. A Space Sun and Warp Drive add extra dimension to the strategy in this game variation.

GAME 11

Each player controls a Star Ship and attempts to connect with a color coordinated Space Module. This galaxy has a Space Sun and galaxy boundaries.

GAME 12

Galaxy boundaries are present in this galaxy. Each player controls a Star Ship and attempts to connect to the same Space Module.

GAME 13

Each player controls a Star Ship and attempts to connect with the Space Module that is color coordinated to the Star Ship. Galaxy boundaries are featured.

ONE-PLAYER GAMES

GAME 14

One player controls a Star Ship and attempts to connect with the Space Module. This galaxy features Warp Drive.

GAME 15

A Space Sun and Warp Drive are featured in this space galaxy. One player steers the Star Ship to connect with the Space Module.

GAME 16

One player controls a Star Ship and attempts to dock it with the Space Module. Galaxy boundaries are present in this playfield.

GAME 17

A Space Sun and galaxy boundaries could affect one player's strategy to connect the Star Ship with the Space Module.

Just like learning to drive a car, it takes a bit of practice to learn how to control your Star Ship. The following exercises will help you gain proficiency in controlling your Star Ship. Game 14, a Space Shuttle game, is an excellent practice field.

EXERCISE 1

After cycling to Game 14, push the game reset button. Push the joystick to the left to make the Star Ship rotate counterclockwise (left). Push the joystick to the right to make the Star Ship rotate clockwise (right). Practice rotating your Star Ship in both directions and notice how the Star Ship looks when it is each position.

EXERCISE 2

Push the game reset button. By pushing the joystick forward (toward the TV screen), give your Star Ship three quick short bursts of "thrust". Notice that your Star Ship is now travelling in a forward motion toward the bottom of the playfield. By turning the Star Ship either clockwise or counter clockwise, turn the Star Ship so it is facing away from the forward motion.

Give the Star Ship three short quick bursts of thrust. Your Star Ship will slow almost to a stop. Push the game reset button again and try again. Practice this exercise until you can completely stop the Star Ship.

EXERCISE 3

Push the game reset button. Turn your Star Ship so it is facing to the right. Give your Star Ship continuous "thrust" by pushing the joystick forward and holding it in position. When the Star Ship is travelling rapidly across the playfield, turn your Star Ship in the opposite direction and push the joystick forward to give your Star Ship reverse "thrust," thereby slowing down your Ship. Practice this exercise until you can bring your Star Ship to a complete halt.

EXERCISE 4

Push the game reset button. Turn your Star Ship so it is facing to the right and down (approximately 45 degrees). Give your Star Ship continuous "thrust" until it is moving rapidly across the playfield.

Alternate using horizontal "thrust" and vertical "thrust" to bring the Star Ship to a near standstill in the middle of the playfield. After mastering these exercises, you should be an experienced Star Ship captain, ready to do battle among the stars!

MAY THE FORCE BE WITH YOU

Take the controls of a sleek starship. Trek for light years with flick of the joystick. Penetrate the boundaries of strange galaxies. Beware the gravity of a strange sun. Drift invisibly through hyperspace.

Blast through 17 games and variations as you make the universe a better place to live in.

Space Combat (game variations 1 to 5) It's a cosmic duel with an alien spacecraft. You may run out of fuel or missiles. Run out of both and you're a sitting duck.

Starbase (game variations 6 and 7) The Starbase has a stockpile of fuel and missiles. Out-maneuver your opponent to get there first.

Space Shuttle (game variations 8 to 17) Your mission is to dock with the Space Module ten times before time runs out. All spacecraft are speeding through hazardous galaxies.

SPACE WAR GAME PROGRAM™

SCORING

During Space War games (1 through 7), a player scores one point when his opponent's Star Ship explodes. A Star Ship will explode when:

- A missile makes a direct hit.
- The Star Ship collides with the Space Sun (games 4 and 5).
- The Star Ship runs out of fuel while in Hyperspace (games 2 through 7).
- The Star Ship attempts to enter Hyperspace when it is out of fuel (games 2 through 7).

In one and two-player Space Shuttle games (8 through 17), one point is scored each time the Star Ship successfully docks with the Space Module.

GAME OPTIONS

GAME TYPE	GAME #	# PLAYERS	FEATURES
Space War	1	2	GB
	2	2	GB & HY
	3	2	WD & HY
	4	2	GB & SS & HY
	5	2	WD & SS & HY
	6	2	GB & HY & SB
	7	2	WD & & SS HY
Space Shuttle	8	2	WD
	9	2	1M & WD
	10	2	WD & SS
	11	2	GB & SS
	12	2	1M & GB
	13	2	GB
	14	1	WD
	15	1	WD & SS
	16	1	GB
	17	1	GB & SS

FEATURES

SINGLE MODULE (IM)

Both players compete to connect with a single Space Module.

GALAXY BOUNDARY (GB)

In some galaxies, your Star Ship can't penetrate the playfield boundaries. Instead, it will bounce off the edges.

WARP DRIVE (WD)

Move your Star Ship off one edge of the galaxy boundary to make it go into Warp Drive, thereby reappearing on the opposite side. For example, move your Star Ship off the right edge and it will reappear on the left edge.

SPACE SUN (SS)

Fight the pull of gravity from the sun in the center of the Space Galaxy. In some game variations, your Star Ship will explode from exposure due to the extreme heat and reset to the starting position.

HYPERSPACE (HY)

Pull the joystick toward you to make your Star Ship enter Hyperspace, becoming invisible in the process. When in this stage, your Star Ship uses more fuel.

It is impossible to get hit by an opponent's missiles or collide with the Space Sun while in Hyperspace. To make your Star Ship exit Hyperspace, pull the joystick toward you.

STARBASE (SB)

Make contact with the Starbase at the center of the galaxy to refuel and resupply your missiles. Your missile and fuel gauges at the top of the playfield will reflect resupplies as your Star Ship resets to the starting point.

DIFFICULTY OPTIONS

The left and right difficulty buttons must be set to position B during all Space War games. In Space Shuttle games, change the button to the A position and you must perfectly match your Star Ship's velocity to the Space Module's velocity. While in the B position, your Star Ship need not travel at the same speed to dock with the Space Module.

SPACE WAR

- Change your Star Ship's position as soon as the game is in the start position. The initial location of the Star Ships makes it easier for players to score a direct hit.
- Always be aware of your opponent's missile supply gauge. Plan your shots so that your opponent deletes his missile supply first, leaving no defense against your missiles.
- Note that missile supplies are automatically replenished only when *both* players have consumed their missiles. Use this feature to you advantage when these three variables occur at once: Your opponent has no missiles; you have missiles; you are playing in a galaxy with a Starbase.
- Leave your opponent without an opportunity to resupply missiles by obtaining all of your missiles at the Starbase before your supplies are completely depleted.

SPACE SHUTTLE

- The easiest way to match your Star Ship's speed with the Space Module's speed is to first stop your ship, then point it in the direction the module is travelling. Apply thrust until the Star Ship and the Space Module are moving at the same speed. After doing so, move the Star Ship toward the Space Module.
- To make your Star Ship contact the Space Module: Your Star Ship must travel at the same speed as the Space Module; your Star Ship must travel in the same direction as the Space Module; you must point your Ship at the Module and apply thrust.

ADVENTURE

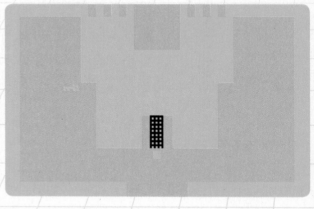

An evil magician has stolen an enchanted goblet. It's hidden somewhere in the kingdom.

Your goal is to find it, but it won't be easy. There are three deadly dragons and a black bat who'll try to stop you. Have no fear, your magic sword will help protect you! Cross the bridge if you can and get the magnet that will attract the goblet.

Oops! The dragon is waiting to eat you. Luckily in this game, reincarnation is as easy as pushing a button.

ABOUT THE GAME

Adventure became one of the first games with a "campaign" of sorts. As the title implies, the game takes the player on an adventure to restore a cherished treasure to its home. *Adventure* was not the first game to follow this theme, but it was definitely the first to do it in this fashion.

Coming from the developer of *Slot Racers*, *Adventure* became a very different game. It was different not only in the obvious gameplay mechanics, but also in the way it was received by the public. The game instantly became beloved by arcade players and home players alike. The terrain within the game was treacherous enough to keep players quite busy for long periods of time. Diving through the trenches and catacombs, even the most skilled players were forced to challenge themselves. And this all happened before you met each dragon!

Adventure helped changed the gaming world by adding considerable depth to the usual arcade action. The cartridge was jam-packed full of data, which meant some things had to be simplified, like the on-screen graphics. For example, the hero is represented by a single dot and most objects in the game are rendered in only one direction. These sacrifices were compensated for by the refreshing gameplay. It's no surprise *Adventure* went on to become an all-time classic.

OBJECT OF THE GAME

The object of the game is to rescue the Enchanted Chalice and place it inside the Golden Castle where it belongs.

This is no easy task, as the Evil Magician has created three dragons to hinder the player from completing this quest. There is Yorgle, the Yellow Dragon, who is just plain mean. There is Grundle, the Green Dragon, who is mean and ferocious.

ATARI NEWS
What The Critics Had to Say

"*Adventure* shatters several video-game conventions. You will never see a commercial-arcade version of this solitaire contest, because it has no scoring system and no time limit."
- *Arcade Alley (Video Magazine), Bill Kunkel & Frank Laney (1981)*

"Truly a classic. It's amazing that this game is still one of my favorites. If you're a fan of RPGs, or just want to play a good old school game, *Adventure* is one you should take a look at."
-*Muchorattler (2003)*

"Gameplay is great for an adventure game you run around a land stabbing dragons and solving the labyrinth on your quest to get the chalice back!"
-*Argo5004 (2013)*

Lastly, there is Rhindle, the Red Dragon, who is the most ferocious of all. Rhindle is also the fastest Dragon and the most difficult to maneuver.

HOW TO PLAY

There are three castles in the Kingdom: the White Castle, the Black Castle, and the Golden Castle. Each one has a gate over its entrance. You can open the gate using the corresponding colored key. Inside each Castle are rooms (or dungeons), depending on the Skill Level of the game.

A series of rooms, pathways, and labyrinths separate the Castles. Common to all the skill levels is the Blue Labyrinth, through which you must find your way to the Black Castle. Skill levels 2 and 3 have more complicated Kingdoms.

GOOD MAGIC

While the Evil Magician has created many hazards to slow you in your quest to rescue the Enchanted Chalice, there is some Good Magic on your side:

- Use the sword to slay the dragons. To do so, you must touch the dragon with it.
- With the right difficulty button set to the A position, all dragons will run away from the sword.

- Use the bridge to pass over the walls of any portion of the kingdom. The bridge cannot be used to pass through any barrier or wall. It also cannot be used to get past a locked castle gate.

- Pick up the bridge as you would any other object. Place the bridge across the wall that you want to pass over and release it by pushing the red controller button. The ends of the bridge must be visible on both sides of the wall for this to work. After releasing the bridge, you can then pass through to the other side of the wall or barrier.

- If you touch the inside of the bridge while passing over the barrier, the bridge will close and you may become trapped in the wall. To escape, press the red controller button. If, for some reason, your magic should fail and you still cannot escape, press game reset and "reincarnate." Use reincarnation as a last resort, especially if you have slain one or more dragons.

- In all games, Yorgle (the yellow dragon) is afraid of the gold key and will run away from it. He will also stay away from the room or area of the kingdom in which the key is located.

- To remove objects that are stuck in a wall and out of reach, use the magnet to affect all inanimate objects (including the bridge). The magnet can be used to move objects in an adjacent part of the kingdom by putting it in front of you before entering that part of the kingdom.

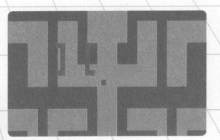

BAD MAGIC

The Evil Magician has cast a spell to make it difficult to succeed in rescuing the Enchanted Chalice. Not only do the dragons rally around and attempt to stop you from getting the Enchanted Chalice, they guard other objects in the kingdom.

- Grundle (the green dragon) guards the magnet, the bridge, and the black key.

- Rhindle (the red dragon) guards the white key.

- Yorkle (the yellow dragon) roams freely about the kingdom when it isn't guarding the Enchanted Chalice. Yorkle will occasionally assist Grundle or Rhindle.

- You cannot pick up and carry a slain dragon.

- In skill levels 2 and 3, the evil magician creates a black bat that carries objects around the kingdom and trades them for an object that you may be carrying. The black bat may trade a live dragon for the sword and leave you defenseless, or it may trade you something for the Enchanted Chalice just as you are ready to put it into the golden castle.

GOOD OR BAD MAGIC

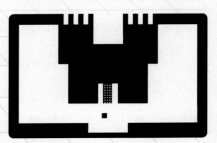

Some magic can be good or bad, depending on the situation.

- You can catch the black bat along with whatever it may be carrying and take it with you. Sometimes, however, the black bat will escape (usually at the most inopportune times).

- If there are four or more objects (including the castle gates) in your area of the kingdom, your magic may or may not work. Sometimes you can slay a dragon, sometimes you can't. However, it is easier to avoid being swallowed by a dragon.

If you have slain a dragon, and he is blocking your path so you cannot get through, you can use this to your advantage by placing one or two objects in the same area and then move through the slain dragon.

Sometimes the black bat can be used to your advantage by getting it to swap for an object you need that may be stuck.

GAME DIFFICULTY

SKILL LEVEL 1

This is the simplest skill level. When you depress the game reset button to begin play, you will see the key to the golden castle. Unlock the castle and enter it. Grundle (the green dragon) guards the key to the black castle. Yorgle (the yellow dragon) is roaming free and may or may not be guarding the Enchanted Chalice, which is hidden with the magnet inside the black castle.

SKILL LEVEL 2

This kingdom is much larger than in skill level 1. There are catacombs, which only allow for partial viewing. The key to the golden castle is hidden in the catacombs. You must pass through the catacombs to reach the white castle. The key to the white castle is hidden in the blue labyrinth. Rhindle (the red dragon) is inside the white castle. There is a secret room in the red dungeon where the key to the black castle is hidden. To find the secret room, you must use the bridge. To access the black castle, you must pass through the blue labyrinth. The grey dungeon is hidden behind the first room of the black castle; it is similar to the catacombs. The Enchanted Chalice is hidden here, guarded by Rhindle (the red dragon). All objects, the dragons, and the black bat will start in the same place in the kingdom each time you play the game at skill level 2.

SKILL LEVEL 3

The kingdom is the same as level 2, but is more difficult as the Evil Magician has placed all objects and the dragons randomly throughout the kingdom. You won't know for sure what is in the next area until you enter it, nor will you know where the Enchanted Chalice is hidden.

NUMBER OF PLAYERS

Adventure is a one-player game designed to take the player on an adventure through castles while slaying dragons along the way.

FEATURES

GAME RESET

If you get "eaten" by one of the dragons, do not despair! Just depress the game reset button to be "reincarnated" and placed back in front of the golden castle. Unfortunately, any dragons you may have slain will also be reincarnated. If you were carrying any object with you, it will remain where it was.

FUN FACTS!

- Won the 1980 Arcade Award for Best Innovative Game.

- Having the dot on the entrance screen to the secret room is not required. The program only checks to see whether or not it's been relocated to any other screen other than where it's originally located. Once moved, the bridge can be used to enter the secret room via the catacombs below it.

- If a dragon eats you, the sword won't have any effect on it. If the bat picks up the dragon (with you in it) and you're still holding the sword, you can actually still kill other dragons if you fly into them. Also, when a bat is carrying you and the dragon, you'll start flying faster all over the kingdom (even into some locked castles) and you might even have a bit of control over which direction the bat flies.

- Use the bridge to get on top of castles. It can also be used to get into the secret room, but you'll be trapped between the two barriers unless you've touched the dot on the entrance.

- There is a room in the white castle's maze that has what appears to be an entrance/exit at the bottom of the screen, but you can't use it.

- You can slow down the music by pressing select after you finish the game.

- Order of magnetism (highest to lowest): gold key ➜ white key ➜ black key ➜ sword ➜ bridge ➜ chalice. Use the magnet to drag items across castle gates, dropping them inside.

- Put the magnet on top of the gold castle, bring the chalice to that screen and drop it, and then leave before it gets pulled across the gate. Wait a few seconds and then return. The game won't end, even though the chalice is now inside the castle! You have to either enter it or press reset.

- With the chalice above you, if you go to enter the gold castle and drop it at the same time it touches the gate, it will end up in the castle and the game will instantly end (no music will play)!

BACKGAMMON

Backgammon, in some version, has been played in various parts of the world for over 5,000 years. It is possibly the oldest war game still being played. It is suggested in early writings that the game was originally designed to train soldiers for combat, as backgammon has all the intricacies of any war game: strategy, position, and timing. It is both a game of skill and luck, which probably accounts for its longevity.

The most ancient possible ancestor to be found so far dates back to the ancient civilization of Sumer. The Egyptian Pharaohs played a similar game. Game boards were found during the excavations of King Tut's tomb that's akin to backgammon. The ancient Greeks and Romans played different forms of the game that were mentioned in many of their writings. A form of backgammon was played in the Middle East during the Crusades. In fact, it is believed that the Crusaders brought the game back to Britain with them, where it flourished in the eighth and ninth centuries.

The earliest written mention of the name "backgammon" was made in 1645 in a description of a game that very much resembles backgammon as it is played today. The rules of today's game were set down by Edmond Hoyle in 1743.

The object of all the variations of the game, from its beginnings to now, is to move your game pieces around the board and bear them off before your opponent does the same.

ABOUT THE GAME

Although hardly a best seller, Craig Nelson's *Backgammon* is arguably the best overall board game implementation on the Atari 2600. The game's color graphics, responsiveness, and feature-set are standouts in comparison to the usual chess and checkers games.

OBJECT OF THE GAME

To win, remove all of your pieces from the board before your opponent.

HOW TO PLAY

Cycle through the Backgammon Game Program variations by pressing Select. For normal play, the left and right difficulty buttons must be in the A position. To begin play, press Reset.

THE BOARD

The backgammon "board" is divided into two halves or tables. The divider is called the bar. The inner table is the portion at the bottom of the playfield, while the outer table is the portion at the top of the playfield.

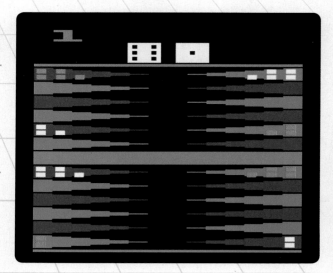

Each table is also divided into halves. The red player's home (or inner) table is on the lower-right side of the playfield; the white player's home (or inner) table is on the lower-left side of the playfield. The red player's outer table is on the upper-right side of the playfield; the white player's outer table is on the upper-left side of the playing field.

Each player's inner and outer table has six "points." The point is the area on which you rest your pieces as you move around the board. Each point is numbered for reference starting in each player's inner table. The white side is numbered 1 to 12 starting at the bottom-right side of the board.

THE MOVES

The moves are governed by "casting the dice." At the start, the players each cast one die (done automatically by the computer). The player with the highest number begins first, using the number count on both dice. On the playfield, the die on the left represents the white player, while the die on the right represents the red player for the beginning roll. The color of the dice corresponds to which player won the roll and will begin the game. After the initial move, each player rolls and moves alternately.

When the right difficulty button is in the A position, the computer will roll the dice. When the button is in the B position, you can use your own dice and then "dial in" the numbers to the computer. Turn the controller knob and the number on the left die changes. When you see the number you want to enter, push the red controller button. Next, dial in the second number on the right die and push the red controller button. The computer will accept the roll and your moves may be made accordingly.

In one-player games, the computer will play red. The white player must move his or her pieces counterclockwise around the board, casting off or bearing off (removing the pieces from the board) from the inner table. The red player must move his or her pieces clockwise around the board, bearing off from the red player's inner table.

The pieces are moved across the points according to the numbers on the dice. Each die must be considered individually, but they can be applied to one piece or two pieces. For example, a roll of 5-3 would allow a player to move one piece five points and another piece three points.

When there is only one piece occupying a point, it is called a "blot." A point with no pieces or a blot is referred to as "open." A point with two or more pieces is referred to as "closed."

If a point is closed, an opposing piece cannot move to that point. However, a player may move past a closed point if there is sufficient count on the dice. If a player has rolled a 5-3 and the five-count point is closed, moving five points and then three points is not allowed. However, moving three points and then five points is permissible.

COUNTING
Players must use the count on both dice whenever possible. If only one die can be used, it must be the die with the higher count.

If you close six consecutive points anywhere on the board, you establish a "prime." Your opponent cannot move past the prime until you break it by moving pieces and creating an open point. The explanation contained in the following section explains why it is a good strategy to build a prime on your inner table.

THE BAR

If a player lands on a blot belonging to the opponent, the opponent's blot is "hit," meaning the piece that occupied that point is removed to the "bar." When a piece gets hit and placed on the bar, it must reenter the board on the opponent's inner table. The white player enters on the lower-right inner table and the red player enters on the lower-left inner table.

A piece must enter the board only on an open point whose number has been cast on the one die. If there is an opposing blot on an entry point, the piece entering hits it and it is subsequently removed to the bar. The sum of the dice cannot be used to enter a piece.

Until all pieces on the bar have been entered, a player cannot move any other pieces on the board. If a roll does not permit entry, the turn passes. Pieces may not enter on closed points.

If a roll does not permit entry, and there are no other pieces on the bar, the remainder of the roll may be used to move other pieces on the board.

A player is said to be "shutout" if all six entry points are occupied, which is why it is a good strategy to build a prime on your inner table.

Then, if you hit one of your opponent's blots, the piece cannot be entered from the bar until the prime is broken. This allows time to move pieces onto your inner table and begin bearing them off while your opponent's remains stuck on the bar.

DOUBLETS

Doublets occur when you roll double numbers (3-3, for example.) When this occurs, a player must move the number shown on one die four times. You can move one piece all four moves, or any other combination of pieces that you choose. If you cannot use all combinations, the dice is passed to your opponent.

BEARING OFF

As soon as a player has all 15 pieces on the inner table, bearing off begins. This is the object of the game. Once borne off the board, a piece never returns to play. The first player to bear off all pieces is the winner.

A piece may be borne off when the number of points remaining is the same as the number on the dice. For example, a roll of 5-3 will bear off a piece from the five-point and the three-point. If the roll is higher than any occupied points, pieces may be borne off from the highest occupied point. If a player has two pieces each on the three and two-points and a 5-3 is made, both pieces from the three-point may be borne off.

A player can use all or part of the roll to move pieces within the inner table instead of bearing them off.

With a roll of 1-2, a player can move a piece from the five-point to the three-point and a piece from the two-point to the one-point. Doublets can also be used in this manner.

If your opponent has pieces on your inner table or the bar and you have begun bearing off, it is to your advantage to leave as few blots as possible. Remember that if you have both the same counts on the dice, it does not matter in which order they are taken.

In this example, you have a blot on your five-point and you roll a 5-1. If you bear off from the five-point with the higher number, you will still be leaving blots on the three-point and the four-point since you must use both numbers of the roll (which means your second move will move a piece from the four-point to the three-point). Instead, your best move is to take the piece from the five-point for the 1-count (putting it on the four-point with your other two pieces) and then bear off using the higher number. This way, you haven't left any blots on your inner table. The point again is that you can play the dice in either order, according to you best moves.

DOUBLING CUBE

Backgammon has enjoyed various degrees of success throughout its history. The game was in a decline in the United States during the early 1900s until the introduction of the "doubling cube" in 1920. Until this innovation, the outcome of a game could be decided in the first few rolls of the dice. Play would continue anyway, since with any dice game, there was always the chance of something unusual occurring. Unfortunately, most of the time, the games became boring.

Backgammon is one the few gambling games in which one can see what the opponent has at all times.

The doubling cube introduced the strategies of "bluffing" and psychological play that are similar to other gambling games. The game of chance is always present because of the use of dice. A skillful player can lose to a less skillful player because of the luck of the dice, but with the doubling cube added, the more skillful player likely won't lose as much.

As a gambling game, backgammon is played for a base "stake," which is agreed upon before beginning play. The doubling cube (represented by the number at the upper-left of the playfield) starts at 1. This means the players are competing for the original stake. Each time the stakes are doubled, this number changes (2, 4, 8, 16, 32, 64). Sixty-four times the original stake is the largest amount possible to wager.

Roll the dice. Make your move. Be sure to cover yourself with two men, or you'll be bumped off the board. And then it's back to the beginning.

With Atari's **Backgammon**, you can use all the strategies you've ever learned, including the use of the doubling cube. Playing against the computer or another player, try to totally overwhelm your opponent and get him to concede.

There's even the popular version of Acey-Deucey, where throwing a one and a two is the name of the game.

Get ready to gammon your opponent in one of the most exciting and newest ways to play one of the oldest Mideastern games ever.

GAMMON YOUR OPPONENT!

BACKGAMMON GAME PROGRAM

After the player winning the first move has completed his or her turn, the computer will ask the opponent "YESdbl " or "NOdbl." By turning the controller knob to YESdbl and pushing the red controller button, the opponent has offered to double the stakes and the doubling cube will now show 2. The first player now has the option of accepting or not accepting the double.

To accept the double, turn the controller knob to YESacc and the push the red controller button. The dice then rolls for your opponent's turn. To reject the double, turn the controller knob to NOacc and push the red controller button. The game will end at that point. To start a new game, Reset.

When you offer to double the stakes and your opponent accepts the double, he or she then "owns" the doubling cube. It will be up to your opponent to redouble at a time when it is advantageous to do so.

If your opponent offers to redouble the stakes and you accept, then you "own" the doubling cube and you can again offer to redouble when you think it is to your advantage. The player who "owns" the doubling cube is shown by the color of the number (representing the doubling cube) at the top of the playfield. If it is red, it belongs to the red player; if it is white, it belongs to the white player.

In one-player games, if the computer decides to offer a double, it asks only YESacc or NOacc. If you own the doubling cube and want to double the stakes against the computer, enter YESdbl when it appears on the screen. The computer will continue to play if it accepts the double, or quit if it refuses the double.

In both one-player and two-player games, if neither player doubles during the game, the doubling cube will remain green and a 1 will appear on-screen. In two-player games, the computer will continue to ask each player in turn if they want to offer a double.

GAMMON AND BACKGAMMON

If a player has borne off all of his or her pieces and the opponent has not borne off any, the game is called a "gammon." The opponent loses twice the stakes (times whatever is showing on the doubling cube).

If a player has borne off all of his or her pieces and the opponent still has pieces on the bar or in the player's inner table, the game is called a "backgammon."

The opponent loses three times the stakes (times whatever is showing on the doubling cube). A backgammon among skilled players is rare. If it appears that you are going to be gammoned or backgammoned, it's best to refuse your opponent's double and retire from the game.

SET UP MODE

It has been mentioned that the left and right difficulty buttons must both be in the A position for normal gameplay. To create a "set up mode" (in which you pick up pieces one by one and place them in various positions around the board), change the left difficulty button to the B position.

Use the controller that corresponds to the color of the dice on-screen when operating in the set up mode. This mode allows you to work out specific problems or strategies. As in regular play, the computer will not allow opposing colors to occupy the same point when you are moving pieces around the board.

Change the left difficulty button back to the A position to start or continue normal gameplay. When the game returns to normal play, the pieces that correspond to the color and count showing on the dice must be moved before the computer rolls the dice again.

ILLEGAL MOVE

Normally, the computer will not allow you to make an illegal move. There is a specific situation, however, in which the computer will illegally allow you to move a piece using the count on one die, even though there are no open points that correspond to the count remaining on the other die. When this situation occurs, the game goes into temporary state of suspension.

If an illegal move happens during a game, there are two possible solutions. One is to use the set up mode (left difficulty button in the B position), return the white pieces to their previous position, and execute the correct move. The other is to press Reset and start a new game.

ACEY DEUCEY

This variation was developed by members of the US Navy. It is similar to some of the game versions played in the Mediterranean area, which suggests that it started in that region. The rules for Acey Deucey may vary from ship to ship and even from player to player. They are not standardized, as are the rules for backgammon.

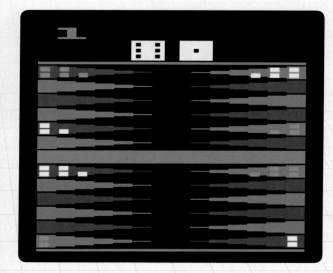

In the Atari version, all the pieces start out on the bar and can be entered at any time with the roll of the dice. A piece need not be entered from the bar before another piece can be moved, even if that piece was hit and sent to the bar.

The other rules of backgammon apply in terms of moving the pieces around the board (open and closed points, hitting a blot, bearing off, and using the doubling cube). A roll of 1-2 (acey deucey) allows a player to choose the most advantageous doublets after making the 1-2 move. After moving the doublets, the player is further rewarded with another roll of the dice.

After rolling the acey deucey, turn the controller knob, "dial in" the number on the left die, then push the red controller button.

Tips & Tricks

◆ If you open with strong rolls, run your pieces toward your home board as swiftly as possible.

◆ By creating four made points in a row, you form a wall that your opponent cannot get past without rolling a five or six.

◆ Leave an anchor point on your opponent's home board to create a safe place to land in case one of your pieces gets sent to the bar or to help provide a threat to your opponent's advancing pieces.

The die on the right will change to match the number on the left die. Push the red controller button again and play your doublets. After the last move on your doublet, the computer will roll the dice again for you and you can make another move.

If, after moving your doublet, you roll another acey deucey, you can again move the 1-2 and choose another doublet. The left difficulty button should be in the A position when playing acey deucey.

GAME OPTIONS

Use Select to choose the game you want to play. There are eight game numbers in total. After selecting the game number, press Reset to start the game. Reset can also be used to reset a game at any time.

GAME TYPE	GAME #	# PLAYERS	FEATURES
Backgammon	1	1	2X
	2	2	2X
	3	1	
	4	2	
Acey Deucey	5	1	2X
	6	2	2X
	7	1	
	8	2	

NUMBER OF PLAYERS

In 2-player games, you and an opponent face off against each other. In 1-player games, the computer is your opponent.

FEATURES

Backgammon and Acey Duecey share one common feature: the Doubling cube (2X). Not all games use the Doubling cube.

FUN FACTS!

● Backgammon games were available on a handful of other videogame consoles prior to 1983, including the Fairchild Channel F (1977), Mattel Intellivision (1979), and Magnavox Odyssey2 (1982). Unlike chess, stand-alone backgammon cartridges were virtually non-existent on consoles after this early smattering of releases.

BOWLING

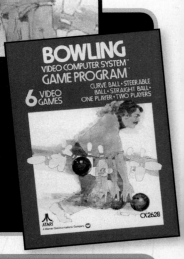

Choose your alley. Pick your spot. Now roll the ball and stay out of the gutter.

It's all part of Atari's *Bowling*, one of the most exciting and challenging ways to bowl.

Your score is automatically kept on-screen, frame by frame. And that includes strikes, spares, and even open frames.

Choose from a selection of six action-packed games. You can roll a curve of a straight ball.

But remember, watch those gutters!

ABOUT THE GAME

Modern bowling games are rightly praised for their level of interactivity, but Atari's *Bowling* was embracing this concept all the way back in 1979! Player choice is the name of the game here, with the ability to position the bowler pre-roll, directly control the ball while it rolls, or make sure it never deviates from its originally determined path. With this combination of options, players can recreate true lane bowling, or direct matches straight out of any bowler's fantasy.

OBJECT OF THE GAME

The objective is to roll as high a score as possible, whether you're playing a one-player or a two-player game.

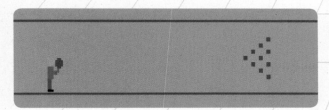

If you knock down all the pins on your first roll, it's called a "strike." An "X" on the TV screen indicates a strike.

FUN FACTS!

The sound engineering for *Bowling* was simple but highly effective. Modest up and down scales were used for most sound effects, such as the sharp "rolling" tones that play as the ball rolls down the lane.

If there are pins standing but you "pick them up" on your second roll, it's called a "spare." A "/" on the screen signifies a spare.

An "open frame" occurs when you fail to knock down all 10 pins after both rolls. A straight horizontal line (-) indicates an open frame.

The ultimate goal of *Bowling* is to roll 12 consecutive strikes for a "perfect" score of 300. See the Scoring section for a more detailed breakdown of point scoring.

HOW TO PLAY

There are 10 "pins" to knock down. You have two tries (or rolls) to knock down the pins on each turn. Each game consists of 10 "frames" (or turns). Move the joystick forward (away from you) and back (toward you) to position the bowler. Press the red button on the joystick controller to release the ball. To start the action:

- **Press the game select button to choose the game you wish to play. The number of each game appears in the upper-left corner of the screen. A 1 or 2 is displayed in the upper-right corner to indicate whether the game is for one or two players.**

- **Press the game reset button to begin play.**

CONTROLS EXPLAINED

Before pressing the red button to release the ball, the joystick controls the positioning of the Bowler. After pressing the red button, however, the joystick controls the direction of the ball as it moves down the "alley."

GAME OPTIONS

GAME #	# PLAYERS	FEATURES
1	1	CB
2	2	CB
3	1	SB
4	2	SB
5	1	NC
6	2	NC

NUMBER OF PLAYERS

In 2-player games, you bowl a frame and then the second player bowls a frame. Games end after each bowler completes 10 frames.

FEATURES

The game features all revolve around control over the bowling ball.

CURVE BALL (CB)

Pressing up or down on the joystick curves the ball in that direction. Only the first touch curves the ball.

STEERABLE BALL (SB)

The bowling ball responds to new controller commands while it rolls down the alley. You must continue to press up or down to guide the ball in a direction. If the joystick is returned to the neutral position, the ball resumes on a straight path.

NO CURVE (NC)

The bowling ball travels in a straight line from the point it leaves the bowler's hand. Positioning your bowler before releasing the ball is vital in No Curve games.

During gameplay, the number of each frame is displayed in the upper-left corner of the screen for one-player and two-player games. In two-player games, the number of the player who is currently up is shown in the upper-right corner of the screen. (Player 1 is blue; Player 2 is green.)

SCORING

In two-player games, the score for the left player is displayed at the top-left corner of the screen; the right player's score is shown on the right. In one-player games, the score is on the left.

You can score anywhere from 0 to 30 points in each frame. However, the difference in your score depends on whether you strike, spare, or leave an open frame.

For instance, the number of pins you pick up (for both rolls) in an open frame is added to your running score.

However, when you pick up all the pins on the second roll (a spare), your running score is not totaled immediately. Instead, the score for that frame remains empty until your next roll. At that time, 10 is added to the number of pins you pick up. This subtotal is then added to your total running score.

After a strike is rolled, your running score is not totaled until after the next two rolls. Ten points are then added to the total number of pins you pick up for those rolls. Therefore, if you roll three consecutive strikes, you score 30 points for the frame in which the first strike occurred.

TENTH FRAME BONUS

If you record a spare in the tenth frame, you get one more roll. The number of pins you pick up—plus 10 because of the spare—is then added to your total score. If you get a strike in the tenth frame,

the pins you pick up for the next two rolls are added to your total score.

DIFFICULTY OPTIONS

With the difficulty button in the A position, the computer makes it more difficult to roll strikes and spares. Use the left difficulty button for one-player games. For the beginning player, it is easier to obtain higher scores when the difficulty button is set to the B position.

- If you're new to the sport of bowling, make sure the difficulty button is in the B position.

- There are two easy ways to get strikes in *Bowling*, assuming you're playing a game mode that allows for ball control as it rolls. The first way is to line up the bowler's feet with the head pin and nudge the ball up or down as it reaches that pin, causing it to hit all of the others.

- The second way is to position the bower all the way at the bottom, and then listen to the "rolling" sounds. On the fourth one, hold the joystick up to make the ball plow through the head pin. It will usually knock down the others in the process.

- Getting spares is fairly easy as well. Simply aim for the lead or middle pin of the remaining pins and adjust the ball as needed.

- The dreaded 7-10 split is the bane of every bowler. Fortunately, positioning the bowler at the top and pressing down on the joystick as the ball reaches the top pin should allow it to hit the bottom pin as well.

CANYON BOMBER

With just a press of a button, you're in control of unloading bombs into the canyon. Careful now. An itchy trigger finger may cost you the war.

In Canyon Bomber, play against the computer or another player. Blast away the boulders with either a set or an unlimited number of bombs.

In Sea Bomber, blow away the carriers, tankers and ships. Your goal is to reach 1000 points before your opponent.

OBJECT OF THE GAMES

For Canyon Bomber games, press the red button on the paddle controller to drop bombs from the plane into the canyon. Note that the controller knob is inoperable during Canyon Bomber games.

For Sea Bomber games, turn the controller knob to move the dashed depth indicator up and down the playfield. This sets the depth at which the charge explodes. Press the red controller button to release the bomb.

In one-player games, play continues until six misses are recorded against you. Or, you (or the computer) score 1000 points in a game with unlimited bombs. In two-player Canyon Bomber games, play continues until both players miss six times in games with unlimited bombs. Or, one player scores 1000 points in games with unlimited bombs.

GAME I: CANYON BOMBER (ONE PLAYER)

Test your skill against the computer. It's not an easy task. You have six chances to match wits with the computer for a higher score. Each time the bricks in the canyon are hit, the remaining bricks "fall" to a lower level rather than remain stationary in their original position. Bricks that fall to a lower level are worth the points designated for that level.

ABOUT THE GAME

Famed programmer and game designer David Crane created the Atari VCS version of *Canyon Bomber*. After working for Atari, he would go on to establish Activision and create games such as *Pitfall!*.

Canyon Bomber was based on the popular arcade version of its namesake. Sea Bomber, meanwhile, has reported roots in *Depth Charge* by Gremlin and Atari's own *Destroyer*.

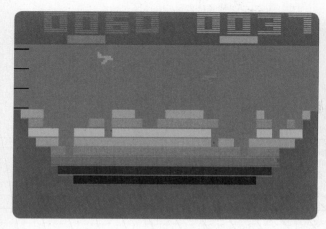

Between Canyon Bomber and Sea Bomber, programmer David Crane managed to pack two arcade games in a single 2KB Atari VCS cartridge. This is an utterly microscopic amount of memory space compared to the beefy '70s arcade hardware that originally featured these games!

Keep an eye on the solid bar beneath your score on the upper-right side of the screen. It is a "miss indicator" and gradually decreases in length each time you miss until six misses are recorded and the game ends. The bar is also color-coordinated with your planes and score.

Set your sights for 1000 points. Although the game will not end if you reach that total, it's an excellent goal to set since it will be very difficult to obtain.

GAME 2: CANYON BOMBER (TWO PLAYERS)

This game differs from Game 1 in that you compete against another player rather than the computer. Play ends when six misses are recorded against both players. The player with the highest score wins. Don't forget to keep an eye on your opponent's "miss indicator" as well as your own.

GAME 3: CANYON BOMBER (ONE PLAYER)

This game variation is the same as Game 1 with one exception. Rather than falling to a lower level, the bricks in the canyon stay "suspended" in their original position when the surrounding bricks are hit.

GAME 4: CANYON BOMBER (TWO PLAYERS)

You compete against another player in this game variation. This time, however, the bricks remain suspended instead of falling to a lower level.

GAME 5: CANYON BOMBER (TWO PLAYERS)

Prepare for a test of your endurance and concentration. The first player to score 1000 points wins. There is no time limit and no constraints on the number of bombs or misses. Falling, as opposed to suspended bricks, are programmed into this game. Also, there isn't a "miss indicator" on the screen in games with unlimited bombs.

GAME 6: CANYON BOMBER (TWO PLAYERS)

This game variation is identical to Game 5, except that the bricks stay suspended.

GAME 7: SEA BOMBER (ONE PLAYER)

Set the level, release the bomb, and you're ready for action against the computer. Although it sounds easy, the computer's a real steady competitor. If you score 1000 points before the computer, you win!

GAME 8: SEA BOMBER (TWO PLAYERS)

This time you compete against another player in a race to the 1000-point mark.

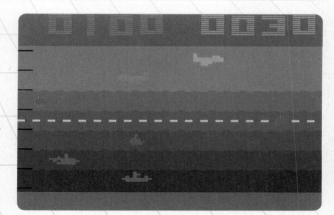

GAME OPTIONS

To choose the game type, depress the game select button. The number for each game is displayed in the upper-left corner of the screen.

GAME TYPE	GAME #	# OF PLAYERS	FEATURES
Canyon Bomber	1	1	FB & LI
	2	2	FB & LI
	3	1	SB & LI
	4	2	SB & LI
	5	1	FB & UN
	6	2	SB & UN
Sea Bomber	7	1	UN
	8	2	UN

BOMBS AWAY!

There are eight bars of bricks that extend across the canyon. Each brick in the first two bars is worth one point, while the bricks in the third and fourth bars are worth two points. The bricks in the fifth and sixth bars are worth three points and the bricks in the bottom two bars are worth four points.

If a player (or the computer) eliminates all of the bricks in the canyon, a new canyon appears and play continues.

FEATURES

FALLING BRICKS (FB)

When bricks as destroyed, bricks from the layers above fall down to fill in gaps.

SUSPENDED BRICKS (SB)

Bricks remain in their original layer until destroyed.

LIMITED BOMBS (LI)

The game ends after six misses. Misses are recorded for bombs failing to strike a brick and when your aircraft crosses the screen without dropping a bomb.

UNLIMITED BOMBS (UN)

There is no bomb limit, regardless of the number of misses.

DIFFICULTY OPTIONS

When the difficulty button is in position A, you must wait until a bomb runs its course before firing again. Change the button to position B and it's possible to recover and fire a bomb again by pressing the red fire button. This allows you to correct a bad shot or fire at a different target, if your opponent hits the original target. There is no limit to the number of times you can recover and launch a bomb again while your plane is making one run across the screen. Additionally, the computer plays much tougher when the game is set to the B position.

SCORING: CANYON BOMBER

In one-player Canyon Bomber games, you compete against the computer for the highest score. A miss is recorded each time you fail to hit a target in the canyon. A miss is also recorded if your plan travels across the canyon without dropping a bomb.

SCORING: SEA BOMBER

In both Sea Bomber game variations, the game ends when a player (or the computer) scores 1000 points. In general, the lower the ship is positioned on the screen, the more points you score. Point values for the five levels are 20, 30, 40, 50, and 60 points.

Tips & Tricks

◆ In Canyon Bomber, keep track of your bomb trajectory. It's important to time your button presses to make sure your bomb doesn't travel along the same path it did on an earlier attempt.

◆ In Sea Bomber, you must think fast during each fly-by. Decide on a target and launch your bomb so that it lands where the target will eventually be, not its current location.

HUMAN CANNONBALL

Carefully judge angle, speed, and distance to launch your human cannonball to the target.

ABOUT THE GAME

Despite its kinetic cover image, *Human Cannonball* is a puzzle game that tests memory skills more than twitch reflexes. In most types, you adjust a single variable. Successful shots become a matter of remembering where to set that variable, based on the variables beyond your control.

The end result is a nice progression of difficulty in *Human Cannonball*. Start with either of the first two games to pick up the basics. Game 3 provides the most customization. The difficulty in game 4 is the result of eyeballing the placement of the cannon. In the other game variations, you adjust numbers that are plainly visible.

The addition of the barrier in the second set of games increases the challenge. During this variation, you must time the launch of the human cannonball to cross the barrier when the window is in position. In Moving Tower, you only need to set numbers correctly. The last step up in difficulty is hard mode (set the button to B), which halves the size of the target tower.

OBJECT OF THE GAME

The objective is to launch the man from the cannon into the target tower. Your man must enter the tower from the top. Hitting the side of the tower results in a painful fall.

One-player games end after seven successful shots or seven misses. In two-player games, the first player to record seven successful shots is the winner. However, the second player gets one more attempt if the first player reaches seven first.

HOW TO PLAY

Dropping the human cannonball into the target tower is a tricky task. There are three variables to consider before launching your daredevil from the cannon.

Depending on the game type you play, these variables are either set by the computer before each attempt or adjustable by you.

The first is the distance from the cannon to the target tower. In games where the cannon's position can be adjusted, push up to move the cannon slowly to the right, or push to the right to move quickly to the right. Push down to move the cannon slowly to the left, or push left to move it quickly to the left.

The second variable is the speed (MPH) at which the cannon launches the human cannonball. The maximum speed for all games is 45 MPH. It is possible—but not practical for scoring purposes—to adjust the speed down to 0 MPH. In games where the speed can be adjusted, push left to decrease the speed by 1 MPH or push right to increase the speed by 1 MPH.

The final variable is the angle of the cannon, which is the number below the MPH value. The minimum cannon angle for all games is 20 degrees, while the maximum angle is 80 degrees.

What The Critics Had to Say

"The sound track is fair at best, with the exception of the effects of bouncing your man off the tower, or straight to earth, which are amusing. The lo-res graphics are unfortunately weak, and overall, I'd have to say the game is just below par."

-The Book of Atari Software 1983

In games where you can adjust the cannon angle, push up on the joystick to increase the angle 1 degree, or push up-left to increase the angle 10 degrees. Push down on the joystick to decrease the angle 1 degree. Push down-left to decrease the angle 10 degrees.

In one-player games, you score one point for each successful shot. The computer records one point against you for each miss. Your score appears at the top-left corner of the screen. The number of misses is shown at the top-right corner of the screen.

The game ends after seven successful "shots" or seven misses. In two-player games, each player scores one point for a successful "shot". Misses have no effect on scoring.

DIFFICULTY OPTIONS

The target tower is half as wide while in the B position as it is when set to the A position.

GAME OPTIONS

GAME TYPE	GAME #	CANNON POSITION	SPEED	CANNON ANGLE
Movable Tower	1	FX	RN	AD
	2	FX	RN	AD
	3	RN	AD	AD
	4	AD	RN	RN
Moving Window	5	FX	RN	AD
	6	FX	RN	AD
	7	RN	AD	AD
	8	AD	RN	RN

FEATURES

In games 1, 2, 3, and 4, you can move the water tower back and forth after the man is launched from the cannon. Push left on the joystick to move the tower left, or push right on the joystick to move the tower right.

Games 5, 6, 7, and 8 have a scrolling barrier with a "window" in front of the tower. Time your shot so that the daredevil flies through the window in the barrier on the way to the tower.

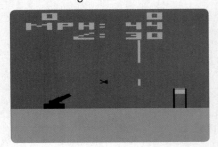

CANNON POSITION

Cannon position is either fixed (FX) or adjusted by the player (AD).

SPEED

The speed at which the human cannonball is launched is either assigned randomly by the computer (RN) or adjusted by the player (AD).

CANNON ANGLE

The angle at which the human cannonball is fired is either assigned randomly by the computer (RN) or adjusted by the player (AD).

Tips & Tricks

◆ For games 1 and 5, the cannon always appears at mid-screen. In games 2 and 6, the cannon is always positioned at the maximum distance from the target tower.

◆ Movable Tower games are more forgiving than Moving Window, so use the first four game variations to learn the nuances of *Human Cannonball*.

◆ The ultimate challenge is game 8 with the difficulty button set to B. The game sets the speed and angle of the cannon. You must move the cannon to the proper location before launching your daredevil through the barrier and into the tower.

MINIATURE GOLF

Get your golf grip down pat. Line up the ball to the cup. (Ask your caddy for assistance, if you must.) Now putt away and sink it!

You'll be putting through a nine-hole course with *Miniature Golf*. It includes two exciting game modes with moving obstacles and all. Stroke by stroke, your score is automatically kept, so as you shoot for the cup, you'll be shooting for par.

ABOUT THE GAME

According to Guinness World Records, *Miniature Golf* was the first ever golf-themed game to be released commercially and the earliest miniature golf game to be released. Such an esteemed title comes at a cost, however, as the primitive nature of the game is apparent in the graphics. The ball, traps, and even the club are rendered as simple rectangles. *Miniature Golf* did not perform well after its release and Atari stopped production of the game later in the same year.

OBJECT OF THE GAME

Hit the ball in the hole using the fewest shots possible, all while avoiding various obstacles. Ideally, your goal is to match or beat par for each hole. The lower your score the better.

HOW TO PLAY

There are nine "holes" in which to hit the ball into the "cup." A "stroke" is counted each time you hit the ball. Although you have an unlimited number of strokes to hit the ball into the cup, each hole has a designated "par" score. Par represents the number of strokes you are ideally supposed to take to complete the hole.

Use the joystick to position the club. Press the red button on the controller to release the club and hit the ball. To position the club more accurately, remember that it moves at a slower speed when travelling close to the ball.

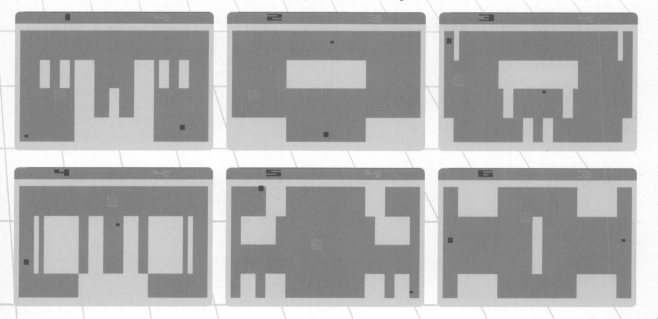

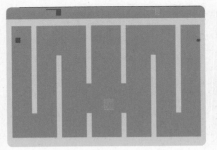

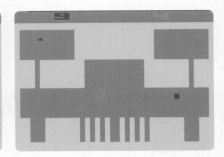

GET INTO POSITION

The club obscures the view of the ball at the beginning of each hole. Your first step, therefore, is to move the club into a hitting position away from the ball. The farther away you move the club, the longer the ball will roll when hit.

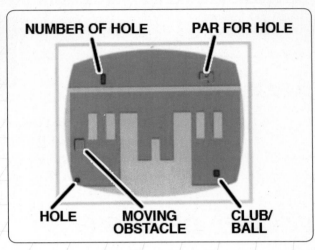

NUMBER OF HOLE   PAR FOR HOLE

HOLE   MOVING OBSTACLE   CLUB/ BALL

DIRECTION OF TRAVEL

After the ball is struck, it travels along the same line of trajectory already established by the club.

DIRECTION OF TRAVEL
BALL
CLUB

JUST REMEMBER...

You can position the club anywhere on the playfield—regardless of course boundaries—before releasing it to hit the ball. Remember, however, that the ball must travel around all boundaries, including moving obstacles.

Game 2 is for two players. The left player goes first. After the first stroke by each player, the respective scores are displayed at the top of the screen until the hole is completed. These score totals replace the hole number and the par as in Game 1. To begin the game, press the game reset button.

DIFFICULTY OPTIONS

The ball travels further when the difficulty button is in the A position. Use the left difficulty button for one-player games.

GAME OPTIONS

To select a game, press the game select button for a one or two-player game. A "1" will appear in the upper-left corner of the screen for a one-player game; a "2" will appear for a two-player game.

Game 1 is for one player only. At the beginning of each hole, before the first stroke, the number for that hole is displayed in the upper-left corner of the screen. The par for that hole is shown in the upper-right corner of the screen. After the first stroke, the player's running score replaces the hole number. A "0" replaces the par until the beginning of the next hole.

IT'S IN THE HOLE!

Players must hit the ball into the cup to complete the hole before the game will move to the next hole or the next player's turn.

SCORING

Each time you hit the ball, the computer records one stroke. Your running score is displayed at the top of the screen.

The score for the left player is displayed at the top-left of the screen, while the score for the right player is displayed at the top-right of the screen.

◆ If your ball gets stuck in a corner, try to aim your next shot toward the nearest wall to make the ball to bounce in the desired direction.

SKY DIVER

You're ready for the big jump! The longer you can wait to open your parachute, the more points you score. Steer your parachute against the wind to guide yourself toward the bull's-eye.

GERONIMO-O-O

ABOUT THE GAME

Mastering most games on the Atari came down to deft joystick handling or familiarity with patterns. You use a bit of both here, but ultimately *Sky Diver* is a test of nerves.

In game variations 1-4, your real competition is the conditions. Once you learn how to adjust for the wind or moving platforms, and the precise timing to earn a maximum score on each drop, your totals will consistently reach the 90s.

Game variation 5 is the ultimate *Sky Diver* test of dominance. The single landing pad scores only for the first person to land on it. Like many of the best Atari cartridges, you'll quickly forget about blocky graphics and limited audio options because you're lost in a tense contest where fractions of a second are the difference between a big score and your skydiver turning into a pancake.

OBJECT OF THE GAME

Guide your skydiver onto the landing pad and score points. To win a game, you must score more points than your opponent.

HOW TO PLAY

You and your opponent (all five game variants are designed for two players) are challenged to score points during a series of nine jumps. The right and left scores on-screen represent the right and left players, respectively. The white number in the lower-left corner is the number of rounds remaining in the current game.

There's a brief pause before the planes start moving and initiate each scoring round. Both planes fly across the screen simultaneously, starting from opposite corners. Press the red button to release your skydiver from the plane and push down on the joystick to deploy your skydiver's parachute. Once the parachute opens, guide your skydiver by pushing left or right on the joystick. You retain control through the entire descent, meaning you can change direction at any time.

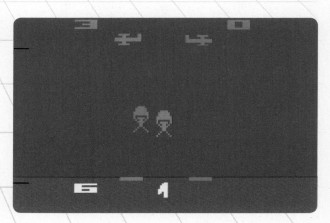

Your skydiver keeps a bit of the momentum from the plane's motion, but its overall effect is negligible. Ultimately, the wind has a greater impact on your ability to successfully complete a landing. Since skydivers fall quickly, the wind doesn't really affect them until the parachutes are deployed.

If you're playing games 1, 2, or 5 (there's no wind in games 3 or 4), check the white windsock at the bottom-center of the screen. The windsock indicates the wind's direction and speed, which obviously changes between jumps. Continue to check the windsock while your skydiver floats to the landing pad, as the wind may shift during a jump.

When there is no wind, your skydiver moves in the direction you push the joystick. At its strongest, the wind blows skydivers with the same force as if you were pushing the joystick. That means if the wind is at full-force and you push the joystick in the opposite direction, the skydiver—with the parachute deployed—falls straight down.

STRONG WIND   NO WIND   STRONG WIND

Each jump is worth between -4 and 11 points. The maximum score in all games is 99. You score points only when your skydiver lands squarely on the pad of the same color with an open parachute (except in game 5, which has a single pad). As long as any part of the skydiver's foot is touching the pad, even if most of his foot is outside of it, points are awarded.

When your skydiver hits the ground with an unopened chute, you are treated to an amusing sound and a much shorter skydiver! You lose up to 4 points (your score never goes below 0).

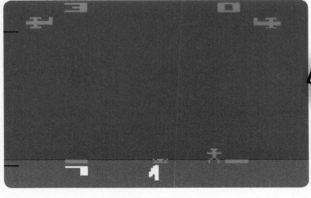

If you neglect to release your skydiver from the plane, or miss the landing pad, you score zero points for that round. If the skydiver hits the landing pad safely, your score is determined by how close to the ground the parachute was deployed. However, if you wait too long, it becomes impossible to open your parachute.

DIFFICULTY OPTIONS

In the A position, the planes fly significantly faster across the screen. It is possible for one player to have fast planes (using the A position) and the other player to have slow planes (using the B position) in the same game. The difficulty buttons have no effect in Game 5, as both planes fly at the faster speed.

GAME OPTIONS

Games 1 and 2 are identical with one exception. Each landing pad in game 2 is narrower, making it more difficult to score points. The landing pads change locations between each jump, as well.

In games 3 and 4, the landing pads move from left and right. The landing pads in game 4 are half the size of those in game 3. Neither game variation includes wind in this instance.

FUN FACTS!

- *Sky Diver* is the home version of an Atari coin-op arcade game called *Skydiver*.

- The Tele-Games version of *Sky Diver* was known as *Dare Diver*.

SKY DIVER®

You're ready for the big jump. The longer you can wait to open your chute, the more points you'll score. Steer your chute against varying wind velocities as you guide yourself to the landing pad. Land on the bull's-eye and get more points.
But, if your chute fails to open - SPLAT!

Five games
Two players
CX2629

Game 5 adds a twist to gameplay. There's only one landing pad in the middle of the screen. The first player to land on the pad scores points. The second player receives no points, even if their skydiver lands squarely on the pad.

What The Critics Had to Say

"Graphics: B / Playability: C"

- *Electronic Fun with Computers & Games (December 1982)*

"Graphics/Sound: B / Difficulty to learn: Easy / Overall Rating: C"

- *Software Report Card, Video Games Player (Fall 1982)*

Game 1 and game 3 landing pads.

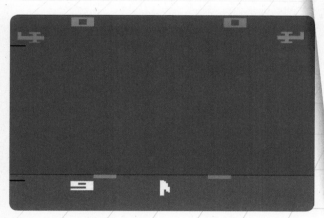

Game 2 and game 4 landing pads.

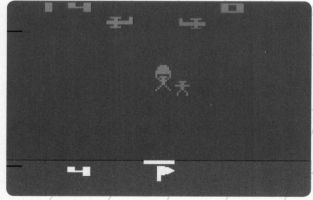

Game 5 landing pad.

SKY DIVER GAME PROGRAM™

JUMP FOR JOY

You're ready for the big jump. The longer you can wait to open your chute, the more points you score. Steer your chute against varying wind velocities as you guide yourself to the landing pad. Land on the bull's-eye and get more points.

But if your chute fails to open—SPLAT! **5 Games**

Tips & Tricks

◆ To get maximum points (11), slowly count to two before deploying your parachute. It takes some practice to learn the exact timing, but two seconds is a good starting point.

◆ For a different sort of challenge, shoot for a "perfect" score of nine in either of the first two games. The challenge comes from scoring exactly one point for each jump. To earn one point, open your parachute immediately after leaving the plane. You must watch the windsock carefully since you'll be fighting the wind during the entire drop.

◆ Getting to the landing pad first in game 5 is all that matters, but there's more to it than opening your parachute at the last second. Being first out of the plane is a huge advantage. Test how much you can adjust your skydiver's pre-parachute descent to determine the earliest possible drop point. Check the windsock before each round and adjust your drop point accordingly.

SLOT MACHINE

Imagine yourself in Las Vegas. Plug your coins into a 3-wheel, 20-stop slot machine — just like the ones in gambling casinos.

But don't put in too many! With *Slot Machine*, you start with a stake of only 25 "coins." Once they're gone, you're broke!

There are eight different and exciting games to choose from. How is *your* luck? Try to hit the jackpot and see for yourself.

ABOUT THE GAME

Slot Machine was programmer David Crane's second game at Atari. A significant challenge Crane faced with the development of *Slot Machine* was creating the art typically associated with the popular casino game. Familiar slot machine staples like lemons, cherries, or oranges became almost impossible to distinguish from one another when rendered in a single color. Crane had to scrap some of the traditional art and instead use angular objects that were much more recognizable when drawn with monochrome pixels. This is why you see familiar objects like bars and bells and some completely new objects, such as table and chairs, cacti, cars, and television sets.

OBJECT OF THE GAME

Place your bets, pull the lever, and win big! The object of *Slot Machine* is to get as many points as possible by putting your own coins on the line. The more you bet, the more you can win!

HOW TO PLAY

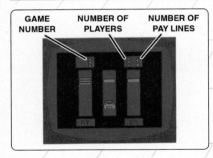

Press the console's game select button to choose the particular slot machine you want to play. Each "machine playfield" features a specific number of players and "paylines." The game number appears in the upper-left corner of the machine playfield. The first number in the upper-right corner refers to the number of players, while the second number refers to the number of paylines.

Press the game reset button to start play. The numbers in the upper-right and left corners change to 25 during games 2, 4, 6, and 8, which are two-player games. This represents the number of coins each player receives in their "bank" to begin betting. During games 1, 3, 5, and 7, which are one-player games, the number in the upper-left corner changes to 24.

This occurs because the computer has made its initial bet and subtracted one coin from the original 25-coin bank. The numbers in each lower corner of the machine playfield show how much each player is betting. A question mark appears in each player's betting square.

BETTING

Use the red controller button to place your bet. You can bet up to five coins each time. Games 3, 4, 7, and 8 have a maximum of five paylines. Each bet of one coin increases the chances of adding to your bank. For example, bet three coins and you could win a jackpot on either the first, second, or third paylines.

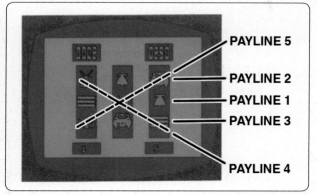

PAYLINE 5
PAYLINE 2
PAYLINE 1
PAYLINE 3
PAYLINE 4

Games 1, 2, 5, and 6 only "pay" on the center line (or payline). In these game variations, the more you bet (up to five coins) the more you can add to your bank.

After placing a bet, pull back on the joystick to spin the reels of the slot machine. In two-player games, both players must do this to spin the reels. The game ends when one player's bank is "broke." To continue play, press the game reset button once to add 25 coins to each player's bank. The game may end with one player going broke, while the other player has coins remaining. When the game reset button is pressed once, the player who went broke is given 25 coins but the player with coins remaining receives 25 additional coins.

You compete against the computer in a one-player game. The computer makes a random bet for each play. The game ends if you, or the computer, go broke. To continue play, press the game reset button once to add 25 coins to each bank. As in two-player games, the player with coins remaining when the game ends does not lose those coins. Press the game reset button twice to reset each player's bank to 25 coins for all one- and two-player games.

GAME OPTIONS

GAME TYPE	GAME #	# PLAYERS	FEATURES
Jackpot	1	1	CL
	2	2	CL
	3	1	U5
	4	2	U5
Payoff	5	1	CL
	6	2	CL
	7	1	U5
	8	2	U5

FEATURES

CENTER PAY LINE (CL)
Only the center line pays off.

UP TO 5 PAY LINES (U5)
The more you bet, the more paylines become eligible to win.

SCORING

Your Slot Machine "pays off" in the same manner as a 3-wheel, 20-stop, slot machine found in a gambling casino.

The score for a one-player game is displayed in the upper-right corner of the screen, while the computer's score appears on the left. In two-player games, the right player's score is on the right and the left player's score is on the left.

ANY BAR	ANY BAR	ANY BAR	20
▬	▬	▬	100
🚗	🚗	🚗	200

For Jackpot Games (Games 1 to 4).

For Payoff Games (Games 5 to 8).

2
5
10
10
14
14
18
18
100
200

VIDEO CHESS

It's your 22nd move of the game. Your defense is set with a tight King position. You move in your Queen and capture your opponent's Rook—his only defense—checkmate!

Sharpen your wits and prepare to become a "master" with *Video Chess*. It's you against the computer in one of the most sophisticated approaches to the classical thinking man's game.

ABOUT THE GAME

As one of man's oldest games, chess is believed to have originated in India between 350 and 400 AD. The first written record of the game was 700 AD. There are many variations of chess played throughout the world.

The game of chess was a classic far before gamers even knew about the Atari gaming system. However, the ability to play against a computer was rather difficult before the advent of *Video Chess*. The fact that players could play against a computer (or even a friend) on the TV screen was the real draw to this game. Despite the graphics, *Video Chess* was a marvel to the gaming industry due to the various difficulties and levels of computer response.

Video Chess can be played for your own entertainment, or to train yourself in chess. To this day, games have been designed to contain gradual increases in difficulty and, even though the game's mechanics generally don't change too much, they do change enough to keep it interesting. In *Video Chess*, the only thing that changes as the difficulty increases is how much smarter the computer gets. This forces you to think about your moves a little more each time. There is one drawback to the difficulty setting feature. Due to the number of calculations the computer must do at higher difficulties, it can take a long time to make a decision. At level 7, for example, each turn can take up to 10 hours!

OBJECT OF THE GAME

In any chess game, the object of the game is to capture the opponent's king.

HOW TO PLAY

The computer sets up the pieces on the board in their proper order. Each player begins with 16 pieces. They include: one king; one queen; two rooks; two bishops; two knights; and eight pawns. Each piece has its own distinctive move.

KING

The King is the most important piece in the game. The king isn't very mobile, as he can only move one square at a time. However, you can move the king in any direction—on the rank (sideways); on the file (forward or backward); or diagonally.

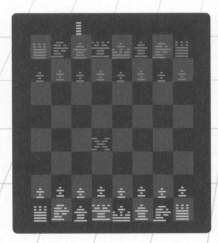

All other pieces should be sacrificed to save the king. The computer will not allow the king to move to a square that is under attack by an enemy piece.

QUEEN

The queen is the most mobile and versatile piece on the board, making her the most powerful. She moves in any direction and for as many open squares as desired. The queen combines the powers of the rook and bishop.

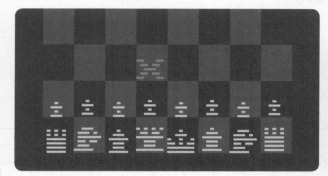

ROOK

The rook moves on the rank or file (forward, backward, sideways) for as many open squares as desired. The rook is usually considered next in importance to the king and queen.

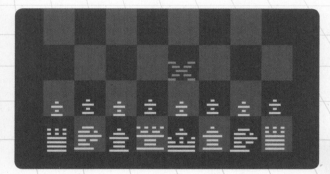

BISHOP

The bishop moves back and fourth in a diagonal line and can move as many squares as the board offers unless blocked by another piece in its way. The two bishops on each side are set such that one is tied to the light blue squares, while the other is tied to the dark blue squares. A bishop is considered slightly more important than a knight, depending on its board position.

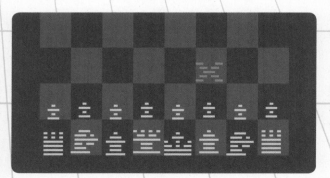

KNIGHT

The knight moves from point to point, following the "one up and two across" or "two up and one across" pattern, which makes an "L" shape. The knight is unique in that it cannot be blocked. It can jump over the other pieces provided its destination is an open square, or one in which it can take and capture an opponent's piece.

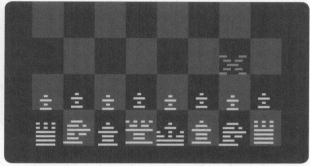

PAWN

The pawn moves straightforward one square at a time; it cannot move backward. If desired, the pawn can advance two moves but only on its initial move. The pawn can capture opponent pieces by taking them on a diagonal move, which is the only time the pawn can move diagonally. (With one exception, see "Double Moves.") Although the pawn is sometimes considered the least important piece, it is the "foot soldier" of chess and is vital in holding territory.

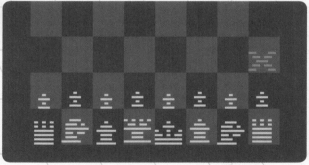

PAWN PROMOTION

If you advance a pawn safely to the last or eighth square (eighth rank) on the opposite side of the board, it can be "promoted" to any other piece except a king. The computer will automatically promote your pawn to a queen, since it is the most powerful piece. Press the left difficulty button to the A position, simply press the red controller button to exchange the queen for any other piece except a king.

CAPTURING PIECES

Pieces (except pawns) can capture in the same manner as they move. If a piece can move to a square that is occupied by an enemy unit, that unit can be captured. The captured piece is permanently removed from the board, and the capturing piece occupies that space. Capturing is optional; you are not required to capture enemy pieces.

Pieces cannot displace or capture pieces of their own color. When capturing or moving, none of the pieces are allowed to jump over other units—except the knight. Traditionally, the capture of the king is never actually carried out. If the king is under attack but has room to escape, it is said to be in "check." The computer in *Video Chess* has a distinct method of showing when a king is in check. If the king cannot escape, it is said to be "checkmated" and the game ends.

DOUBLE MOVES

There are two "double moves" allowed in chess. One is known as "castling," the other is known as "en passant." The computer opponent (as well as regular players) in *Video Chess* can use either or both during the course of a game.

CASTLING

Castling can be an offensive or defensive move. To castle, the squares between the king and one of the rooks must be clear. The king or the rook may not have been previously moved. This move protects the king and moves the rook to the center of the board where it can be more effective.

When this situation occurs, move your king two spaces to the right or left (depending on which way you are castling), and push the red controller button. The computer will automatically bring the rook around the king, thereby completing your castling move. The computer will then determine its next move.

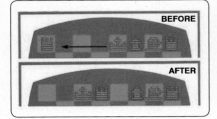

Castling

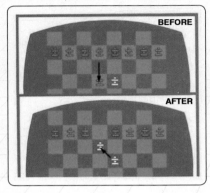

En passant

CASTLING

If you move the king toward the rook on its side of the board, it is called "castling to the king's side." If the king is moved toward the queen's side, it is called "castling to the queen's side."

A player cannot use the castling move when the king is in check. Additionally, a player can't castle to the king's side if any of the squares between the king and the rook are threatened. The former example is called "castling out of check"; the later example is known as "castling across the check."

EN PASSANT (IN PASSING)

This move is used to counteract the enemy pawn's initial double move on an adjacent file. To carry out the en passant, advance your pawn to the fifth rank. Your opponent then has the option of moving his or her pawn one square (where it would be under attack) or two squares. If your opponent elects to move two squares, the "en passant" move allows you to take that pawn by diagonally moving your pawn to the square that was skipped over.

KEEP IN MIND...

There may be some occasions in which the computer will not allow a player to use en passant to move out of check. If this should occur, use the set-up move to complete the sequence.

The en passant capture must be made immediately, meaning when the opportunity is first available or not at all. It cannot be executed during a later turn.

DIFFICULTY OPTIONS

In the A position, the computer plays white pieces and moves first. In the B position, the human player controls the white pieces and moves first. The color of the number at the top of the playfield (also denoting skill level) indicates which color you're playing. If it is white, for example, then you're playing the white pieces.

While in the A position, you can set up the board for a particular problem or situation. Move the cursor to the square where you want to place a particular piece. Each time you press the red controller button, the computer puts a different piece on that square, starting with the computer's king, and cycling through the player's pawn. After placing the piece on the board, move the curser to the next position and repeat the process.

To remove a piece from the board, place the cursor over the piece and cycle past the player's pawn. An "X" will appear and that piece will be removed from the board. When the board is set up properly, press the left difficulty button to the B position and begin play. At this point, you must move first, whether or not the right difficulty button is in the A or B position.

GAME SELECT BUTTON

Depress the game select button to choose the game's level of difficulty. Level 8 is a learning level for beginning players. It is the least difficult, so it makes for good practice for beginners. After practicing at level 8, beginning players should move to level 1. Levels 1 through 7 become progressively more difficult, with level 7 being the most difficult. You can change the level of difficulty any time during a game by depressing the game select button.

GAME RESET BUTTON

Depress the game reset button to start or restart a game. If the computer is playing the red (black) pieces, it is not necessary to depress this button when turning on the game.

If the computer is playing the white pieces, though, you must depress the game reset button before the computer makes its first move.

SKILL LEVELS

There are seven progressively harder skill levels in *Video Chess* and one level for beginners. As the levels increase from 1 to 7, the computer will take longer to compute its next move.

LEVEL	TIME
LEVEL 1	15 SECONDS
LEVEL 2	30 SECONDS
LEVEL 3	45 SECONDS
LEVEL 4	2 MIN. 45 SEC.
LEVEL 5	3 MIN. 15 SEC.
LEVEL 6	12 MINUTES
LEVEL 7	10 HOURS
LEVEL 8	10 SECONDS

The times listed below for each skill level are an average, since the length of time depends on the complexity of the board and the level chosen.

NUMBER OF PLAYERS

Video Chess can be played as a single-player game against the computer or against a live opponent on the second controller.

- According to Larry Wagner, *Video Chess* was developed as a direct result of a customer who complained that the original VCS system box showed a picture of chess, but no chess game existed.

- Atari developed a bank switching ROM cartridge for earlier prototypes of *Video Chess* that were larger than four kilobytes in size. Ultimately, the released version fit the standard 4K size. This technology was later used for other Atari 2600 titles.

- If you checkmate the computer, the game doesn't actually end. Instead, you'll hear a buzzing sound and you can take the king and keep playing. If you can promote a pawn afterwards, it may become the computer's (Queen) piece.

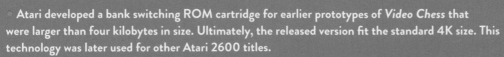

- On game 6 or 7, the computer will start moving pieces around if the controls are not touched for an extended period of time.

- According to the game manual, the computer may not let you use "en passant" to move out of check. If this occurs, you must go into the set-up mode to correct it. If after setting up a chess problem and your initial move is to "castle," the computer may not accept it as a legal move.

3D TIC-TAC-TOE

Put your thinking cap on for this one. Examine the board. Carefully plan your strategy. Then make your move. The object here is to place four Xs and four Os in one horizontal, vertical, or diagonal row on one plane or through all the planes. To win, you must complete your row before your opponent or the computer.

ABOUT THE GAME

Programmer Carol Shaw chose the superior 4x4x4 variation of *3D Tic-Tac-Toe* over the original 3x3x3 variation. The former avoids the latter's problem of the first player always winning if they choose a center square. Although not one of the Atari 2600's more beloved titles, *3D Tic-Tac-Toe* certainly ranks amongst its most distinctive.

OBJECT OF THE GAME

In this game, there is a perspective drawing of four square boards (or planes) displayed on-screen, which is intended to create a three-dimensional effect. Each board is a 4 x 4 grid. The object of the game is to place four Xs or four Os in one horizontal, vertical, or diagonal row. To do so, you can use one plane or all four planes. You must place four markers in a row before your opponent does (or before the computer) to win.

HOW TO PLAY

To move the "cursor" (the blinking X or O) right or left, move the joystick right or left. This causes the cursor to wrap around (disappear on one side of the level or plane and appear on the other side). Move the joystick forward to move the cursor up from square to square, or to a new level as it reaches the top of a plane.

To move the cursor down in the same manner, move the joystick back. Put the joystick in a diagonal position and the cursor moves diagonally on the screen and from one level to another.

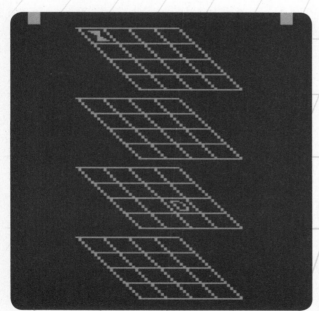

To place an X or an O on-screen, press the red controller button when the cursor is in the square you wish to occupy. The last move made is indicated by a blinking X or O in the appropriate square.

The computer will not allow a move to an occupied square. It will sound an error message when a player presses the controller button in an attempt to move into a square that is already occupied.

In total, there are 76 possible ways to win. It is not possible to win by using two or three planes, you must use one or all four.

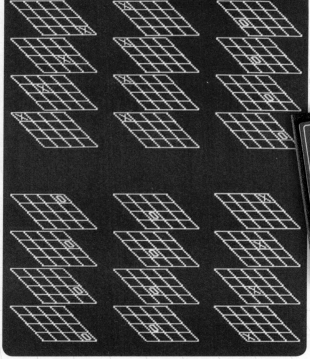

A page from the game's original manual describing some of the possible ways to win.

It has been proven that the first player to move can always win, provided he or she plays a perfect game. The computer, on the other hand, has a degree of randomness programmed into its play, so it will not always play a perfect game, even at the highest skill level (8). This gives the opponent a chance to win, if he or she is a skillful player.

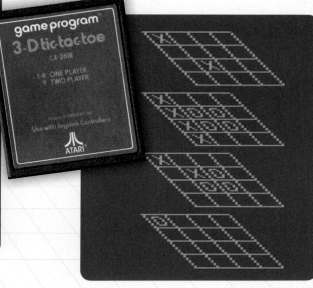

X has won.

STRATEGY

To beat the computer or another player, you must place two three-in-a-rows so that the opponent cannot block both of them. Occasionally, you may win when an opponent fails to see that you have three-in-a-row, but that method involves more luck than strategy.

At higher skill levels, placing three-in-a-row becomes difficult. One of the secrets to playing winning tic-tac-toe is to play in the 16 "strong" squares at the beginning of a game. The 16 strong squares are the eight outside corner squares and the eight inside center squares.

Try to take over or dominate planes. The four tic-tac-toe boards represent horizontal, vertical, and diagonal planes. When you place three or four markers in one plane and your opponent has none, you can probably win.

Continue to force the opponent to block until you have two three-in-a rows that cannot both be blocked in one move.

When planning your moves during a game, don't lose sight of the fact that your opponent is doing the same. Blocking your opponent's markers is equally as important to establishing your own strategy.

DIFFICULTY OPTIONS

The right difficulty button determines who begins the game. For one-player games with the button set to the A position, you start; when the button is in the B position, the computer starts. In two-player games the right difficulty button determines whether X or O starts.

In the A position, the X player, or the player using the joystick plugged into the first controller port, starts. In the B position, the O player (using the second controller port) starts.

The left difficulty button can be used to create a "set up" mode on the screen. To do this, press the button to the A position. You may then use the joystick plugged into the first controller port to place Xs or Os anywhere on the screen. Press the controller button to place markers. Hold the button down and the cursor alternates between Xs, Os and blinks on the screen so that you can place whichever you wish in the desired square.

When you place the left difficulty button in the B position, tic-tac-toe is ready for normal gameplay. After using the set up mode, either X or O may play first. This is determined by the position of the right difficulty button, the same as at the start of the game.

GAME OPTIONS

When the game starts, the display shows the four square boards (or planes) and the number 1 appears on each side of the top of the screen.

The left number 1 represents the game number (or skill level); to change it, press Select. Choose between game numbers 1 through 8, with each higher number a progressively higher skill level. Game 9 is a two-player variant.

The right number 1 corresponds to the number of players for each game. This number changes automatically to 2 when the ninth game is selected.

Press Reset to begin a new game. The game number remains the same when Reset is pressed. The game number only changes when the Select button is used, or when the power is turned on and off.

DIFFICULTY LEVEL	NUMBER OF MOVES THE COMPUTER LOOKS AHEAD	COMPUTER'S APPROXIMATE MOVE TIME
1	1	0.5 seconds
2	2	3 seconds or less
3	3	1 minute or less
4	4	3 minutes or less
5	5	10 minutes or less
6	6	10 minutes or less
7	9	10 minutes or less
8	9	20 minutes or less

The computer moves quickly and is fairly easy to beat at level 1. At level 8, the computer may think, or "compute," for as long as 20 minutes before making its move. At this level, it is very difficult to beat.

When the computer is working on its next move, the tic-tac-toe boards are not displayed. Instead, various colors appear on-screen. Pressing Reset or changing the difficulty buttons when this occurs will have no effect on the game. However, pressing Select causes the computer to move almost immediately, without changing the game number.

If the computer is not computing its next move, the skill or game may be changed by pressing Select.

- Depending upon which part of the world you reside, "tic-tac-toe" might instead be referred to as "noughts and crosses" or simply "Xs and Os."

- Parker Brothers produced a 3D Tic-Tac-Toe board game called *Qubic* in 1964, which received a reissue in 1972.

- Although there were several computer versions of *3D Tic-Tac-Toe* created, the Atari 2600 plays host to the sole console version.

3-D TIC-TAC-TOE
GAME PROGRAM™ (AVAILABLE SOON)

X MARKS THE SPOT

Put your thinking cap on for this one. Examine the board. Carefully plan your strategy. Then make your move. The object here is to place four X's or four O's in one horizontal, vertical or diagonal row on one plane or through all the planes. To win, you must complete your row before your opponent does or before the computer does.

3-D Tic-Tac-Toe

Tips & Tricks

◆ Unlike traditional tic-tac-toe, which favors corner squares, the odds of winning are greatly increased in *3D Tic-Tac-Toe* if the player who goes first chooses a center square as his or her first move.

CHAMPIONSHIP SOCCER

Soccer is a game of skill and strategy. It takes a lot of practice to play a winning game. And what's true on the field is true on your Atari Video Computer System. Pele's *Championship Soccer* challenges you every inch of the way. Passing. Dribbling. Kicking. Blocking. Attacking. Defending. You choose the level of difficulty you want to play and, with 54 separate games from which to choose, even Pele will find plenty of challenge. It's more than a video game. It's a game of skill and strategy for the whole family.

Okay, soccer fans, the Atari Championship Soccer Team challenges you to a game. The Atari computer team is waiting impatiently inside your Game Program cartridge for you to select one of the single-player games (Games 28 through 54). They want to show you their stuff. Here's a brief rundown on each player, so you'll know who you're up against.

"Crash" Morgan, the galloping goalie, is the fastest man on the team. "Crash" got his nickname because he is forever slamming into the goal posts chasing after the ball. Fortunately, the goal posts are never damaged, but sometimes you can score a goal on him before his ears stop ringing.

Nick Danger, the frantic forward, is mean and nasty and just loves to blast the ball into your goal shouting, "Eat leather, chump." Don't let his bad manners bother you; it's just his way of rattling the opposition.

"Lumpy" Duran, the left back, is without a doubt the clumsiest player in the world of soccer. Penalized twice for stepping on the ball instead of kicking it, he was finally thrown out of one game for toe-kicking the referee!

Alexie Putsnowski (Putsy), the right back. What can we say Putsy? A real ladies man, a great soccer player, a sore loser. Even though "The Puts" has kicked and gouged his way to soccer stardom, he has been voted the "least liked" player for three years in a row.

ABOUT THE GAME

With 56 different play modes, *Championship Soccer* is a game that has a nearly endless amount of gameplay. Within the different play modes, there are several variables that create difficulties ranging from the computer's skill to unique challenges.

Championship Soccer has a high entertainment value, however, it does fall short of having quality in the detail between each play mode. Yes, there are many play modes with a great amount of different options, however, quantity does not mean quality. If all you are looking for a soccer game that works and is not so shallow that you can at least show off some skill, this game will do it for you. So, for being one of the first sports games to be released on the Atari 2600, Championship Soccer provides for a great blueprint toward the perfect soccer game.

OBJECT OF THE GAME

The object is to score points by kicking the ball into your opponent's goal. One point is scored for each goal. The team with the most points wins the game.

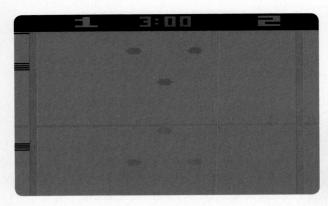

HOW TO PLAY

TEAM MOVES

Each team consists of three players (a Forward and two Backs) and a goalkeeper. The fielders, who are controlled by using the joystick, always move together in the direction the joystick is pressed (up, down, right, left, or diagonally).

The goalie moves from side to side within the goal area. While the ball is in play, the computer controls the goalkeeper and keeps him in front of the ball. You can make him move faster by moving the joystick left and right. When the goalkeeper takes possession of the ball, you gain control of him.

THE REFEREE

The black lines that appear on the left side of the screen represent the referee and the linesman. The referee blows the whistle to start and stop play and positions the ball for kickoffs and penalties.

THE CLOCK

A game of *Championship Soccer* takes place over the course of two halves. A half lasts from 3 to 5 minutes, depending on the Team Speed of the game you select. The clock (located at top center of the screen) starts counting down the seconds to the end of the first half when you press down the game reset button.

There is no break between the first and second half. As soon as the first half ends, it resets and starts counting down the time remaining in the second half. The referee's whistle signals both the end of the first half and the start of the second.

THE OPENING KICKOFF

At the start of the game, the ball is placed on the centerspot and both teams line on either side of the centerline. Use the left joystick to control the Red team. Use the right joystick to control the Blue team.

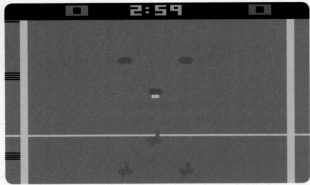

The Red team's Forward kicks off. The kickoff is a kick backward to one of the same team's Backs. Move the left joystick diagonally back left or right to start the kickoff. There's no need to press the red button to start the kickoff, but you can kick faster if you move the joystick and then quickly press the button.

THE GAMEPLAY

After the opening kickoff, the Red team (the attacking team) dribbles and kicks the ball toward the Blue team's goal. The Blue team (the defending team) attempts to steal the ball and attack the Red team's goal. In *Championship Soccer*, the defending team has an advantage because it moves faster than the attacking team.

When an attacking team is within range of the opponent's goal, the attackers attempt to kick the ball past the goalkeeper into the goal. If the goalkeeper catches the ball, he attempts to kick the ball upfield to a teammate. The attackers try to intercept and make a goal.

THE SECOND HALF

The teams switch sides at the half. The Blue team's Forward kicks off to one of the team Backs to continue the game.

HORIZONTAL LIMITS

If your Forward is playing the ball close to a sideline, one of your Backs will be positioned over the sideline. This is perfectly legal in all games, including games with sidelines out of bounds.

VERTICAL LIMITS

Teams can approach the goal line close enough to trap the ball, but they cannot cross the goal line.

OUT OF BOUNDS - PENALTY PLAYS

Each time an out-of-bounds infraction occurs, the referee blows his whistle. The team against which the penalty is called flashes, indicating that it forfeits the ball. One of three penalty plays results: a Throw-In, a Goal Line Kick, or a Corner Kick.

THROW-IN

The Throw-In penalty play results when a team puts the ball over a sideline. The ball is then thrown in to a player at the point at which the ball went out of bounds. To receive a Throw-in, move your player up to the ball and touch it. The ball will jump from the sideline and your receiver will trap it. The ball is back in play as soon as the Throw-in is completed.

GOAL LINE KICK

When an attacking team maneuvers the ball over the defending team's goal line, the referee calls a penalty against the attacking team. The referee places the ball on the goal line in front of the defending team's goalkeeper and the goalkeeper traps the ball. He then kicks it upfield to a teammate. The attacking team can intercept the kick, since the ball is back in play as soon as the goalkeeper kicks it.

CORNER KICK

If the defending team maneuvers the ball outside its own end line, the referee calls a penalty against the defending team. The referee places the ball at the corner close to the defending team's goal. The attacking team then kicks it upfield to a teammate. The defending team cannot intercept the ball until after the attacking team touches it, or it rolls to a stop.

To perform a corner kick, position the attacking team to receive the ball and press the button on the joystick.

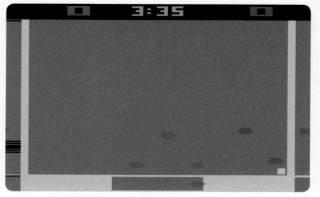

The ball will sail from its spot at a 45-degree angle, as long as you hold in the button. If you release the button, the ball will cut in front of the goal line, at which time you can attempt to kick a goal.

BALL CONTROL

DRIBBLING

Use the joystick to dribble the ball. Move your team up to the ball until a player traps it. After doing so, quickly move the joystick in the direction you want the ball to go.

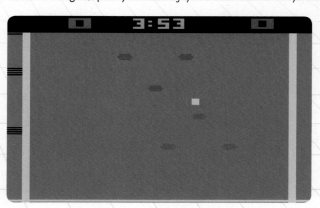

The ball will move a short distance and stop, unless it is intercepted before it stops.

Important Reminder: When sending your players after the ball, remember that you can touch the ball and immediately take off in any direction. You don't have to go around the ball to establish the direction you want to move; think of it as "touch and go".

KICKING

To kick the ball after your player traps it, move the joystick in the direction you want the ball to go and press the red controller button. The longer you hold the button, the longer the kick will be. To avoid kicking the ball in the wrong direction, always move the joystick before pressing the button. If you press the button without moving the joystick, the ball is kicked straight upfield, or straight downfield, depending on whether your player is above or below the ball when the kick occurs.

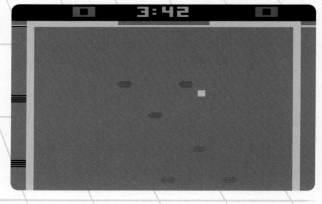

TOE KICK

The toe kick is fast and powerful, making it the most effective way to drive the ball toward the goal. This kick extends your player's trapping range and moves the ball downfield very fast. This technique enables you to out-distance the defending team and keep control of the ball.

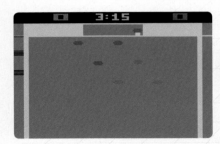

To execute a toe kick, move a player within a short distance of the ball, push the joystick in the direction you want the ball to go, and press the red button. You can use the toe kick while your team is moving across the field, as well as when it is moving upfield or downfield.

GAME DIFFICULTY

Games are normally played with the left and right difficulty buttons set to the B position. To give yourself a handicap, set the difficulty button to the A position. This makes the goal larger, making it harder to defend and easier for your opponent to score.

GAME OPTIONS

CHOOSING A GAME

Select your game number from the Game Select Matrix. The matrix describes each of the 54 games variations in *Championship Soccer*. Games 1 through 27 are two-player games against the computer.

The Game Select Matrix describes two-player games in terms of how fast the teams move (Team Speed), the size of the goals (Goal Size), and which penalties apply, if any (Penalties).

Some two-player games have no out-of-bounds penalties (Penalties N in the Game Select Matrix). In these games, the ball rebounds from boundaries (sidelines and goal lines). In other two-player games, the ball rebounds from goal lines but there is a penalty if the ball crosses a sideline (Penalty S). In the remaining two-player games, there are penalties if the ball crosses either a sideline or a goal line (Penalties SG).

The easiest two-player game is Game 1. The teams move slowly (S), there are no penalties (N), and the goals are larger (L). The most difficult two-player game is probably Game 27 with fast teams (F), out-of-bounds (SG), and small goals (S).

There are no penalties in single-player games.

2-PLAYER GAME #.	1-PLAYER GAME #	GOAL SIZE	TEAM SPEED	PENALTIES (2-PLAYER ONLY)	COMPUTER DIFFICULTY (1-PLAYER ONLY)
1	28	L	SL	NP	EZ
2	29	M	SL	NP	EZ
3	30	S	SL	NP	EZ
4	31	L	SL	SP	MD
5	32	M	SL	SP	MD
6	33	S	SL	SP	MD
7	34	L	SL	SG	DF
8	35	M	SL	SG	DF
9	36	S	SL	SG	DF
10	37	L	MF	NP	EZ
11	38	M	MF	NP	EZ
12	39	S	MF	NP	EZ
13	40	L	MF	SP	MD
14	41	M	MF	SP	MD
15	42	S	MF	SP	MD
16	43	L	MF	SG	DF
17	44	M	MF	SG	DF
18	45	S	MF	SG	DF
19	46	L	FA	NP	EZ
20	47	M	FA	NP	EZ
21	48	S	FA	NP	EZ
22	49	L	FA	SP	MD
23	50	M	FA	SP	MD
24	51	S	FA	SP	MD
25	52	L	FA	SG	DF
26	53	M	FA	SG	DF
27	54	S	FA	SG	DF

NUMBER OF PLAYERS

Depending on the game variation, you can play against an opponent using the other controller, or you can play against the computer. There are many difficulties in either of these modes.

FEATURES

GOAL SIZE

The goal's width is set to large (L), medium (M), or small (S).

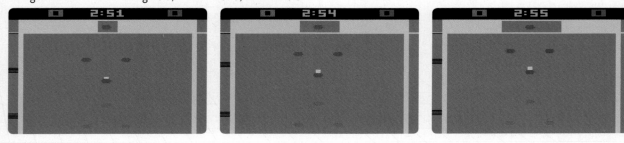

TEAM SPEED

Team Speed affects both the speed of your players and the length of each half. Slow (SL) teams play three-minute halves. Moderately fast (MF) teams play four-minute halves. Fast (FA) teams play five-minute halves.

PENALTIES

Penalties apply only to two-player games; all one-player games use no penalty (NP) rules. A penalty is called in Sideline penalty games (SP) when the ball goes over a sideline.

Penalties are called when the ball crosses a sideline or the goal line in Sideline and Goal Line penalty games (SG). Penalties result in out-of-bounds plays.

COMPUTER DIFFICULTY

The computer play ranges from easy (EZ) to moderately difficult (MD) to difficult (DF). The computer will play harder as your lead grows, or it will ease up if it takes a lead, regardless of the starting difficulty.

FUN FACTS!

○ *Championship Soccer* is the first game to have a scrolling playfield, and the first to feature a "celebration" screen.

○ The HMOVE lines, which are the black lines at the side of the screen where code is stored, are referred to as referees in the manual.

○ If you score over 110 points, the first digit will become garbled and will change every 10 points thereafter. To do this, play game #19 and keep scoring against your team.

○ Sears released the Tele-Games version as *Soccer*.

○ *Championship Soccer* was later re-released as *Pelé's Soccer* by Atari in 1981 and was one of the first sports games that was endorsed by a star player. Pelé even appeared in television commercials for the game!

○ Championship Soccer was an Honorable Mention for Best Sports Game in the 1982 Sportie Awards.

Tips & Tricks

◆ Maintaining Control Over the Ball: When your team is attacking, use evasive moves to control the ball. Pass the ball from player to player and dodge and weave around the defending players to avoid losing the ball. Since the defending team moves faster than the attacking team, it is easier to intercept the ball when the ball is dribbled and kicked straight toward the goal.

◆ Scoring a Goal: A straight kick into the goal will almost always get blocked, because the goalkeeper is always in front of the ball. That said, position your player for a diagonal kick.

◆ Defending Your Goal: Shift your attention from your regular players to your goalkeeper. Position your Forward and Backs so they can harass the attackers and block goal kicks, but keep your eye on the ball and concentrate on your goalkeeper. Use the joystick to make him move faster within the goal area.

◆ Turning the Play Around: Always look for a chance to steal the ball. If you can steal it, pass it to your goalkeeper. Remember that as long as he has the ball, you control the play. Don't kick the ball to another player until you find the right opportunity. Back your players away from the goal line, dodge the attackers, and look for a chance to kick the ball to someone with open space.

◆ Scoring a Goal on a Corner Kick: Success depends upon position, speed, and surprise. Position your Forward as if you were going to make a forward attack on your opponent's goal. Press and hold in the button on your joystick. This will cause the ball to leave its spot at a 45-degree angle. Quickly release the button to make the ball cut across the goal line.

CIRCUS ATARI

How good are your reflexes? To find out, try to pop the balloons by bouncing the clown on the teeter-totter. Red, white, and blue balloons are all worth different points. The more difficult to "pop," the more you score.

ABOUT THE GAME

Demanding both quickness and precision from its players, Mike Lorenzen's *Circus Atari* is one of the more demanding paddle controller-based games. Although graphically simple, Lorenzen was able to animate a surprising amount of personality into the little clown stick figures.

OBJECT OF THE GAME

POP! POP! POP! Pop the balloons and score points. A wall of red, blue, and white balloons appears at the top of the screen. You must pop balloons by catching a clown on the teeter-totter and bouncing him up to the balloons. Use the controller to move the teeter-totter across the screen to catch the clowns.

Each time a clown pops a balloon, the balloon disappears and you score points.

HOW TO PLAY

Each player receives five clowns (or turns). If you fail to catch a clown on the teeter-totter, he will crash and disappear from the playfield. Press the red controller button to make another clown bounce off the trampoline from the right or left corner of the playfield. The game ends after five clowns have crashed. The clowns may land on any point of the teeter-totter except where the other clown is sitting, which causes them to crash.

Use the paddle controller to move the teeter-totter across the screen. Press the red button on the paddle controller to start a turn, or press the red button to make a clown bounce on the trampoline. Pressing the red button while the clown is in the air changes the direction of the teeter-totter. This is helpful in preventing the airborne clown from crashing into the other clown on the teeter-totter.

SCORING

The first point is scored as the clown leaves the trampoline. Once the clown starts the bouncing motion, one point is scored each time he hits the trampoline or the teeter-totter. Additional points are scored as the clown pops the balloons.

Remember, the higher the balloon the clown pops the more points you score, so it is best to catch him on the edge of the teeter-totter for the highest bounce.

You receive an extra clown (or turn) each time you pop an entire row of red balloons. The top-right corner of the screen will show an "X" to indicate an extra clown or turn. Although scoring can be infinite, there is only space for four digits on the screen, so when you become a pro, your score will read 0000 again when you pass 9999.

At the end of each game, final scores appear at the top of the screen; left player to the left and right player to the right in two-player games.

ATARI NEWS
What The Critics Had to Say

"*Circus Atari* is basically the same as Atari's *Breakout* cartridge - only better."

-How to Win at Home Video Games book, 1982

DIFFICULTY OPTIONS

When the difficulty button is in the A position, the clowns bounce faster after contact with the balloons and the teeter-totter. While in the B position, you have better control over the clowns because they don't move as fast. For one-player games, use the left difficulty button.

GAME OPTIONS

To choose a game, press Select. There are eight game variations. The game and the number of players appear in the upper-middle part of the screen, with the game number to the left and the number of players to the right. To begin a game, press Reset.

One or two players can play Games 1 through 6, but Games 7 and 8 are two-player games only.

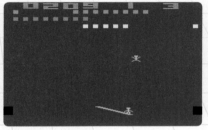

Circus Atari Game 1.

GAME 1: BREAKOUT CIRCUS

As the clown pops balloons, he rebounds from one balloon to the next both horizontally and vertically. After popping a full row of balloons, a new row appears and you receive bonus points. Simply pop the top row of red balloons to receive an extra clown.

GAME 2

This game is similar to Game 1, except the playfield has an additional wall of barriers added below the balloons, which makes the game more difficult.

GAME 3: BREAKTHRU CIRCUS

In this game variation, the clown does not rebound off the balloons. Instead, he continues to move in a horizontal direction off the balloons. This version is somewhat easier for a beginning player. Scoring is the same as in Game 1.

GAME 4

This version is Breakthru Circus with a row of barriers added to the playfield below the balloons.

GAME 5

This game is also similar to Breakout Circus, except the balloons do not "restore" after the full row has been popped. You must pop all balloons on the screen to get three new rows of balloons. Once this happens, you receive 170 bonus points and an extra clown.

GAME 6

The same as Game 5, but with an additional row of barriers added below the balloons.

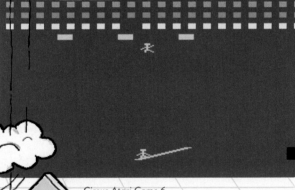

Circus Atari Game 6.

GAME 7

Game 7 is for two players. Both players share the same wall of balloons. The computer tracks each player's score individually.

GAME 8

This variation is the same as Game 7, but with the addition of barriers below the balloons to make the game more challenging.

GAME TYPE	GAME #	# PLAYERS	FEATURES
Breakout	1	1-2	1L
	2	1-2	1L & BA
Breakthru	3	1-2	1L
	4	1-2	1L & BA
Breakout	5	1-2	FC
	6	1-2	FC & BA
	7	2	FC
	8	2	FC & BA

FEATURES

SINGLE LINE CLEAR (IL)

A new row appears each time a full row of balloons is popped.

FULL CLEAR (FC)

To receive a new row of balloons, all balloons on the screen must be popped.

BARRIERS (BA)

A row of barriers appears below the rows of balloons.

FUN FACTS!

Circus Atari was a clear derivative of an Exidy arcade game from 1977 called *Circus*, which was a variation on Atari's own *Breakout*.

Tips & Tricks

◆ For the best chance to pop several balloons at once, make sure the clown leaps in the opposite direction to the one in which the balloon row is traveling.

◆ In the versions of the game that resets each row of balloons individually after it is cleared, focus on the red balloons since they are worth the most points. Remove just enough lower point balloons to create a gap to enter and pop all of the red balloons. This should take care of most, if not all, of the balloons below it.

Circus Atari as described on the front cover of issue number 10 of The Atari Owners Club Official Bulletin from 1980.

DODGE 'EM

It's you against the crash car. Accelerate. Change lanes. Each driver gets three heats. A crash ends the heat. If your score looks too good, another crash car comes on course. Levels of difficulty keep the game a constant challenge.

ABOUT THE GAME

Dodge 'Em was programmed by Carla Meninsky, one of the era's most notable female engineers and creator of another Atari hit, *Warlords*. In terms of design, it is a close relative to Sega and Gremlin's *Head-On*, which was released in the previous year.

OBJECT OF THE GAME

Steer your racecar counterclockwise on the four-lane track. The objective is to score as many points as possible by running over the dots that appear on the track's lanes.

At the end of a game, the scores alternately flash on-screen. In one-player games, try to beat your previous score. In two-player games, the player with the highest score after three heats is the winner.

HOW TO PLAY

Each player controls a car: red car, left controller player; green car, right controller player; blue car, computer controlled (except in Game 3).

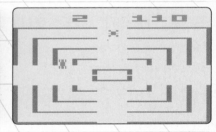

In all games, your racecar automatically moves forward/counterclockwise around the four-lane track. To steer your car right or left, move the joystick forward or backward (toward yourself). The red controller button acts as the vehicle's gas pedal.

The computer car races clockwise around the track and tries to crash into your car. When a crash occurs, you lose a turn. If you run over two sets of dots, two computer cars will appear on the track.

To avoid the computer car and score points, timing is important. Use the accelerator and your skill at steering from one lane to another to win.

You can change a maximum of two lanes at a time, except when accelerating. When accelerating, you can only change one lane at a time.

In one-player games, try to score as many points as possible during your three turns.

There are two two-player games:

◆ You and an opponent take turns scoring while the computer controls the other car (Game 2).

◆ You and an opponent go for it at the same time. The player using the left joystick starts as the point-scoring car (moving left to right on-screen); the right player controls the crash car with one speed and no point scoring. When a crash occurs, the roles are reversed (Game 3).

The number at the top-right corner of the screen represents both players' scores; it changes color according to the color of each car.

SCORING

Each player receives three turns, or "heats," during a game. Each turn ends when your car crashes—three heats, three crashes! When you run over all the dots on the track, you score eight bonus points and another set of dots appears. However, you are only allowed five sets of dots per turn. The number of your remaining turns is displayed at the top of the playfield.

GAME/DIFFICULTY OPTIONS

GAME 1:
One player.

GAME 2:
Two players; the computer controls one car.

GAME 3:
Two players alternately control a point-scoring car and a crash car.

GAME SELECT BUTTON

Use this button to select the game number you want to play. The number of each game appears momentarily at the upper-left corner of the screen.

LEFT DIFFICULTY BUTTON

In the A position, the computer car (or cars) travel at twice their normal speed after the first and third sets of bonus points are awarded. In the B position, the car (or cars) travel at a slower or normal speed.

RIGHT DIFFICULTY BUTTON

In the A position, the computer car begins game play in different playfield positions. In the B position, the computer car always begins next to your racecar.

GAME RESET BUTTON

Use this button to start gameplay.

After *Dodge 'Em* was released, Atari contacted Carla Meninsky about doing a version to market garbage trucks for Mercedes. While it was apparently completed, it is still an unreleased, "lost" game.

FUN FACTS!

Tips & Tricks

◆ For reliable lane switching, hold the direction you want to change lanes just before coming to the gap, as opposed to the moment you reach the gap.

◆ Unless you're a pro player, use acceleration sparingly. It's great for zipping through a road to get dots if you see the computer dragging its heels.

◆ The speed of the computer car(s) will always remain constant. Use this to plan your strategy on-the-fly.

GOLF

It's nine holes of golf where you control the direction and the power of your shot.
Watch out for the hazards!

GOLF
VIDEO COMPUTER SYSTEM™
GAME PROGRAM™
9 HOLE COURSE
ONE TO TWO PLAYERS
ATARI
A Warner Communications Company
CX 2634

ABOUT THE GAME

Videogames were still a relatively new phenomenon when the Atari launched. Parents at that time had not grown up playing them, which is why a game like *Golf* was important in homes where parents were perhaps reluctant about buying a home system. Properly handled, *Golf* became a bargaining chip to get parents to try Atari. Convince them there was a game for them and parents became more likely to buy an Atari for the house.

The case for *Golf* was simple. It's a familiar game, unlike the others that featured shooting and driving and loud noises. And whereas other Atari sports games depended on quick reflexes, Golf allowed the player to take his or her time to line up potential shots.

OBJECT OF THE GAME

When playing a one-player game, try to match or beat par. In two-player games, the player with the fewest strokes is the winner. The left player's stroke count appears in the upper-left corner of the screen, while the right player's score (two-player game only) is displayed in the upper-right side of the screen.

HOW TO PLAY

A stroke occurs each time you hit the ball. Although the number of strokes you take to hit the ball into the cup is unlimited, each hole has a designated par score. In two-player games, player one plays the entire hole, then the second player completes the same hole before the first player moves to the next hole.

Par represents the number of strokes you ideally need to complete the hole. Total par for the course is 36. Par for each hole appears as a red number next to the hole number. Your total stroke count appears to the left of the hole number.

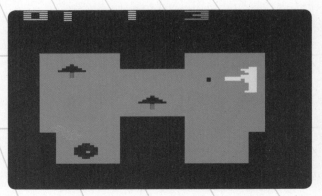

In this image, 01 is total stroke count, 1 is the hole number, and 3 is par for the first hole.

Move the golfer around the course by using the joystick. The golfer's club always points toward the ball. To change the angles of the club (in relation to the ball), position the tip of the club over the ball and walk the golfer around the ball. When you find the desired position (see "Examples of Ball Direction" image), leave the tip of the club over the ball and press the controller button to start a backswing.

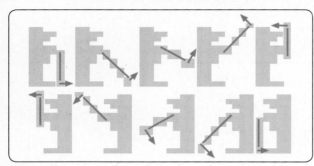

Examples of ball direction.

Hold down the red controller button to begin your backswing. A longer backswing results in the ball traveling further when hit. Release the red controller button to start your forward swing. If any part of the club (or the golfer) hits the ball while the forward swing is in progress, the ball is set in motion.

The direction in which the ball travels is set the moment the backswing begins. You cannot change the direction once the swing has started in motion. If you begin your backswing prematurely, move your golfer away from the ball. There is no penalty stroke for missed swings.

When the ball stops on the green, the screen changes to a close-up view of the green. With an accurate shot, it's possible to sink the ball from the fairway view without going into the close-up view.

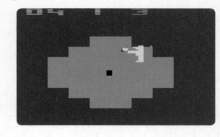

Depending on the difficulty setting, the ball slows down and becomes invisible when entering the "rough" (the blue area on the screen that surrounds each fairway or green). Move the golfer and club through the rough and note the direction the club points. When hitting the ball from the rough, it starts with one-half the normal momentum.

Hazards (such as sand traps, trees, and water) are a different story. Given enough power or momentum and a certain distance, the ball can fly over or pass through hazards.

Sand traps are similar to the rough. A ball that lands in a sand trap loses momentum and becomes invisible. Balls hit from a sand trap also lose half their momentum.

When a ball hits a tree without sufficient momentum it bounces directly backward.

When a ball lands in a water hazard, it returns to the fairway closest to the point of entry and a penalty shot is added to your score.

ATARI GOLF COURSE LAYOUT

The computer automatically tracks your score. Each time your golfer hits the ball, one stroke is recorded by the computer. A ball that lands in a water hazard adds one penalty stroke.

HOLE #	1	2	3	4	5	6	7	8	9	TOTAL
Par	3	5	4	4	4	5	4	3	4	36

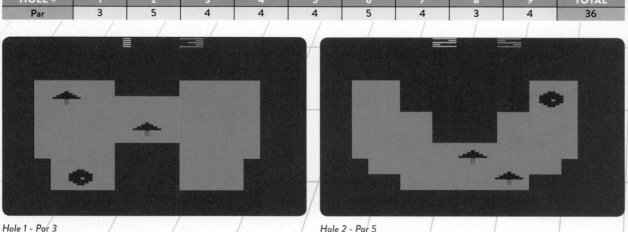

Hole 1 - Par 3

Hole 2 - Par 5

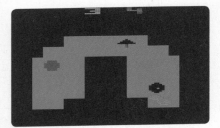

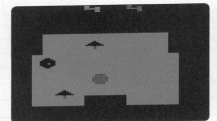

Hole 3 - Par 4

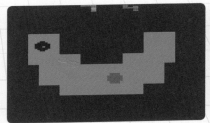

Hole 4 - Par 4

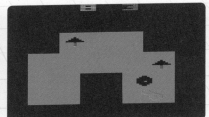

Hole 5 - Par 4

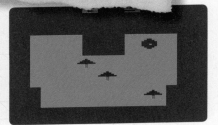

Hole 6 - Par 5

Hole 7 - Par 4

Hole 8 - Par 3

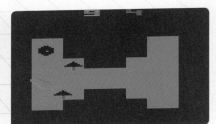

Hole 9 - Par 4

DIFFICULTY OPTIONS

When the difficulty is set to the B position, each hole's cup is large and the ball stops at the edge of the rough. In the A position, each hole is smaller. Also, the ball travels off the course and into the rough when hit off target.

Tips & Tricks

- The golfer moves slower when close to the ball, which allows you to set up your shot more accurately and—more importantly—allows you to locate your ball in the rough and sand traps.

- If you start your backswing too soon and want to avoid hitting the ball, remember the following two things. First, keep the red controller button pressed until your golfer is clear of the ball. Second, always move directly away from the ball. If any part of your club (or the golfer) touches the ball after releasing the red controller button, the ball will go somewhere you don't want it to go and your stroke count will go up.

- Exercise restraint on the greens. If you putt the ball too hard, it will pass through the hole instead of dropping into it.

STEEPLECHASE

Welcome to the video arcade stables. It's time for you to meet the lively thoroughbreds waiting inside this game cartridge. This spirited bunch of hoofers never misses a race.

In the lane at the top of the playfield is "Little Dictator." Little Dictator has a mean streak which surfaces every now and then. Once, after losing a race, he ate the entire grandstands!

The horse in the next lane was aptly named. "Just Missed" just missed every race he had ever entered before coming to our stables. Now he's as dependable as a horse could be. He doesn't win every race, but he never misses one.

"Absent Mind" occupies the third lane down. He tends to forget things occasionally. One time during a race, he completely forgot what he was supposed to be doing and ended up selling programs to the spectators lined up at the railing.

The horse at the bottom of the playfield is the pride and joy of video arcade stables. "Lucky Devil" is his name. He's become so wealthy from winning races that he now lives at the infamous "Horse Heaven Penthouse." At Horse Heaven, he sleeps in a hoof-shaped waterbed, dines regularly on caviar-flavored oats and carrots, and drinks champagne while lounging in his Gucci loafers and satin dinner jacket.

ABOUT THE GAME

A classic before the release of the Atari VCS, *Steeplechase* was known by other names and lived in an arcade cabinet far before hitting the home console. Originally, *Steeplechase* was a six-player game that simulated horse racing at the racetrack. Each player would control their own horse and compete against each other to get from one side of the screen to the other.

This is simply a racing game that takes you in a very linear path that allows for great at-home competition with your friends. As a game that lasted for years in the arcades, this was a game that had a lot of flair and promise, however, not as much delivery as one might hope. Since the game required the use of the paddle controllers, the controls were a little difficult. Due to limitations of the console, the number of players that could compete against each other was also decreased, which changed the experience a bit.

Tips & Tricks

- At first, it may be difficult to focus your attention on the horse and the height indicator bar. You may have a tendency to keep your eye on the horse rather than the bar. To avoid this problem, set the height indicator bar to its highest position and leave it there for the entire race. This allows you to get the hang of jumping the hurdles without having to worry about the bar. When you feel more comfortable about jumping, switch your attention to the height indicator bar.

- Also, try to change your concentration from the horse to the bar and back to the horse. The trick here is not to linger too long on the bar and miss the hurdle. Another method you might try is to keep your attention mainly on your horse and use your peripheral vision to follow the bar. This method can be especially helpful once you are used to adjusting the controller to move the bar.

ATARI NEWS
What The Critics Had to Say

"The only fault with *Steeplechase* is that the jump height indicator is on the far right, and it's tough to keep an eye on both that and your horse. But if you're looking for some unique four-player action, *Steeplechase* is worth checking out."
-Video Game Critic (2001

"The multi-player modes offer some enjoyment initially, but then the game gets old very quickly. Perhaps if there was another track or two or some different kinds of obstacles."
-Brett Allan Weiss (20

OBJECT OF THE GAME

The object of *Steeplechase* is to be the first player to advance your horse to the right side of the screen.

HOW TO PLAY

Each horse gallops at a given speed from left to right. While the horse gallops, hurdles of different sizes approach from right to left. Obviously, your task is to jump and clear the hurdles.

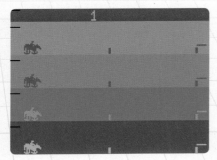

While jumping, your horse actually has no motion from left to right. When you hit a hurdle, your horse loses some horizontal position (distance) while it falls to the ground and gets up. The higher the horse jumps, the easier it is to clear a hurdle. The higher you jump, however, the more time it takes to clear the hurdles, thereby increasing the time it takes to reach the right side of the screen.

The height of a jump can be set by adjusting the height indicator bar. There are four height settings. Each horse has its own height indicator bar.

The speed of the race starts off slow and increases when the leading horse gets about one-third of the way across the screen. Additionally, the speed increases again when the leading horse gets approximately two-thirds of the way across the screen.

A game automatically ends when the game clock reaches 3:00 and none of the horses have made it to the right side. All six game variants are playable by one to four players.

If fewer than two players choose a horse before a race begins, the computer will control the other horse(s).

If players want to compete against each other only, they should play against the computer horses in games 1 and 4. In these games the computer horses' performance rating is "poor," so they won't pose much of a threat. If one or more players want to race against the computer, play against the computers' horses in games 2 or 5 ("good" performance rating) and games 3 or 6 ("excellent" rating).

GAME VARIATIONS

GAMES 1, 2, 3

The spacing between hurdles in these games is uniform, meaning that the distance between all hurdles is the same. In Game 1, the computer horse's racing ability is poor. In Game 2, the computer horse's ability is good and in Game 3 it is excellent.

GAMES 4, 5, 6

In these game variants, the spacing between hurdles is random, meaning that the hurdles appear with varying distances between them. In Game 4, the computer horse's racing ability is poor, it's good in Game 5, and excellent in Game 6.

GAME OPTIONS

One, two, three, or four players can play all six games.

GAME #	COMPUTER PERFORMANCE RATING	HURDLE SPACING
1	Poor	Uniform
2	Good	Uniform
3	Excellent	Uniform
4	Poor	Random
5	Good	Random
6	Excellent	Random

NUMBER OF PLAYERS

Steeplechase is playable by two players only. You can play against one player while the computer controls the other horses.

FEATURES

COMPUTER PERFORMANCE

The computer's race performance will be poor, good, or excellent.

HURDLE SPACING

Hurdles are either uniformly spaced or randomly placed.

SCORING

There is no scoring in this game. You either win the race or you don't. There are no points for second place.

FUN FACTS!

Steeplechase was one of the three games Atari created exclusively for Sears and their Tele-Games line-up.

VIDEO CHECKERS

Learn winning checkers. *Video Checkers* offers you nine levels of difficulty in a game that has challenged young and old for centuries. At level one, the computer plays beginning checkers. At level nine, you're playing a master of the game.

ABOUT THE GAME

Video Checkers wasn't just an algorithmically advanced electronic version of the popular board game, it offered a new game mode, giveaway checkers, and an optional color scheme used in professional games. Developed at Atari by Carol Shaw, one of the industry's first female video game designers, *Video Checkers* could outplay the competition. One of those competitors was Activision's version for the Atari 2600 created independently by Al Miller. Al Miller was a familiar name to Carol. Al interviewed Carol for her job at Atari!

OBJECT OF THE GAME

Capture all your opponent's pieces before your pieces get captured.

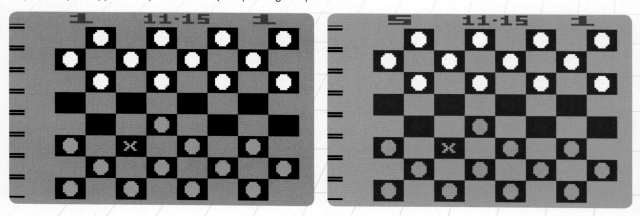

HOW TO PLAY

The computer plays by the standard rules of checkers. The most important rules are:

◆ **A player must jump when able.**

◆ **A piece that jumps into the king row and is promoted to a king cannot continue jumping on the same turn.**

◆ **The game ends when one player cannot move. This could occur because the player is blocked, or because the player has no pieces left.**

The checkers are usually referred to as "black" and "white", regardless of their actual colors. In *Video Checkers*, the pieces are red and white. In amateur games (level 1 through 4), the board has black and red squares. In pro games (level 5 through 9), the official colors of green and buff are used. Buff is normally referred to as a moderate orange-yellow or a light to moderate yellow. The joystick is used to move the cursor and/or the checkers around the board. The cursor is a red or white "X." The color of the cursor indicates whose turn it is. The cursor can only be moved diagonally on the black squares.

To move one of your checkers, push the red controller button when the cursor is in the same square as the piece you wish to move; this "picks up" the piece. Next, move the checker to the square you wish to occupy. To complete the move, push the controller button again. This "drops" the piece. Before you drop the piece, though, the computer will allow you to return it to the square from which it came and move a different piece. While it is your move, you may use the set-up mode to take back moves or rearrange the board. After you make your move, the computer will make its move.

To perform a jump, pick up the piece to be moved as described previously. After doing so, move the piece over the piece being jumped to the next empty square and push the controller button. For a multiple jump, continue jumping by moving to the appropriate square and pushing the button again.

The computer will not allow you to pick up a piece that cannot make a legal move or move a piece to the wrong square. Instead, it will make a buzzing or "razzing" sound. If you must jump, the letters "JP" for jump will flash at the top of the screen.

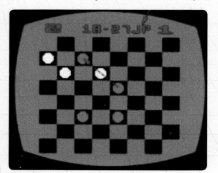

Jump signal.

When the left difficulty button is set to the A position (set-up mode), the left controller button is used to select the piece to be placed in each square. First, move the cursor to the desired square. Next, hold the controller button down or press it several times until the desired piece appears.

KING ME!
The computer will automatically convert a piece to a king when it is placed in the appropriate king row.

DIFFICULTY OPTIONS

LEFT DIFFICULTY BUTTON

Use the B position for normal gameplay; use the A position to set up the board. In set-up mode, use the left joystick to place pieces on the board wherever you want. Move the cursor to the square where you want to place a piece; it does not matter if the square is empty or occupied. Press the button on the joystick and the pieces of each color will flash in that square. When the piece you want is flashing in the square, release the button. To continue gameplay, change the left difficulty button to the B position.

The left difficulty button is not "checked" while the computer is working on the next move. This means that changing the button when the computer is computing a move has no immediate impact on the move.

RIGHT DIFFICULTY BUTTON

In the B position, the left player in a two-player game, or a single player in a one-player game, is "black" and starts the game. In the A position, the right player in a two-player game or the computer player in a one-player game is "black" and starts.

Changing the right difficulty button when it is your turn to play will cause you to trade sides with the computer. The computer will take over your pieces and make the next move.

COMPUTER MOVE

The length of time the computer takes to move depends on the difficulty level and the number of possible moves. The times given in the Game Table are approximate. The actual time for a move varies, depending on the current situation.

While the next move is being computed, the board will disappear from the television screen and different colors will flash on-screen. When the computer completes its move, the board reappears. The computer's move is indicated by a blinking "X" of the computer's color and a blinking computer piece. The jumped pieces, if any, will also blink. Your cursor will appear in your color. As soon as you move the joystick or press the controller button, the computer's piece will stop blinking and the jumped pieces will disappear.

GAME OPTIONS

In Games 1-9, the computer plays regular checkers. The computer's skill level increases as the game number increases. Game 10 is for two players. The number of players for each game is displayed in the upper-right corner of the screen.

Games 11-19 are losing, or "giveaway," checkers. As in Games 1-9, the skill level increases as the game number increases. The object of giveaway checkers is to be the first player to be unable to move by losing all of your pieces or by being blocked.

The game select button can be used in the middle of a game. When this occurs, the computer will continue to play using the new game difficulty level or variation. When the computer is computing its next move, the game select button has no effect.

GAME RESET BUTTON

Use this button to set up the checkers on the board for a new game or reset a game at any time. If the computer starts the game, it will pick its first move at random. To clear all pieces off the board, press the game reset button with the left difficulty button in the A position (set-up mode). Use the game reset button at any time, even while the computer is computing its next move.

Use the game select button to cycle through the games (displayed at the upper-left corner of the screen). If the game number is white, then the human player (or the left player) controls the white pieces on the board. If the game number is blue, then the human player is red.

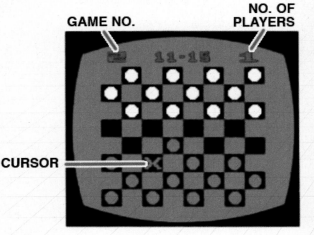

GAME NO.

NO. OF PLAYERS

CURSOR

GAME NUMBER	NUMBER OF PLAYERS	# OF MOVES COMPUTER LOOKS AHEAD	APPROXIMATE TIME FOR MOVE
1	1	1	1.5 sec
2	1	2	2 sec
3	1	3	3 sec
4	1	4	5 sec
5	1	5	10 sec
6	1	6	30 sec
7	1	7	1 min
8	1	8	4 min
9	1	9	15 min
10	2	--	--
11	1	1	1.5 sec
12	1	2	2 sec
13	1	3	3 sec
14	1	4	4 sec
15	1	5	6 sec
16	1	6	14 sec
17	1	7	30 sec
18	1	8	2 min
19	1	9	8 min

Tips & Tricks

◆ Try to control the center of the board.

◆ Protect your king by keeping pieces in squares 1 and 3 or 30 and 32.

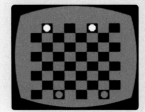

◆ Try to obtain the first king and make good use of it.

◆ Set up a series of jumps that leave you one or two pieces ahead (called 2-for-1 shots, 3-for-2 shots, and so on).

◆ When you're ahead, don't be afraid of trading down (losing more pieces than you take), since two kings can win against an opponent's lone king. When you are behind, avoid even trades (losing a piece for every piece you take).

COMPUTER METHOD

When computing its next move, the computer does what is called a "tree search" using "alpha-beta" pruning. What this means is that the computer picks a move, then picks a countermove by its opponent. Depending on the difficulty level, the computer continues making moves and countermoves. At some point, it evaluates the board to see how many pieces each side has and the position of the pieces. The computer does this for various combinations of moves and picks the move that will be most advantageous of itself, assuming its opponent will do the same. Alpha-beta pruning is a technique that is used to reduce the number of moves that must be examined.

The game number determines how many "plies" (or moves) deep the computer goes in the tree. One "ply" is a move by one player; technically, a "move" is considered to be two-ply (one move by each player). For example, in Game 1 the computer only looks one ply deep. However, if there is a jump, the computer keeps searching until there are no further jumps, regardless of the game number.

The computer becomes progressively more intelligent as the difficulty level increases. At level 1 (Game 1), the computer does no positional checking. It simply counts the number of pieces on the board, giving extra weight to kings. At level 4 and above, all of the positional checking is brought into play, including king row protection and center and double corner control.

While the next move is being computed, the board will disappear from the television screen and different colors will flash on-screen. This is done to speed up the computer since the design of the Atari Video Computer System makes it difficult to do extensive computations and display the board at the same time.

VIDEO PINBALL

Okay, pinball wizards, get set for the ultimate pinball challenge, complete with sounds and flashing colors. Pull back the plunger, release the spring, and shoot the ball. Hit bumpers, spinners, targets, and rollovers to rack up points. You get three balls to start with. Hit the Atari rollover four times to receive an extra ball.

You can nudge or apply body English, but be careful you don't tilt or you're out of action. So flip your flippers and catch the fever. Play against the computer to try your wizardry

So take a deep breath, turn up the stereo, and jump right into *Video Pinball*. One more thing... Better get yourself a piggy bank for all those quarters you're going to save.

ABOUT THE GAME

The Atari 2600 was created as a way to bring the arcade to players' homes for unlimited plays and the ultimate quest for the highest score. *Video Pinball* is—and was—the perfect example of this concept, as it brought the best version of a digital pinball machine to your home.

The design of this game is a rather simple one, but it can become very addictive. There are only a few objects to use to score points, but that is what keeps the game from becoming too complicated. This precise fact is exactly what makes the game so addicting. *Video Pinball* has enough of a challenge to pinball friends to compete, but it's not too difficult for beginners either.

There are all kinds of bonuses to accomplish and unlock while playing *Video Pinball*, which adds to the excitement of the game. Depending on your skill level, or how much you practice, you may be able to find most of the bonuses which will help increase your score even further.

Video Pinball wasn't meant as a replacement for a classic pinball machine, however, it was probably the closest thing to it in 1980.

This 4K cartridge will never be as highly praised as some of the other classic arcade ports, but it is still a great game that is still at the top of the list of "must-own" games for the Atari 2600.

OBJECT OF THE GAME

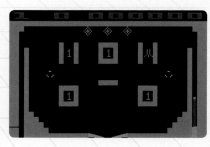

The object of the game is to keep the ball in play as long as possible and score as many points in the process. It is a game of skill and chance. Each player starts with three balls.

HOW TO PLAY

USING THE CONTROLLER

Use the joystick to start the game. Pull the joystick down (toward you) to bring the plunger back. Press the red controller button to release the spring and shoot the ball into the playfield.

You can also use the joystick to "nudge" (or apply "English") on the ball. These terms refer to forcing the ball to go in a particular direction. To do so, hold down the red controller button while pushing the joystick in the desired direction go. All game variations allow you to nudge the ball.

To select a game, press the game select button. The number of players for each game appears at the upper-left corner of the screen. The game number appears to the right of the player number.

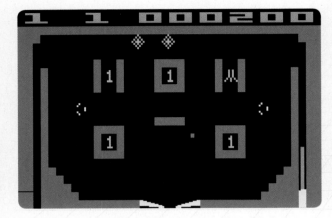

After selecting the game, press the game reset button to start the action. The game starts over each time the game reset is pressed. When gameplay starts, the player number and the ball number appear at the top of the screen (to the left of the score).

GAMEPLAY TIPS

Every time you hit the Atari rollover four times, you receive an extra ball. The large "X" at the bottom of the screen signifies an extra ball. Playing *Video Pinball* requires skillful control of the flippers, which are located at the bottom-center of the screen. When the ball drops here, send it back into the playfield by using the flippers. The flippers are controlled by using the joystick controller. It's your job to guide the ball within the playfield hitting bumpers, spinners, targets, and rollovers to score points.

Use the joystick to "nudge" the ball, but don't do it too much or you'll cause a "tilt". If you tilt the game, you won't score any more points and lose any extra balls.

GAME VARIATIONS

Video Pinball has four exciting game variations. There are two games for one player and two games for two players.

GAME 1

Game 1 is a one-player game that allows you to nudge the ball. Too much nudge will cause you to lose a ball ("tilt") and any extra balls are lost. During Game 1, the bumper values are accumulated for an entire game.

GAME 2

In this two-player variant, each player takes a turn playing one ball at a time. The turn lasts until the ball is lost. Each player's score appears at the top of the screen with each turn. The left player is always number one.

GAME 3

This variant is a one-player game that is similar to Game 1, except that the bumper values are not accumulated. The bumper values are reset with each new ball. Game 3 is also just a bit more difficult than Game 1. For a real challenge, try Game 3 with the difficulty set to position A.

GAME 4

A two-player version of game 3, each player takes a turn playing one ball at a time. The turn lasts until the ball is lost. Each player's score appears at the top of the screen with each turn. As is the case with Game 2, the left player starts the game.

DIFFICULTY OPTIONS

The A difficulty setting in *Video Pinball* is for expert pinball players, known as "pinball wizards." The B setting is for novice players. The A difficulty level has two extra drain holes at the bottom of the playfield. Each *Video Pinball* player can select his or her own difficulty level. In a one-player game, use the left difficulty button. For two-player games, the left player uses the left difficulty button while the right player uses the right difficulty button. Difficulty levels may be changed at any time during gameplay.

FUN FACTS!

○ It is possible to roll the number counter over 28 times (up to 255 numbers), after which the counter bonus resets back to 0. If this occurs, the counter likely won't go back to 1 when you lose a ball.

○ When the ball is moving fast enough, it will occasionally cross over the bonus rollovers without registering. The same thing can happen with the drop targets at the top.

○ On rare occasions, the ball may go through the Atari rollover and the symbols won't appear on the playfield (although the score counter will register it).

NUMBER OF PLAYERS

Just as in the arcade versions of pinball, *Video Pinball* has options for one-player and two-player games.

SCORING

You score points each time your ball hits targets, bumpers, rollovers, or spinners. The scoring happens quickly; listen for special electronic sounds as points are scored. The screen flashes when bonus points are scored. Scores are posted at the top-right of the screen. In two-player games, each player's score appears after each turn. At the end of a two-player game, both player's scores alternate at the top of the screen.

OBJECT NAME	POINTS
Spinners	1 point
Bumpers	100 times their current value. The value inside the bumper increases each time all of the diamond-shaped drop targets are knocked down.
Drop Targets	100 points each time a drop target is hit.
Atari Rollover	100 points. After hitting the Atari rollover four times, you receive an extra ball. Each time it rolls over, the bonus multiplier increases by one. Only one extra ball can be awarded with each turn. The number of Atari rollovers hit is indicated at the bottom of the screen by one Atari symbol for each hit.
Left Rollover	100 points each time it rolls over. Its value increases by one with each hit. When the ball drains, you receive 1,000 points for each time it has rolled over, (up to 4,000 points).
Special Lit Target	This target lights up for only four seconds. It is located between the two lower bumpers. Each time it is hit, the screen flashes and you score 1,000 points.

The bonus multiplier is tallied at the end of the turn. This rapid scoring is accompanied with a "whirring" sound. If you happen to score one million points, the score rolls over and starts again. When this happens, you don't lose the additional 999,999 points; they remain part of your score.

What The Critics Had to Say

"Video Pinball is a surefire classic in my book. Even though it's real simple in most ways, it is just as fun as any other pinball video game I've ever played, and I've played a good number of them. It's one of my favorite Atari 2600 games, and even though I'm not big on listing favorite games of all time, I'll go ahead and state that *Video Pinball* is one of those too. Play it and you'll see why."

-Retro (2001)

"1981's Video Pinball is a very strong title on par with such fine games as *Dodge 'Em* or *Othello*. I doubt it motivated anyone to purchase a 2600, but it's certainly a nice game to pull out and play every now and then. Yeah, the graphics aren't exactly pretty and the sound borders on obnoxious, but the game is terribly addictive."

-Ethan C. Nobles (2005)

◆ **Tilt:** Nudge the ball too much and the game will tilt. When a tilt occurs, the top portion of the screen turns red, your flippers are frozen, you cannot score points, and eventually the ball is lost through a drain. If an extra ball was earned before a tilt, you lose it. You still retain the bonus earned from the left rollover.

◆ **Nudge:** Nudging can be helpful in preventing a lost ball. If the ball gets too close to a drain, use a nudge to move the ball away from a drain. Nudge the ball by holding the red controller button down while pushing the joystick in the desired direction. You can also use a nudge to score points by nudging the ball toward a rollover or target.

◆ **Flippers:** Use the flippers to maneuver the ball so that it rebounds off a bumper, rollover, and so on.

◆ **Plunger:** Try pulling the plunger halfway back, all the way back, or anywhere in between. You may find you have better control over the ball with a particular plunger setting. Sometimes, a combination of plunger setting and nudging will send the ball in the direction of the Atari rollover.

ASTEROIDS

On a quiet serene evening, the Cosmic Space Patrol sets out for the usual night cruise through the boulevards of space. This beat was always the same; calm, no action, and no excitement. For some reason, this night feels different. Shortly before 0200 hours, some form of intergalactic material is sighted through the visual particle counter. The material is too large a mass to measure. It's drifting closer. Look out, it's a giant asteroid boulder and it's headed straight for the Cosmic Spacecraft! The only chance for survival is to dodge the boulder or destroy it. Destroying it doesn't mean just breaking it up, it means vaporizing it. Small asteroid boulders are equally as fatal as large ones.

Whew, the boulder just missed colliding with the Cosmic Spacecraft, but suddenly the Cosmic Space Patrol find themselves surrounded by thousands of the deadly asteroids! The Cosmic Space Patrol must act quickly to save their spacecraft and spare their lives. The spacecraft is equipped with photon torpedoes, hyperspace, shields, and flip control.

The Cosmic Space Patrol is highly trained to handle this situation. Could you do as good a job as the Cosmic Space Patrol? How would you protect yourself if you were caught in a deadly asteroid belt? This is your big chance to fly throughout the dimensions of space and fend against asteroid boulders. The longer you survive, the more space hazards you'll encounter.

ABOUT THE GAME

After *Asteroids* took the arcade by storm, Atari began work on the home version. With advance orders as far back as a year before its release—complete with $5 deposits—Atari knew it was going to have a hit on its hands. The only catch was how they were going to deliver.

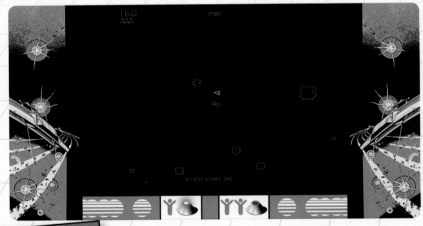

The original vector-based Asteroids arcade game as emulated on the Xbox One version of Atari Flashback Classics Volume 2 (2016).

Atari previewed the Atari 2600 version at several trade shows in early 1981. Unfortunately, reaction was mixed at best. Despite the addition of color over the black-and-white vector-based coin-up, the graphics were considered overly blocky and the feel of the play not-quite-right. Heading back to the drawing board, Atari made the fateful decision to develop a bank-switching technique that allowed the 2600 to work with twice as much data as previously possible. This extra room did the trick for programmer Bradley G. Stewart.

With the extra memory, *Asteroids* was finally the game everyone expected it to be.

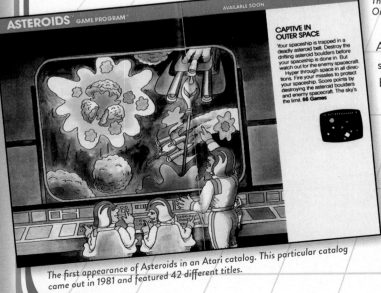

The first appearance of Asteroids in an Atari catalog. This particular catalog came out in 1981 and featured 42 different titles.

With gameplay that matched the arcade original, a plethora of game modes, and a colorful presentation that took advantage of the Atari 2600's strengths, it's no wonder that *Asteroids* would go on to become one of the platform's best sellers. With 3.8 million copies sold on the Atari 2600, *Asteroids* ranks third after *Pac-Man* (7.7 million) and *Pitfall!* (4.5 million), beating out both *Missile Command* (2.76 million) and *Space Invaders* (2.5 million) in the top five.

OBJECT OF THE GAME

The object of the game is to destroy asteroid boulders and keep your ship in space for as long as possible. Use the joystick controller to maneuver your ship through space and press the red controller (fire) button to shoot photon torpedoes at the asteroid boulders. When an asteroid is hit, it may break up into smaller boulders, or it may be completely pulverized. In some game variations, you'll face additional space hazards such as satellites and UFOs (unidentified flying objects); both of which may fire torpedoes at your ship.

HOW TO PLAY

Use the joystick controller to aim the spaceship and fire photon torpedoes at the asteroids. Move the joystick right to rotate the ship clockwise; move it left to rotate the ship counterclockwise. Push the joystick forward to thrust (propel) the ship through space (the ship moves only in the direction it's pointed).

Pulling the joystick down causes the ship to perform different functions such as hyperspace, shields, or flip depending upon the game variation selected. After aiming the spaceship with your joystick, press the fire button to shoot photon torpedoes at the asteroid boulders. Continue to press and release the fire button as fast as possible to quickly destroy all the asteroids.

If the game variation you're playing includes satellites and UFOs, use the joystick to aim and press the fire button to shoot torpedoes at them just as you would for the asteroid boulders.

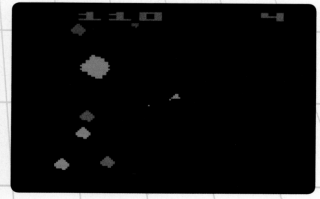

Asteroids with Scanlines turned on.

FUN FACTS!

• *Asteroids* was the first Atari 2600 game to use a technique called bank-switching, which allowed it access to more than the usual 4KB ROM limit. As an 8KB game, *Asteroids* was larger than any other Atari 2600 game released to that point.

• According to the Winter 1981 issue of *Electronic Games* magazine, gamers were pouring 10 million quarters into *Asteroids* arcade machines every single day!

• As reported in *Atari Age* magazine, May/June 1982, Andy Beyer, aged 15, of Chicago, scored 142,910 points in two games to win first place and a $5,000 scholarship at the Atari International Asteroids Tournament in Washington, DC. All games were played on game 6, skill level A.

DIFFICULTY OPTIONS

Asteroids has two difficulty levels, A and B. The B level is normal game play for beginning players. The A level offers a greater challenge with the addition of UFOs and satellites. UFOs are tough to hit, but each one is worth 1000 points.

Satellites are larger and easier to destroy. UFOs and satellites may fire back at your ship, so be on the lookout for their stray artillery. UFOs usually don't attack until you accumulate between 7,500 and 15,000 points, and always after. When satellites and UFOs sneak up and attack, you'll hear their engines. The satellites have a low-pitched engine sound and the UFOs have a high-pitched sound.

GAME OPTIONS

To select an *Asteroids* game, press the game select button. The game number and the number of players appear at the top of the screen. The game number is on the left, while the number of players is on the right.

After selecting a game number, press the game reset button to start the action. The game starts over each time game reset is pressed down. After the game starts, the score appears at the top of the screen. To change game numbers quickly, hold down game select and game reset together.

There are 66 game variations for one or two players.

1-PLAYER GAME #	2-PLAYER GAME #	SPEED	EXTRA LIFE	FEATURES
1	34	S	5	H
2	35	F	5	H
3	36	S	10	H
4	37	F	10	H
5	38	S	20	H
6	39	F	20	H
7	40	S	N	H
8	41	F	N	H
9	41	S	5	SH
10	43	F	5	SH
11	44	S	10	SH
12	45	F	10	SH
13	46	S	20	SH
14	47	F	20	SH
15	48	S	N	SH
16	49	F	N	SH
17	50	S	5	FL
18	51	F	5	FL
19	52	S	10	FL
20	53	F	10	FL
21	54	S	20	FL
22	55	F	20	FL
23	56	S	N	FL
24	57	F	N	FL
25	58	S	5	W
26	59	F	5	W
27	60	S	10	W
28	61	F	10	W
29	62	S	20	W
30	63	F	20	W
31	64	S	N	W
32	65	F	N	W
33	66		CHILDREN	

FAST/SLOW

Fast/Slow (F/S) refers to the speed at which the asteroids travel.

LIVES

Lives is a feature that allows you to earn extra spaceships. Game variations provide an extra ship every 5000, 10,000, or 20,000 points, depending on the game number chosen. The tougher game variations don't provide any extra spaceships. You'll hear a beeping sound when an extra spaceship is earned.

FEATURES

Depending on the game variation chosen, you can save your spaceship from destruction by using one of the game features of *Asteroids*.

NO FEATURES

W refers to games without features.

HYPERSPACE

Hyperspace (H) is a feature offered in games 1 through 8 for one player and games 34 through 41 for two players. By moving the joystick down (or towards you), hyperspace makes your spaceship disappear and reappear at some other place on the screen. Hyperspace is helpful as a quick getaway when an asteroid or boulder is headed toward your spaceship, but it may also be a hindrance if your spaceship reappears in the path of an oncoming asteroid boulder.

Making a quick, but risky escape with Hyperspace.

SHIELDS

Shields appear in games 9 through 16 for one player and games 42 through 49 for two players. They allow you to protect your spaceship by surrounding it with protective shields (SH). Pull the joystick back (or towards you) to put up shields, but don't use shields for more than two seconds or your spaceship will blow up.

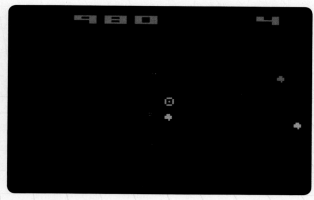

Using the Shield.

FLIP

In game variations featuring Flip (FL), you can flip your spaceship around 180 degrees, which aims it in the opposite direction. Flip is a great way to attack asteroids coming from behind. Flip is a feature in games 17 through 24 for one player and games 50 through 57 for two players.

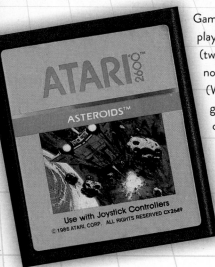

Games 25-32 (one-player) and games 58-65 (two-players) have no optional features (W). This makes these game variations more challenging and you must depend solely on your quick skill and coordination.

YOUNG CHILDREN'S VERSIONS

Games 33 through 66 are easy versions for young children. These games feature slow asteroids, hyperspace, and an extra ship every 5000 points.

SCORING

OBJECT	POINT VALUE
Small Asteroids	100
Medium Asteroids	50
Large Asteroids	20
Satellites	200
UFOs	1000

◆ When the screen becomes clear of asteroids (just before a new group of large asteroids appears), avoid placing your spaceship close to the right or left edge of the screen. New asteroids almost always begin from these edges.

◆ It is often helpful to remain in the center of the screen throughout the game, aiming your spaceship right or left in a circular motion.

◆ If you're close to earning an extra ship, and your spaceship is about to crash, you may want to cause your spaceship to collide with a small asteroid, UFO, or satellite. You'll earn points even if you crash, and this may be just enough points to earn that extra ship.

◆ Try to hit the faster and smaller asteroid boulders. This will give you more protection and points.

◆ If a UFO appears on-screen, you can make it disappear by immediately changing the difficulty button to the B position.

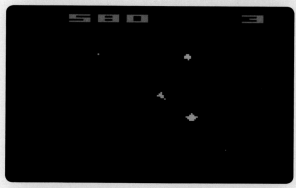

If you can keep the UFO from destroying the last asteroid, you can really start to ramp up your score.

◆ If you eliminate all but one asteroid, bonus satellites and UFOs will keep coming. Take advantage of this situation to add to your high score.

MISSILE COMMAND

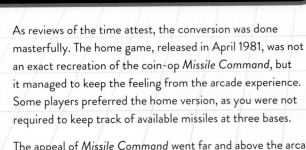

Aliens from the planet of Krytol have begun an attack on the planet Zardon. The Krytolians are warriors, out to destroy and seize the planet of Zardon. Zardon is the last of the peaceful planets. The Zardonians are skillful and hardworking people. Their cities are built-up and rich in resources. It is truly a planet void of crime and violence.

Zardon has built a powerful defense system. Several anti-ballistic missile bases have been established within the cities of Zardon. The Zardonians are ready for this attack and prepared to fight to save their cities.

As base commander, it is your responsibility to protect and defend six cities on the planet of Zardon. The Krytolians have begun firing interplanetary ballistic missiles. They are aiming at your cities and missile bases. Your only defense is to fire back with anti-ballistic missiles. But watch out, the Krytolians are sly—they also have cruise missiles. Cruise missiles look like satellites, but they are just as deadly as the interplanetary ballistic missiles.

Use your anti-ballistic missiles (ABMs) to stop the enemy before your happy and harmonious planet is destroyed.

ABOUT THE GAME

Missile Command took the coin-op arcade world by storm when it was released in 1980. Atari eventually produced over 17,000 arcade uprights and cocktail cabinets of *Missile Command*. The game's popularity made it an obvious choice for a conversion to Atari's home system. However, the coin-op game employed a track ball controller and three buttons for firing ABMs from different bases, so the programmer faced a challenge in modifying the game to fit the limitations on the home console and its controllers.

As reviews of the time attest, the conversion was done masterfully. The home game, released in April 1981, was not an exact recreation of the coin-op *Missile Command*, but it managed to keep the feeling from the arcade experience. Some players preferred the home version, as you were not required to keep track of available missiles at three bases.

The appeal of *Missile Command* went far and above the arcade and home console. Beyond the obligatory merchandise, such as t-shirts, *Missile Command* was used in fast food promotions, for model kits, and even as a Halloween-themed costume.

Missile Command has appeared in movies and television shows beginning at the height of its popularity through today. Hollywood icon Steven Spielberg is such a fan of the game that a photograph of him from the 1980s book *Invasion of the Space Invaders* includes his personal *Missile Command* cabinet.

Nostalgia, retro-gaming consoles, and software collections have created a modern market for merchandise based on older games. Recent offerings include clothing, drinking glasses, and even a *Missile Command*-themed Hot Wheels vehicle. It's safe to say that interest in *Missile Command* will never die out completely.

If an incoming missile hits the center of your missile base, it destroys any remaining ABMs in the base. However, any ABMs in the underground dump remain unaffected.

OBJECT OF THE GAME

The object of the game is to defend your cities and missile base. The game ends when all the cities are destroyed.

HOW TO PLAY

The enemy fires interplanetary ballistic missiles and cruise missiles, both aimed at your cities and missile base. There are two types of cruise missiles. Dumb cruise missiles descend in a pre-set path. Smart cruise missiles, which first appear in Wave 6, attempt to evade any anti-ballistic missiles (ABMs).

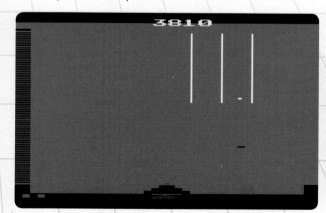

The enemy attacks in waves that may vary in the number of incoming missiles. Each consecutive wave moves faster. The faster the wave, the more difficult it is to defend the cities and the more points an incoming missile is worth.

There are 30 ABMs available during each wave. Your launching missile base, which appears in the center of the playfield, holds 10 ABMs at a time. As each set of 10 ABMs is exhausted, you automatically receive 10 more from an underground missile dump. After launching 30 ABMs, you are defenseless until the next wave begins.

The joystick controls the blinking cursor that acts as your target control. Press the red controller button to launch an ABM at the point where the cursor is located when the button is pressed.

Your ABMs are not direct-fire weapons. Instead, they fly to the target location and then explode and destroy anything caught inside the explosion. ABM explosions build gradually, so aim ahead of the path of incoming missiles. The explosion must make contact with the tip of an enemy's missile to destroy it. Smart missiles actively avoid explosions and may require multiple ABMs to eliminate them.

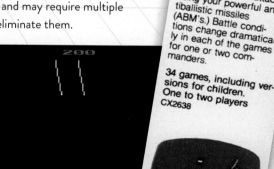

You score points by destroying ballistic missiles and cruise missiles. Unused ABMs and saved cities are tallied at the end of each wave. Between each consecutive wave, the cities fall and rise again when the next wave starts.

A bonus city is awarded every 10,000 points. If your score reaches the next 10,000 point value at the end of a wave and all six of your cities were destroyed during the wave, you will receive a bonus city. Bonus cities are saved if none of your cities are destroyed.

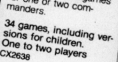

DIFFICULTY OPTIONS

The B setting is for normal game play, while the A setting is for skilled players. When the difficulty button is in the A position, your ABMs move at a slower pace, making it more difficult to defend your cities and missile base.

GAME OPTIONS

INITIAL WAVE	1-PLAYER GAME #	2-PLAYER GAME #	FEATURES
1	1	18	FT & DM
	2	19	SL & DM
	3	20	FT & SM
	4	21	SL & SM
7	5	22	FT & DM
	6	23	SL & DM
	7	24	FT & SM
	8	25	SL & SM
11	9	26	FT & DM
	10	27	SL & DM
	11	28	FT & SM
	12	29	SL & SM
15	13	30	FT & DM
	14	31	SL & DM
	15	32	FT & SM
	16	33	SL & SM
N/A	17	34	CHILDREN

FEATURES

Missile Command allows skilled players to skip slower waves. Use the Initial Wave column to choose the missiles' speed at the start of the game. Other features change the speed of your target control and the behavior of cruise missiles.

FAST TARGET CONTROL (FT)
Your target control moves quickly around the screen.

SLOW TARGET CONTROL (SL)
Your target control moves slowly around the screen.

DUMB CRUISE MISSILE (DM)
Incoming cruise missiles travel in a straight line and won't evade your ABMs.

© ATARI, INC., 1980

ATARI

SMART CRUISE MISSILE (SM)

Incoming cruise missiles detect and evade your ABMs.

CHILDREN

Incoming attacks use dumb enemy cruise missiles, slow target control, and the enemy attacks at a slower rate with fewer missiles.

SCORING

EVENT	BASE POINT VALUE
Destroy Ballistic Missile	25
Destroy Cruise Missile	125
Unused Anti-Ballistic Missiles	5
Saved Cities	100

SCORING MULTIPLIER

WAVE	MULTIPLIER
1-2	1x
3-4	2x
5-6	3x
7-8	4x
9-10	5x
11+	6X

To see the initials of the game's programmer, select game 13. Allow the incoming missiles to destroy all of your cities. Empty your missiles reserves without scoring any points. The city on the right side changes into "RF", which are the initials of programmer Rob Fulop.

Featured in books *The Player's Strategy Guide to Atari VCS Home Video Games* (1982) and *The Winners' Book of Video Games* (1982).

Voted Best Solitare Game and honorable mention for Game of the Year in the 1982 Arcadie Awards.

Electronic Games magazine ran a monthly survey called E.G. Readers Pick Their Favorite Games. Over the first year of the magazine's printing (Holiday 1981 to December 1982), *Missile Command* appeared in the top 10 Most Popular Videogame Cartridges every month, most often at #2 behind either Asteroids or Pac-Man.

◆ The changing colors of the sky and cities indicate increased missile speed and score multiplier.

 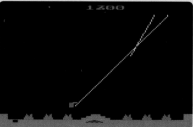 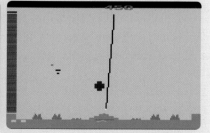

◆ You can fire up to three defense missiles simultaneously. After pressing the red controller (fire) button, move to the next enemy site and fire again. Do not wait for the explosion before moving.

◆ Once a city is destroyed you can no longer defend it, so concentrate only on your missile base and saved cities. Ignore enemy fire aimed at cities already destroyed.

◆ Smart enemy cruise missiles are easiest to destroy if your target control is directly on them. When this is the case, the enemy cannot detect your ABMs.

STELLAR TRACK

It is 2000 years since the unification of our planet and we "Terrans" have peacefully excelled in art, philosophy, and science. Our technology has mastered all but one problem: the hyperwarp drive (which would allow us to travel to other planets). Trapped in our own solar system for lack of the hyperwarp drive, there seems to be no way out until we are discovered by extraterrestrial life. These "Aliens" are anxious to trade their hyperwarp technology for Terran art and science to revitalize their stagnant culture.

As time passes, we Terrans expand our empire through interstellar trade and the use of hyperwarp technology. Increasingly, the Terrans and Aliens compete over the riches of the universe. We develop phased energy weapons and force shields, while the Aliens insist on escorting their merchant envoys with warships. Tension begins to grow.

The Terran government, directed by the House of Viceroys, decides to build an indestructible Starfleet and two Galactic Starbases to ensure cosmic military supremacy. With the invention of a deadly photon-launcher and the virtual invisibility of the starbases (their location is a closely guarded secret), we Terrans feel that a single Super Warship can keep the scattered Alien fleet in check. You are the captain and sole commander of that warship.

While the Viceroys are relaxing and confident of our military superiority, the Alien Council of Elders rules that the Terran culture must be destroyed. This is to be done before Alien dominance in the heavens is lost. As the commander, you must throw back the Alien invasion.

ABOUT THE GAME

Stellar Track was based on a text-based *Star Trek* game found on college mainframe computers in the 1970s. One of a handful of games sold exclusively at Sears stores, *Stellar Track* was released to a mixed reception. The complexity of the game and relatively simple graphics made it difficult for *Stellar Track* to stand on its own against other games released around the same time.

OBJECT OF THE GAME

The object of your mission is to destroy the Aliens in the galaxy using Photons or Phasers before they destroy you. If you run out of time (Stardates) or fuel (Energy), we Terrans are lost!

> The complexity of *Stellar Track* will make it necessary to periodically refer to this chapter during your first several missions. It's also a good idea to write down vital information during each mission.

HOW TO PLAY

After selecting the mission size, press the red controller button to start. The Galaxy Map command will flash near the bottom of the screen. In total, there are seven commands.

These commands are chosen using the joystick, then entered by pressing the controller button. Each command is displayed (flashing) on-screen as you move the joystick right or left.

You won't know which commands to use (and especially in what order to use them) until you learn more about each one through these instructions. For now, remember that when the command you want to use is displayed on-screen, you must press the red controller button to enter it.

> Keep in mind that you must press the red controller button when you are finished reading a particular display and are ready to continue with another command.

MISSION OVERVIEW

So far, you've been given some basic information on the history of the war, the overall mission objective, how to select the size of a mission, and how to get the mission started.

This information alone addresses only the beginning of the mission. Now you must learn how and when to use each command. You must also learn how to deal with other mission factors, such as the difference between a quadrant and a sector, what a starbase can do for you, and so on.

QUADRANTS/SECTORS

The galaxy is divided into 36 quadrants and each quadrant is subsequently divided into 64 sectors. It may help to think of the quadrants as states and the sectors as cities within those states. The general flow of the mission is as follows:

1. **Use the Long Range (LR) Scan to see which quadrants contain Aliens and/or starbases.**

2. **Use the Warp command to travel or jump among the quadrants and sectors as you pursue Aliens and starbases.**

3. **Use the Short Range (SR) Scan to see which sectors contain Aliens and starbases.**

4. **Use Photon/Phasers to destroy Aliens.**

5. **Use the Status command to track remaining Aliens, time left (Stardates), Energy, and damage to your ship.**

6. **Use Starbases to refuel and repair damage to your ship.**

7. **Use the Galaxy Map to coordinate the entire mission.**

8. **Use a note pad to keep track of all the above.**

If you destroy all the Aliens, your mission is successful and you receive a ranking (Cadet, Ensign, Lieutenant, Captain, Commodore, or Admiral). Ranking is based on how much time and energy it takes to destroy the enemy. The less energy used, the higher your ranking. You're ranked at the end of a mission regardless of how it ends. Naturally, if you save the galaxy, your rank tends to be higher. However, if you waste resources to win, you might still be reduced to Cadet!

If you run out of time (Stardates) or fuel (Energy), the Terrans must surrender to the Aliens.

IMPORTANT
The color of the screen indicates who or what is in the quadrant you are currently occupying.

GREEN	Empty
RED	Aliens
GREY	Starbase

When you are in a quadrant containing both Aliens and a Starbase, the screen will be red. Once you destroy the Aliens in that quadrant, the screen will turn grey.

GALAXY MAP

The Galaxy Map is a 6x6 grid that starts out empty at the beginning of each mission. Each time you scan one of the 36 quadrants, that quadrant will appear on the Galaxy Map the next time it is displayed. A scanned quadrant shows a two-digit number. The left digit indicates the number of Aliens in that quadrant, while the right digit indicates whether a Starbase exists in that quadrant.

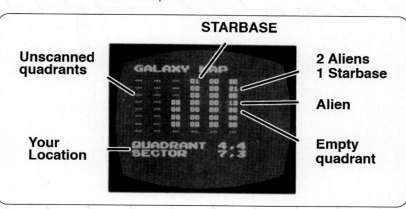

As an example, an entry of 21 reveals two Aliens and a Starbase in the quadrant. Keep in mind that although some commands use time or energy, calling the Galaxy Map is completely free.

LONG RANGE (LR) SCAN

WARNING
The LR SCAN looks similar to the Galaxy Map, so it is easy to confuse them.

The LR SCAN is a 6x6 grid that shows the contents of the current quadrant, plus all adjoining or adjacent quadrants. As with the Galaxy Map, the information is presented as a two-digit number. The left digit shows the number of Aliens in the quadrant; the right digit indicates whether a Starbase exists in the quadrant.

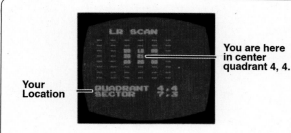

The LR SCAN does not use energy or startime. However, when you are in a quadrant with Aliens, they will fire at you (one by one) after you use the LR SCAN. Note that the LR SCAN shows adjacent quadrants while the Galaxy Map cumulatively displays all the quadrants you have scanned.

SHORT RANGE (SR) SCAN

Each quadrant contains 64 sectors. The SR Scan is an 8x8 grid that enables you to see exactly what is contained in your quadrant by showing what appears in each of the 64 sectors. A SR Scan fills in the Galaxy Map for the current quadrant only.

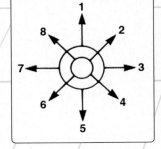

You must use the SR Scan to find out exactly where the enemy a Starbase is located. It does not use energy or startime, but like the LR Scan, any Aliens in your quadrant will fire at you (one by one) after you use it.

WARP

The Warp command is used to move your ship from one quadrant to another, or from one sector to another. Using the Warp command is expensive—it uses Startime and Energy.

WARPING AMONG QUADRANTS

Startime used = one Stardate for each quadrant jumped.

Energy used = 100 units for each quadrant jumped.

WARPING AMONG SECTORS

This maneuver costs 10 units of Energy for each sector jumped, but uses no Stardates. How to Warp:

1. Using the Joystick, display the Warp command on-screen.

2. Enter the Course number, which is the direction you want to travel. This is done by moving the joystick to the right or left. There are eight possible directions to move (with corresponding numbers).

3. When the number you want is displayed (flashing) on-screen, press the red controller button to enter it.

4. Enter the Factor numbers, which represent the distance in quadrants and sectors you want to travel. Move the joystick right or left to change the numbers on-screen. Next, press the red controller button button to enter the numbers. The first (left) number indicates how many quadrants you want to jump. The second (right) number indicates how many sectors you want to jump.

5. Remember, when moving within the same quadrant (sector to sector), you must enter "0" for the first number since you do not want to move quadrants, only sectors.

> **WARNING**
> You cannot Warp through a star in your quadrant. If you attempt to do so, you will lose the Stardates and energy required for the Warp.

When you successfully Warp into another quadrant the Status report automatically appears on-screen. If you fail to Warp, you will hear a loud buzz sound and the screen will remain unchanged (you tried to warp through a star).

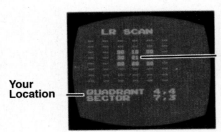

PHOTON TORPEDO

Your Photon Torpedoes are one of two weapons you have to destroy Aliens. The other weapon is your Phasers, explained in the next section.

You start with nine torpedoes. All nine torpedoes are automatically replaced whenever you dock at a starbase.

There are eight different directions (CourseS) to fire Photon Torpedoes. Your ship must be directly in line (right, left, up, down, or diagonally) with an Alien to successfully hit it with a torpedo. You cannot shoot through a star or out of one quadrant and into another.

How to Use:

1. **Select the Photon command using your joystick.**

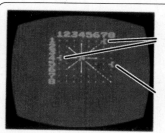

These Aliens in line— Torpedo will hit.

Must WARP to new location to get this Alien in line.

2. **Enter the Course (direction) number in the same manner you enter the Warp Course number.**

3. **Press the red controller button to fire.**

Using your Photon Torpedoes requires no Energy or Stardates. The Alien is always destroyed when hit by a Photon Torpedo. Any undestroyed Aliens in the quadrant will fire back after you use a Photon Torpedo.

PHASERS

Your Phasers are energy weapons. A Phaser blast can cause damage or destroy an Alien if it's strong enough. To destroy and Alien, the Phaser blast energy value must be greater than the energy value of the Alien ship. (All Aliens start with 99 units of energy.)

You do not have to be directly in line with an alien (as with protons) to destroy or damage it with Phasers.

The power for your Phasers comes from your Energy supply. Think of your Phasers as a flashlight beam with great power close and less power further away. The closer the enemy, the less power you need to destroy him.

To use Phasers:

1. **Select the Phasers command using your joystick.**

2. **Assign the energy (Phaser units to fire?) using a three-digit number. You must enter three numbers for it to work. The energy fired will be deducted from your Energy supply.**

3. **After entering the last (third) number by pressing the red controller button, the Phasers will automatically fire. You must fire once for each Alien in the quadrant.**

After firing a Phaser, you receive a message saying "Alien Destroyed," or:

◆ **How much energy hit the Alien (Unit Hit).**

◆ **The coordinates of the Alien that was hit.**

◆ **How much energy the Alien has left.**

If more than one Alien is present, the energy will be divided between them. Any undestroyed Aliens will fire back at you.

DAMAGE

Aliens in your quadrant will fire only after they detect a maneuver on your part. Their sensors are unable to detect when you use the Status or Galaxy Map, so these are the only "free" moves. All other actions antagonize the Aliens to return fire, which can damage one of five ship functions: Launcher; Phasers; Engineers; SR Scan; LR Scan.

Your Status Report will show "OK" if a function is undamaged, a negative number will indicate how many Stardates must be used up before that function is repaired. For example, if a ship function shows -3, then three Stardates must be used up before you may use it again.

Docking at a Starbase repairs all damage to your ship, regardless of Stardates. If you attempt to use a ship function, the computer will respond with a buzz and the command will not be entered. Your Engines are a special case when it comes to damage.

◆ **You cannot leave a quadrant with damaged Engines.**

◆ **To fix damaged Engines, enter a Warp command for the same number of quadrants as Stardates needed to repair the damage.**

◆ **Instead of moving quadrants, your ship will move only the number of sectors entered for quadrants.**

◆ **Although Stardates and Energy will be deducted, your Engines will be repaired and you can leave the quadrant.**

STATUS REPORT

STATUS		
Stardate	11	Number of Stardates left to destroy all Aliens.
Aliens	08	Number of Aliens left in the galaxy.
Energy	1250	Amount of energy left in your ship.
Photons	8	Number of photon torpedoes remaining.
DAMAGE		
Launcher	-3	Photon torpedo launcher.
Phasers	OK	Phasers.
Engines	OK	Ship engines for using Warp command.
SR Scan	OK	SR Scan.
LR Scan	OK	LR Scan.
LOCATION		
Quadrant	4, 4	Which quadrant you're in.
Sector	7, 3	Which sector of that quadrant you're in.

Although it didn't explicitly use the *Star Trek* name, *Stellar Track* did use terms from *Star Trek* lore as well as the likeness of the *Enterprise* for the player ship.

Damage:

◆ OK = There is no damage to report.

◆ -3 = This ship function is damaged and you must use three Stardates to fix it, or dock at a starbase for repair.

Calling up the Status Report does not use any Energy or Stardates.

STARBASE DOCKING

Docking at a Starbase repairs all damage to your ship. This procedure provides you with a new supply of Energy (3000 units). It also replaces all nine of your Photon Torpedoes.

To dock at a Starbase, Warp to the same quadrant and sector as the Starbase. This places you virtually on top of the Starbase.

There are always two starbases in the galaxy. Starbases are randomly placed at the beginning of each mission. They never move or get destroyed.

If your ship receives damage while docked, you must back off the Starbase and then back on to it for more repairs and refueling.

ALIENS

All Aliens start each mission with 99 units of energy. If you leave an Alien in a quadrant and then return later, it will be refueled to 99 units of energy (if damaged) and it is very likely that it will move. When you are in a quadrant with an any Aliens, you and the enemy side take turns:

1. You Warp into a quadrant containing an Alien, then you use your SR Scan to find it.

2. The Alien will then fire at you.

3. You execute another command.

4. The Alien fires again.

5. You execute another command.

6. The Alien fires again and so on.

Each time an Alien fires at you, you receive a report on how much of a hit you took as well as how much Energy remains. If there is more than one Alien in a quadrant with you, each Alien takes its turn before it becomes your turn.

COMMAND SUMMARY

SHIP FUNCTION	COST
Galaxy Map	Free
Status	Free
Photon	Photon & Turn
Phasers	Energy & Turn
Warp	Energy, Stardate(s), & Turn
SR Scan	Turn
LR Scan	Turn

GAME OPTIONS

The game select and reset buttons both have the same function, which is to randomly select the size of a new mission. There are two factors that vary with each mission. One is the number of Stardates you have and the other is the number of Aliens you must destroy to win. Press either button to change and/or select the size of each mission. Continue pressing either button until you select the size mission you want.

HELPFUL HINT
The best missions to start out with are those with approximately 25 to 35 Aliens and the most Stardates you can find.

The right difficulty button controls the shield strength of damage probability. In the Novice position, the probability of damage is lower. In the Expert position, the probability is twice as high.

The left difficulty button controls your Phaser strength. In the Novice position, your Phasers (or energy units) are twice as powerful as the Aliens' Phaser strength. In the Expert position, your Phasers are equal in strength to the Aliens' Phasers.

◆ Don't waste your Warps. They cost Stardates, which are one of the most important mission factors to handle.

◆ Check your Status Report and Galaxy Map often. They do not cost any time (Stardates) or Energy and they are important sources of information.

◆ Remember where the Starbases are located and use them strategically as you journey through the galaxy. Also, don't be in a hurry when making commands. Careful thought, along with some minor calculations, will be valuable assets in your missions.

SUPER BREAKOUT

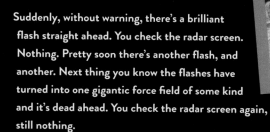

Imagine you're in a one-man space shuttle travelling through the heavens at the speed of light. You and your tiny ship are totally engulfed in darkness, except for the luminance of an occasional passing star.

Suddenly, without warning, there's a brilliant flash straight ahead. You check the radar screen. Nothing. Pretty soon there's another flash, and another. Next thing you know the flashes have turned into one gigantic force field of some kind and it's dead ahead. You check the radar screen again, still nothing.

The colors in this mysterious force field are so bright, they're almost blinding. And they seem to be in layers. But the strangest thing is that nothing shows up on the radar screen. What could that mean? Is it possible to travel through this mysterious force field or will you crash and be destroyed? And what about the layers? If you make it through one, can you make it through the next, and the next?

It's decision time and there are only a few seconds to think about it.

Turn back or blast ahead and try to make it through the layers of the brightly colored force field. It's up to you.

ABOUT THE GAME

Atari produced the arcade version of *Super Breakout* in 1978, changing from its predecessor's discrete logic to a microprocessor-based game. This allowed for an arcade machine that was both easier to produce and featured additional game variations.

Although not breaking the 1 million games sold barrier like its predecessor, many enthusiasts consider the Atari 2600 port of *Super Breakout* a superior experience. Its relatively late 1981 release, which was around the same time as ports of more high-profile arcade games like *Space Invaders* and *Asteroids*, likely resulted in its poorer commercial reception.

OBJECT OF THE GAME

Super Breakout contains the following game variations:

◆ Breakout   ◆ Double   ◆ Cavity   ◆ Progressive   ◆ Children's Versions

Each game variation may be played by one or two players, with the exception of Progressive, which is for one player only.

The object in all of the games is to keep the ball in play (as you knock out bricks) to score the highest number of points possible, or to score more points than your opponent.

HOW TO PLAY

Push the red controller button to serve the ball. To make contact with the ball and keep it in play, turn the knob on the controller—the paddle moves horizontally back and forth across the bottom of the screen. Turn the knob clockwise to move the paddle right; turn it counterclockwise to move it left.

The angle the ball rebounds off the paddle depends on which part of the paddle it hits. The paddle is divided into four sections. During the first eight hits, the ball bounces off the paddle normally.

After the eighth, 16th, and 48th hits, the ball reacts differently and speeds up (except in the Children's Versions). The ball also speeds up after hitting any bricks in the last four rows (or the last eight rows in Progressive).

Whenever you break through the last row of bricks and the ball makes contact with the boundary at the top of the playfield, the paddle is reduced to half its original size (except in the Children's Versions). In Double and Cavity, both paddles are reduced in size. The paddle or paddles return to normal size when a new turn begins.

Each turn ends when the ball is missed and disappears off the bottom of the playfield. In games with two or three balls in play, a turn ends when the last ball is missed.

DIFFICULTY OPTIONS

The difficulty buttons control the size of the paddle in all games. In the B or beginner position, the paddle is twice the size it is in the A position. The A position is for experienced *Super Breakout* players.

Use the left difficulty button for one-player games. For two-player games, the first player uses the left difficulty button; the second player uses the right difficulty button.

Remember that the paddle reduces to half its original size when the ball breaks through the last row of bricks and hits the boundary at the top of the playfield.

GAME OPTIONS

Use Select to choose the game you wish to play. There are nine game numbers in total.

There are eight exciting game sounds programmed into *Super Breakout*. One of these eight sounds is randomly selected each time you begin a new game (when you press Reset, you hear a sample of the sound selected for that game).

After you have selected the game number you wish to play, press Reset to start the game. Reset may also be used to reset a game at any time. When you press Reset, you hear a sample of the scoring sound to be used during the game.

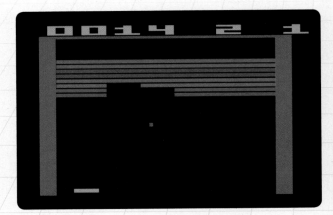

BREAKOUT (GAMES 1 AND 2)

Games 1 and 2 are regular Breakout. Game 1 is for one player; Game 2 is for two players.

As in all two-player games, each player has his own wall of bricks (and corresponding score), which is displayed on the screen during that player's turn.

Each wall of bricks contains eight rows. Bricks in the first two rows are worth one point each. The third and fourth row bricks are worth three points each. The fifth and sixth row bricks are worth five points each, and the seventh and eighth row bricks are worth seven points each.

If you knock out all the bricks (within five turns), a new wall of bricks appears on the screen. Each wall of bricks is worth 416 points.

There is no limit to the number of times a new wall of bricks can be reset during a game.

If a tie occurs in a two-player game, the player reaching that score in the fewest turns is the winner. The maximum score for Breakout is infinite since the wall of bricks resets indefinitely. However, since the screen display has room for only four digits, a player's score resets to 0000 if it exceeds 9999.

DOUBLE (GAMES 3 AND 4)

Game 3 is Double Breakout for one player. Game 4 is Double Breakout for two players.

The playfield in Double is the same as the Breakout playfield, except that there are two paddles and two balls served. The paddles are stacked one on top of the other. The point value of the bricks is essentially the same as Breakout except when there are two balls in play. When this occurs, each brick is worth twice its normal amount.

Doubles.

If you miss the first ball served, it counts as a miss and goes against your allotted serves (turns) per game. Otherwise, the second ball is served. If you miss the second ball (after hitting the first ball), play continues until you miss the first ball. After both balls are in play (have been hit at least once), one may be missed while the other remains in play.

The wall of bricks resets an infinite number of times after the first wall is knocked out. The maximum score for Double Breakout is infinite.

CAVITY (GAMES 5 AND 6)

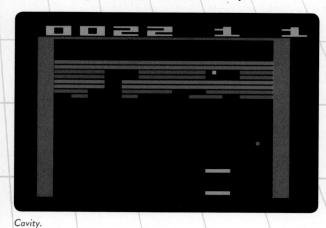

Cavity.

Game 5 is Cavity Breakout for one player. Game 6 is Cavity Breakout for two players.

The Cavity playfield contains slightly fewer bricks to make room for two "cavities", each of which contains a ball. When the game begins, the balls bounce inside each cavity but are held captive for the time being while a third ball is served. There are two paddles, the same as in Double.

Point values of the bricks are the same as the other games (defined by rows) when one ball is in play. When enough bricks are removed to release a captive ball, each brick is then worth twice its normal amount when hit. If the third ball is freed, bricks are worth triple their normal amount when hit.

If any one of the balls is missed, the scoring returns to double points. If the second ball is missed and only one ball remains in the playfield, the point value of the bricks returns to normal.

The wall of bricks resets an infinite number of times, therefore the maximum score possibility for Cavity Breakout is infinite.

FUN FACTS!

- Although the Atari 2600 version of *Super Breakout* has a 1978 copyright date to match the arcade version, it was not actually released until 1981.

- *Flux* magazine, in their April 1995 issue, named *Super Breakout* number 93 in their list of top 100 videogames of all-time.

Challenge Games

ARCADE PINBALL
Score with bumpers, targets, rollovers and spinners.

ADVENTURE
Search for the golden goblet while slaying dragons.

BREAKAWAY IV
Smash through brick walls. Each wall has a point value.

TARGET FUN
Hit clowns, ducks, boats, planes or rabbits.

CIRCUS ATARI•••
Bounce your clown on the teeter-totter and break balloons to score points.

*Indicates a Trademark of ATARI, INC.
•••Indicates a registered Trademark of ATARI, INC.

CANYON BOMBER•••
Bomb a canyon or drop depth charges in the sea to win.

SUPER BREAKOUT•
Deluxe version of Breakaway IV with progressive breakouts.

The Super Breakout page in a 1981 Sears Video Arcade Cartridges catalog, featuring 34 unique game titles.

PROGRESSIVE (GAME 7)

Game 7 is Progressive Breakout for one player only.

The playfield in Progressive is set up somewhat differently than Breakout. When the game begins, the playfield contains four rows of bricks at the top of the screen, followed by four blank rows, and then four more rows of bricks. The point value of the bricks is defined by row numbers, the same as in Breakout.

After game play begins, the brick walls "progress" toward the bottom of the screen. As the bricks are knocked out and the walls progressively move down toward your paddle, new bricks enter the playfield at a progressively faster rate.

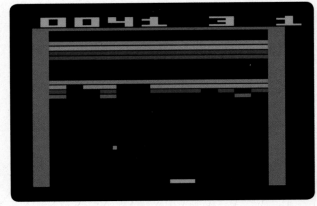
Progressive.

Four rows of bricks are always separated by four rows of blanks. As the brick walls progress downward, their colors change, which gives them a new point value. The maximum score for Progressive is infinite.

CHILDREN'S VERSIONS (GAMES 8 AND 9)

Game 8 is a one-player Children's Version. Game 9 is a two-player Children's Version. Both games are regular Breakout. The game play in these versions is programmed at a slower rate. The ball does not speed up after hitting bricks in the last four rows. Also, the paddle does not reduce to half its original size when the ball reaches the top boundary of the playfield. Scoring and other game play characteristics are the same as normal Breakout.

GAME NUMBER	1	2	3	4	5	6	7	8	9
One-player	X		X		X		X	X	
Two-player		X		X		X			X
Breakout	X	X							
Double			X	X					
Cavity					X	X			
Progressive							X		
Children's Versions								X	X

- ◆ When playing any of the *Super Breakout* games, your best bet is to break out through the right or left corner of the playfield. The corners seem to be the easiest points at which to establish a "groove." Beginners should use the larger paddle size.

- ◆ Be prepared for the ball to return at a faster speed when it hits the bricks in the last four rows (or the upper rows of bricks in Progressive). You can miss a lot of shots simply by not being prepared.

- ◆ Don't panic when the ball reaches the top boundary of the playfield and your paddle reduces to half its original size. All it takes at this point to keep the ball in play is a little more concentration, and a finer touch on the controller. In time you'll have no trouble at all keeping the ball in play when your paddle is reduced in size.

- ◆ Learn to anticipate where the ball is going to be. Anticipation can be a key factor, particularly when the ball bounces off one of the side boundaries near the bottom of the playfield. When the ball is travelling at high speed, you won't always have time to react and move your paddle to the right position. Your paddle must be in the correct position to advance. The only way to accomplish this is to anticipate where the ball will be.

- ◆ In the Progressive game variations, when a brick progresses to the last row at the bottom center of the screen, it stays there for a set amount of time and then disappears. If you hit the brick in the center before it disappears, you may receive a special bonus of 50-150 points!

WARLORDS

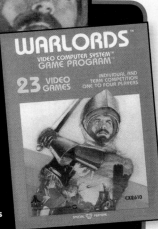

Once long ago in a distant land lived a king named Frederick. He took very good care of his subjects and pretty much let the kingdom run itself. One day King Frederick and his wife, Queen Christina, decided to start a family. To their surprise, Queen Christina soon gave birth to quadruplets. Four healthy sons, all at once. The King and Queen were overwhelmed.

The years passed quickly and Frederick's sons (Dominick, Marcus, Felipe, and Restivo) grew to be strong young men. But they were nothing like their kind and peaceful father. They were just the opposite. The four sons of King Frederick fought constantly over anything and everything. Their fighting was so fierce that even the normally unconcerned Frederick became concerned. Left to his violent and competitive sons, his peaceful kingdom could very well be destroyed after he was gone, or perhaps even sooner.

The solution King Frederick decided upon was drastic, but he knew it had to be. Dominick, Marcus, Felipe, and Restivo were banished from their homeland and sent far away to a forbidden land. There they became warlords, dividing their newly acquired territory into four equal sectors, which incidentally, was the first and last thing they ever agreed upon. They then took to building their own castles, after which the battling resumed and never ended. They stopped catapulting fireballs and lightning balls at one another only long enough to rebuild their damaged and war-torn castles. After repairs were made, the fighting always began again with renewed ferocity.

So King Frederick's warlords have been battling for many centuries and now it's up to you to carry on their long-standing feud. Dominick, Marcus, Felipe, and Restivo have been locked inside this game program. They've stored enough fireballs and lightning balls so that they'll never run out and neither will you. They can hardly wait to do battle. So good luck, you're in for some fierce competition.

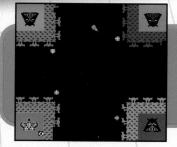

ABOUT THE GAME

Warlords was—and is still—considered to be one of the best group/party games of all time. It's easy to see why. A game of *Warlords* is fast, furious, and strategic, with consequences directly tied to player action at all times. With roots in classics such as *Pong* and *Breakout*, it is also easily accessible to newcomers and those who already spoke the language of games.

According to Carla Meninsky, the game's designer, the VCS/2600 version of *Warlords* was actually worked on prior to the arcade game, with the arcade game then being derived from the console version. Which version was released to the public first is still a point of debate amongst fans and historians. Some differences exist between both versions, such as catching the ball having adverse consequences for your castle in the arcade version.

In the arcade version of the game, computer-controlled players were not the Warlords from the game's lore. Instead, they were Black Knights who still did whatever they could to take down any player-controlled Warlords.

OBJECT OF THE GAME

The object of the game is to destroy the other three warlords before your warlord is destroyed. Use the paddle controller to protect your castle and your warlord. (Your warlord is located inside the castle.) Turn the knob on the controller to move your shield around your castle and block the ball.

HOW TO PLAY

Turn the controller knob to move your shield and block the ball. To use the catch feature, press and hold the red controller button before the ball makes contact with your shield. Release the button to send the ball back toward your opponents at high speed.

If you miss the ball, it knocks out your castle's bricks. As it breaks down, it becomes possible for the ball to hit your warlord, at which time you're out of the battle. Each battle ends when only one warlord remains on the playfield. The first person (or computer player) to win five battles wins the war.

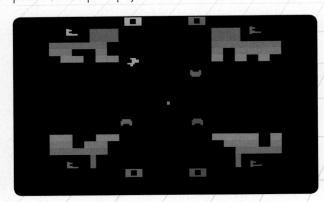

Note that a shield controlled by the computer will move slower than a shield controlled by a human player. To compensate for this fact, the computer player and shield have the power to throw the ball in unexpected directions.

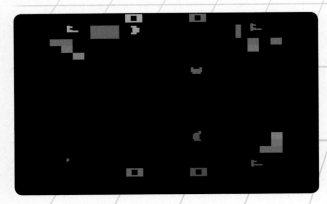

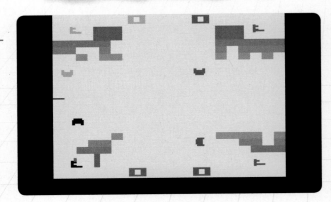

Also, when a warlord gets killed, his ghost will haunt the battlefield. If the ball comes near, the ghost may actually hit the ball in a new direction. If you look closely, you may even catch a glimpse of the ghost and his shield.

GAME VARIATIONS

Warlords has three main game variations:

1. Number of players: **One, two, three, four, or doubles. In doubles (D) games, two players control two shields each. The computer operates any unused shields.**

2. Ball speed: **Fireball/lightning ball. Depending on the game number, the ball speed will either be slow (fireball) or fast (lightning ball). As noted before, when using the Catch feature, the ball bounces off your shield at high speed. Also, when hitting bricks, the darker the wall, the faster the ball will return.**

3. Shields Ricochet/Catch: **Your shields function either with Ricochet or Catch. Ricochet simply means that the ball rebounds off your shield when contact is made. The Catch feature means that the ball sticks to your shield (when you hold down the red controller button) before contact is made. The ball comes off the shield at high speed when you release the button. Use the Catch feature to aim the ball at your opponents, or change the pace of the battle.**

CHILDREN'S VERSIONS

Games 21, 22, and 23 are special versions for young children, as the gameplay is slowed down considerably. All three games feature Ricochet (rather than Catch) and all three have fireballs (slow balls). The only difference in the three games is the number of players (4, 3, or 2).

GAME OPTIONS

GAME #	NUMBER OF PLAYERS	SHIELDS	BALL SPEED
1	4	C	F
2	3	C	F
3	2	C	F
4	1	C	F
5	D	C	F
6	4	C	S
7	3	C	S
8	2	C	S
9	1	C	S
10	D	C	S
11	4	R	F
12	3	R	F
13	2	R	F
14	1	R	F
15	D	R	F
16	4	R	S
17	3	R	S
18	2	R	S
19	1	R	S
20	D	R	S
21	4	CHILDREN	
22	3	CHILDREN	
23	2	CHILDREN	

FEATURES

D in the number of players column indicates Doubles. Two players each control two shields.

SHIELDS

In Ricochet (R) games, shields can only deflect incoming shots. In Catch (C) games, hold down the red button before the incoming shot makes contact with your shield to catch it. When you release the button, the ball comes off your shield at high speed.

BALL SPEED

The ball speed is either Slow (S) or Fast (F).

CHILDREN

The children's games use ricochet shields and slow balls and but the pace of the game is much slower.

GAME SELECT BUTTON

The game number changes at the top-left side of the screen when you press the button. The number to the right is the number of players for each game, which also changes as the game number changes.

Tips & Tricks

◆ When you first start playing the game, choose games with slow ball speed (fireball). This will help you get a feel for the game easier. Also, there are certain positions in which the ball always comes off your shield at the same angle, or in the same direction. Learn these positions and use them to your advantage against your opponents.

◆ Don't be too predictable. If you attempt to shoot from the same angle or position too often, your opponents will know what to expect. Vary your attacks to keep the other players off guard.

◆ Study your opponents' weaknesses. You can learn a lot by studying the habits of the enemy. You may find, for example, that one opponent moves very well in one direction when attempting to block shots, but has trouble moving in the opposite direction.

CENTIPEDE

Once upon a time in a misty, enchanted forest, there lived a colony of good elves. These elves had a major problem, though. Their prized mushroom garden was infested with pests—a giant Centipede, a poison-spreading scorpion, a mischief-making spider, and a pesky flea. The good elves tried everything they could to rid their garden of these bugs, but nothing worked.

One day, an elf named Oliver was hacking away at a poisoned mushroom in the garden. Suddenly, he saw an unusual stick gleaming in the dirt. Just as Oliver picked up the stick, a spider jumped out from behind a mushroom and rushed at him. When Oliver waved his hands wildly to try to scare the spider away, sparks flew from his stick and the spider disappeared!

"How did that happen?" Oliver wondered out load. "Could this be a magic wand?"

Soon Oliver had another chance to try the wand. When the scorpion scurried across a row of mushrooms, poisoning every mushroom it touched, Oliver pointed the wand at the scorpion and shouted, "Be gone!" Instantly, the scorpion disappeared and the poisoned mushrooms were transformed back into normal mushrooms.

"This is great! This is the tool we need to clean up our mushroom garden!" Oliver shouted ecstatically. With his newfound magic wand, Oliver hid behind a mushroom.

"OK, you great big Centipede," he said. "Come out wherever you are. I'm ready for you now!

ABOUT THE GAME

Centipede is a game that most people are familiar with. Not only did it become an instant classic, it also became a game that was created and recreated several times throughout the ages. However, this version of *Centipede* on the Atari 2600 was the first of its kind outside of the arcade, although it is the same version.

As one of the few games to come to the 2600 that was meant for a single player to enjoy, the game proved incredibly successful.

Ed Logg and Dona Bailey developed *Centipede* and, since Bailey was one of the few game programmers in the industry at the time, this game holds a very special place in development history. *Centipede* was also one of the first arcade, coin-operated games to have a significant female player base. *Centipede* may have changed the world of gaming demographics forever.

Not only was this game recreated multiple times throughout the years, it was also re-released on the Atari consoles that released after the 2600. Centipede isn't easy to master, but it keep your adrenaline pumping as the difficulty increases rather quickly and only gets harder the longer you play.

OBJECT OF THE GAME

Use your magic wand to score as many points as possible. Use strategy and quick thinking to avoid the paralyzing insect bites. The Enchanted Forest is a challenging but dangerous region. By learning about the dangers that lurk behind every mushroom, you can become a skilled and heroic wand wielder.

HOW TO PLAY

The Centipede consists of nine body segments. It attacks from the top of the screen and winds down toward the bottom. Each time you hit a segment, it becomes a powerless mushroom and the body segment behind that mushroom becomes the head of a new centipede.

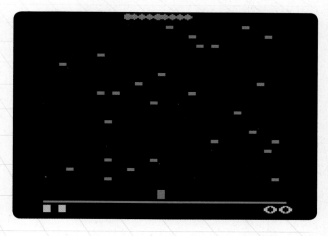

The centipede has eight different attacks. In wave 1, the Centipede is composed of a head attached to eight body parts. In wave 2, it has a head attached to seven body parts, plus a detached head. Wave 3's centipede is composed of six body segments with one attached head and two detached heads. The centipede continues to transform a body segment into a head until wave 8, at which time it has nine independently moving heads.

You must eliminate the wave 1 centipede just once. Until your score passes 40,000 points, you must destroy each subsequent centipede wave twice. First as the centipede moves slowly toward you and then as it moves quickly. After you score over 40,000 points, you must defeat each centipede only once.

When you shoot every segment of the insect, the centipede briefly disappears and then reappears at the top in a new and fiercer attack formation.

- Shoot away mushrooms in a straight line up the screen to create a "corridor" of sorts. When the centipede reaches this "gap," it will fall straight down the battlefield, making it easy to defeat.

- Since the flea doesn't appear until you have eliminated most of the nearby mushrooms, you can set up a shield to prevent this pest from striking. Just leave at least five mushrooms on the lower third of the screen. After you score 120,000 points, you'll need to leave 10 mushrooms.

- Shoot centipede heads to create new heads out of the body segments left behind. Since heads are worth 10 times the point value of body segments, you'll score more points.

- Each creature makes a distinct sound. By becoming familiar with these sounds, you will know—without looking—what is attacking and where it is on-screen.

ATARI NEWS
What The Critics Had to Say

"*Centipede*, without a doubt, is one of the most successful and enjoyable arcade games of all time. The game was a major hit for Atari, and variations of it roll out for various consoles even today. Still, little or no improvements have been made to the formula which made the game an almost instant classic, and the folks at Atari retained the thrilling gameplay in Centipede for the good ol' 2600."

- Ethan C. Nobles, The Atari Times (2003)

"The premise in *Centipede* is really basic yet it works… Not only are the controls very accurate but the game even looks just like the arcade game."

- Ryan Genno, The Atari Times (2005)

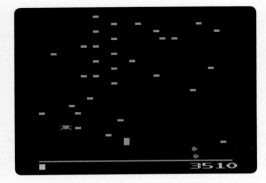

MUSHROOMS

Dotting the forest floor are mushrooms. The Centipede slides horizontally in one direction. When it touches a mushroom or the edge of the screen, it drops down to the next row of mushrooms and reverses direction. It takes three consecutive hits to eliminate an entire mushroom.

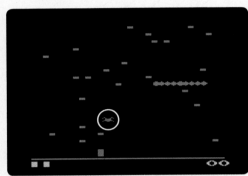

SPIDER

The spider jumps all over the battlefield, eliminating some of the mushrooms it touches. You score 300, 600, or 900 points when you zap the spider. The closer the spider is to your wand, the greater the score. When you hit it, the spider's score lights up on-screen.

FLEA

The flea appears after you shoot away most of the nearby mushrooms. It drops straight down, creating mushrooms as it falls. You must hit the flea twice to make it disappear. Warning: After the first shot, the flea drops twice as fast!

SCORPION

Sometime after you clear three *Centipede* screens, the scorpion will scurry across the battlefield, poisoning every mushroom it touches. If you zap the scorpion before it runs across an entire row of mushrooms, however, the spell of poison is broken and the mushrooms remain normal.

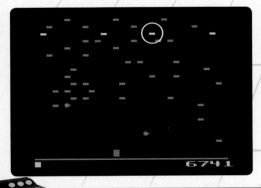

POISONED MUSHROOMS

The scorpion creates the poisoned mushrooms of a deadly white color. When the centipede bumps into a poisoned mushroom, it goes wild and plunges straight through the field of mushrooms toward you. As is the case with normal mushrooms, you must hit a poisoned mushroom three times in succession to destroy it. Each time you lose a wand, poisoned mushrooms transform back into normal mushrooms.

GAME DIFFICULTY

Centipede offers two game variations: Easy Play for beginners and children and Standard Play for skilled players. In Easy games, you do not lose a magic wand when the flea or spider touches you. The centipede always starts the attack in a single formation, never with detached heads.

NUMBER OF PLAYERS

Centipede is a one-player game with the goal of obtaining the highest score possible. You can track your score and use it to compete against other players, however, the game itself does not include a multiplayer function.

SCORING

In a standard *Centipede* game, you can score a total of 999,999 points before the score rolls back to zero. In the Easy game variation, you can score a total of 99,999 points

CENTIPEDE BODY SEGMENT	10 POINTS
Centipede head	100 points
Spider (distant range)	300 points
Spider (medium range)	600 points
Spider (close range)	900 points
Flea	200 points
Scorpion	1,000 points
Mushroom	1 point (estimated)
Mushroom (wounded or intact at end of turn)	5 points for every 2
Poisoned Mushroom	1 point (estimated)
Poisoned Mushroom (wounded or intact at end of turn)	5 points for every 2
Bonus Wand	Every 10,000 points

FUN FACTS!

Some graphics from the game *Galaxian* are in the code, specifically the player's ship and one of the Galaxians. According to the GCC programmer Mark S. Ackerman, game data tables were usually partially overwritten with data tables from other games in an effort to save bytes.

The game is incompatible with some 7800 consoles.

DEMONS TO DIAMONDS

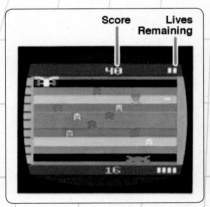

You and your best friend are spending a super Saturday at the Cosmic Carnival. So far, you've done all the usual things. Now you're restlessly looking around for a new thrill—something exciting and different, some competitive skill sport. Suddenly, you hear a taunting voice coming from the vicinity of Target Skill Gallery.

"Whoa, let's see what that's about!", you say as you make a sharp left and jog off in the direction of the high-pitched speech.

The non-stop voice belongs to a squat, two-foot tall demon parading back and forth in front of a huge, vertical, shooting range.

"Hey, you!" squeaks the demon, pointing directly at you. "Would you like to command a laser base? Like to hit targets and score points? Are you looking for fun, excitement—a game in which you must dodge danger? We are the demons and we dare you to try your laser-sharpshooting skills on us! We're full of surprises. We sidestep all over the shooting range. We yak at you until you shut us up. We change into new target forms—precious diamonds or deadly skulls. Hit a diamond and you'll score a small fortune in bonus points. But beware of skulls!"

"So, come on, reach for your laser, exercise your trigger finger on us. Put us through our paces and we'll dazzle you with demonic tricks!"

ABOUT THE GAME

Demons to Diamonds utilizes core concepts from previously popular shooter games. Atari attempted to offset the similarities to the games *Demons to Diamonds* borrowed from with the introduction of new gameplay elements, such as updated animations and graphics from artist Alan Murphy, enemy movement in multiple directions at once, and the added challenge of a competing second player on the opposite side of the screen. Players not only had to shoot the enemy demons, but also avoid hitting the opposing player's targets.

Even with the advanced graphics, animations, and new gameplay elements, *Demons to Diamonds* released to mediocre reception.

OBJECT OF THE GAME

The objective in *Demons to Diamonds* is to score as many points as possible while losing as few lives as possible.

HOW TO PLAY

You start the game with five lives; four of which are displayed on your side of the screen in the far-right corner. The lives resemble white rectangles, as shown here.

Use the joystick to move your laser back and forth across the top or bottom of the playfield. Press the red controller button to fire at demons. The longer you press the red button, the further the laser will extend up or down the screen. The laser disappears when it hits a demon, a skull, or any other object on-screen.

Score — Lives Remaining

Hit demons that are the same color as your laser base to score points. Demons first appear in the middle two rows. When you hit a demon of your color, it eventually changes into a pulsating diamond.

If you (or your opponent) can hit this diamond before it disappears, the one who hits it scores bonus points. When you hit a demon of your opponent's color, it transforms into a skull that shoots in both directions. Watch out for these skulls! You lose a life each time you are struck by a skull's bullet. In some game variations, you also lose a life when your opponent shoots your laser base.

Skulls disappear after a short period of time. The image here shows a typical *Demons to Diamonds* game playfield with demons, skulls, and bonus diamonds.

Bonus Diamond   **Demon**

Laser Base   **Skull**

Demons move back and forth across the screen, changing color when they bump into either side of the wall. After hitting a wall, they may move up or down the screen into new rows. Each time you shoot all the demons on-screen, a new wave of the little devils appear.

The screen flashes briefly to signal the end of one wave and the start of the next. At first, the demons move slowly and the skulls are stationary. As the game progresses, though, the demons pick up speed and the skulls move around.

In single-player games, skulls spontaneously appear in the first wave. At first the skulls don't move, but by wave three they move up and down the screen, making it difficult to dodge their deadly fire. In two-player games, the skulls appear in wave five and move during wave seven.

When a skull's bullet hits you, you will know. An echoing sound plays and everything on-screen momentarily stops.

In two-player games, you score bonus points for lives that remain after your opponent loses all his lives. A high, bell-like sound chimes for each remaining life as your bonus points are added.

DIFFICULTY OPTIONS

Difficulty buttons control the speed of the skulls' bullets in all games. In the A position, the bullets fire almost twice as fast as in the B position.

Use the left difficulty button for one-player games. For two-player games, the bottom player uses the left difficulty button and the top player uses the right difficulty button.

GAME OPTIONS

Use the game select button to choose the game variation you want to play. The game number appears at the top-center of

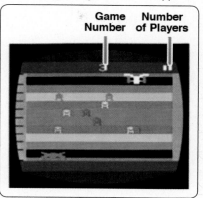

Game Number   **Number of Players**

the screen, while the number of players for that game appears at the top-right as shown in the screenshot to the left.

There are six game numbers in total.

GAME #	# PLAYERS	FEATURES
1	1	FB
2	2	FB
3	2	FB & AT
4	1	SB
5	2	SB
6	2	SB & AT

FEATURES

FAST BULLETS (FB)
Skulls fire bullets that travel at normal speed, shoot often, and move quickly up and down the screen.

SLOW BULLETS (SB)
Skulls fire bullets that travel slower, don't shoot as often, and take longer to move up and down the screen.

ATTACK OPPONENT (AT)
Your attacks can destroy your opponent's laser base.

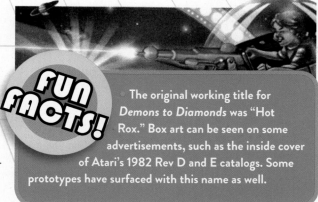

FUN FACTS!

The original working title for *Demons to Diamonds* was "Hot Rox." Box art can be seen on some advertisements, such as the inside cover of Atari's 1982 Rev D and E catalogs. Some prototypes have surfaced with this name as well.

SCORING

DEMONS

Every time you hit a demon of your own color, you receive from 1 to 8 points, depending upon which row the demon occupies. For example, a demon in the row nearest your laser base is worth 1 point, while a demon in the third row from your laser is worth 3 points.

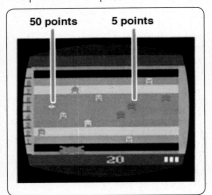

50 points   5 points

DIAMONDS

Each pulsating diamond is worth 10 to 80 points, or 10 times the value of the row it occupies.

BONUS LIVES

Any remaining lives after an opponent loses all five of his lives are credited to your score. The value of a bonus life increases with each wave, as shown in the following table.

WAVE NUMBER	1	2	3	4	5	6	7	8
Points Per Life Left	10	20	30	50	100	150	200	250

WAVE NUMBER	9	10	11	12	13	14	15	16
Points Per Life Left	300	350	400	500	750	1000	1500	2000

Tips & Tricks

◆ Create skulls as far as possible from your laser base; these are more likely to hit your opponent than you.

◆ Aim at demons of your own color that are as far away as possible; they are worth more points than the closer ones. But beware of your opponent hitting your bonus diamond. He gets those points, too!

◆ Try to hit the diamonds whenever possible. They are worth a lot of points and, if you can hit them consistently, your score will quickly rise.

◆ Spontaneous skulls usually appear at the edge of the rows. Don't spend too much time in this vicinity. The safest position is just to the right or left of the center.

◆ Take care when firing into the center of the screen. This is where demons first appear and you can inadvertently hit an opponent's while aiming at your own color. The same thing can happen when you try to hit your own color at the edge of the screen. Since demons change color when they bump into the right and left sides of the screen, you can potentially end up hitting an opponent's and creating a skull there.

Safe Laser Base Position Skull

HAUNTED HOUSE

Many years ago in the small town of Spirit Bay, there lived a mean old man named Zachary Graves. Old man Graves was not a very well liked person. He rarely left the old mansion and spent most of his life brooding about the decaying four-story house. When he died, the house was condemned and locked up.

The townspeople claim that old man Graves knew the whereabouts of a magic urn, a family heirloom of the first family of Spirit Bay. It seems that the mansion was the family's first home and that the magic urn, which broke into several pieces during the earthquake of 1890, is still in the old house.

To this day, no one has mustered the courage to search the mansion for the pieces of the urn. It is common knowledge that the ghost of old man Graves still haunts the mansion. Some of the neighbors claim to have seen lights flickering in the windows. Some say that they have heard eerie sounds, doors slamming, and heavy footsteps. Some even claim to have seen shadows running through the mansion.

The mysterious mansion has 24 rooms connected by long corridors and staircases. Some of the rooms have been locked for over 50 years. There is supposed to be a master key hidden somewhere in the mansion. Without the key, it might be impossible to travel from room to room. There is also an ancient scepter hidden in the mansion. Old man Graves always carried this scepter. He believed it scared off evil spirits.

Do you dare enter the frightening old mansion? If you do, remember to carry matches; the *Haunted House* is very dark.

ABOUT THE GAME

Haunted House was the first of several horror games released for the Atari 2600 and one that many would argue is perhaps the best in this genre released in the first few decades of home videogames. This game looked great on the Atari 2600, plus the sound design was extremely detailed. As most critics will say, it is incredibly easy to tell what you are looking at the entire time while also being spooked by the sounds affected by your actions.

The game is simple in the sense that there seem to be only a few different directions to run and the rooms are rather wide open. However, it is quite the opposite. There are eight different hallways, some with locked doors, others with stairs, and still others that will take you to a floor with a creature ready to pounce. There is also a great amount of strategy needed in order to play *Haunted House*.

The game will most definitely keep you on your toes, as one minute you are concentrating on what to do next and then the next minute you are running for your life.

OBJECT OF THE GAME

The object of the game is to find the three pieces of the magic urn and carry them back to the mansion's main entrance before losing all nine lives. Your score is based on the number of matches and lives used during your search.

HOW TO PLAY

So far, we've told you some of the things to expect while inside the *Haunted House*. The following section reveals information to help you understand the objects and characters in the game, as well as the progressive levels of difficulty.

The urn pieces are randomly scattered throughout 24 rooms. There are four floors, each with six rooms. Staircases connect the floors, while corridors and doorways connect the rooms. Some of the doors are locked, so you must find the master key (also hidden in the mansion) to unlock them.

What makes finding the urn so difficult is the fact that the mansion is so dark. To see your way around, you are given an unlimited supply of matches, which you light by pressing the red controller button.

Once you can see, be warned that you'll encounter several types of creatures in the mansion. Be prepared to see a vampire bat, hairy tarantulas, and the ghost of old man Graves himself! Each time a creature touches you, you'll be "scared to death" and—consequently—lose a life.

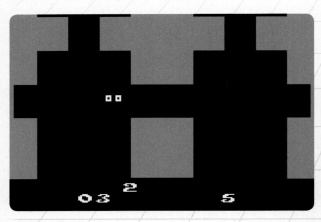

OBJECTS

The urn is broken into three pieces. To see the pieces and other objects, you must light a match. To pick up a piece of the urn, you (the eyes) must touch it. When you touch it, the piece appears at the bottom-right corner of the screen. The urn pieces automatically attach to the other pieces once new ones are found. They eventually bond together to form the entire urn as one object.

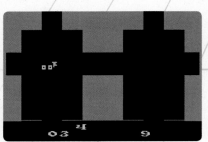

If you are carrying one object and pick up a new one, the new object will replace the old object. You will quickly learn that you can only hold one object at a time. When you have successfully put the three pieces of the urn together, you must return to the mansion's main entrance with the urn.

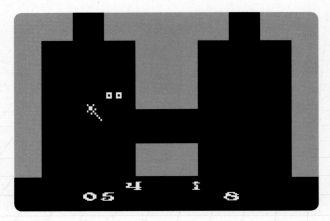

THE SCEPTER

The scepter is a magic stick used to make you invisible to all creatures in the mansion. To use the scepter you must drop any other object and touch the scepter. As long as you hold the scepter, you cannot be "scared to death."

Like all other objects, while you are holding the scepter, it appears at the bottom-right corner of the screen.

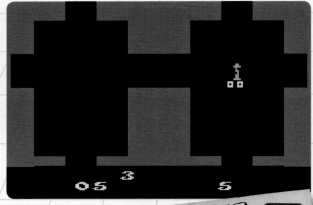

LOCKED DOORS

Games 3 through 9 include locked doors that connect some of the rooms. To open these doors, you must find the master key. It is hidden in one of the unlocked rooms. To use the key, you must touch it. When you hold the key, it appears at the bottom of the screen. As is the case with other objects, you cannot hold anything else while holding the key.

DOORWAYS

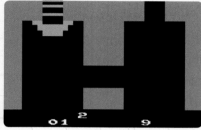

As you travel through the mansion, you'll encounter several doorways. Some are locked, while others aren't. To see the doorways in Games 2 through 9, light a match.

TARANTULAS

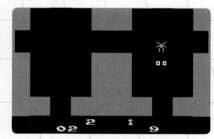

Tarantulas are giant, hairy spiders that slowly move around the mansion. If a tarantula touches you, you lose a life unless you are carrying the scepter.

VAMPIRE BATS

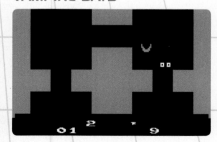

Vampire bats fly quickly around the mansion. If touched by a vampire bat, you lose a life unless you're carrying the scepter.

GHOSTS

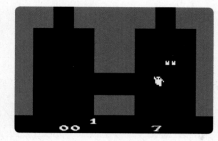

There is one very fast ghost in the mansion. It can pass through locked doors and walls to chase you. If the ghost touches you, you will get "scared to death" and lose a life. Carrying the scepter in Games 1 through 7 will protect you from the ghost.

> **SCARED OF THE DARK?**
> When any creature enters a room, your lighted match is blown out but the creature's body still glows in the dark.

SOUNDS

The game sounds in *Haunted House* provide important gameplay clues. You will hear a sound when you run into walls or locked floors. You will hear and see flashes of lighting. If the wind blows, don't be surprised if it blows out your match. When you walk through doorways, you'll hear the doors open and shut.

The mansion is so creaky you can hear your own footsteps. When you climb up or down stairways, you will even hear a spooky tune. A tune plays low musical notes to high notes while ascending stairs. As you go downstairs, the tune plays high notes to low notes.

CONTROLS

Move the joystick up, down, right or left to move around the house.

Your eyes (the player character) will move in the same direction as you move the joystick. Press the red controller button to light a match. When you light a match, a circular area around you becomes visible. All game variants have an unlimited supply of matches.

To pick up an object, use the joystick to guide the eyes to touch the object. To drop an object, use the joystick to touch another object. The two objects will automatically change places. You can also drop an object by pressing the red controller button if a match is lighted.

Use the joystick controller to move up or down stairways. Each stairway travels only in one direction: up or down. Stairways leading down start with large steps decreasing in size, while stairways leading up start with small steps increasing in size. To change floors, use the joystick to move to the end of the stairway and then move the joystick in the opposite direction to enter the room.

Each floor is numbered and color-coded. The number is located in the lower-left portion of the screen. The number changes as you move from one floor to the next. The entire lower portion of the screen changes colors with each of the four floors in the house.

GAME OPTIONS

GAME 1

Game 1 is the beginning level. It includes lighted walls to help you see the rooms. There are no doors, so no key is required, but you need to light matches to see objects. There are three creatures on the prowl: one bat, one tarantula, and one ghost.

GAME 2

In Game 2, the mansion is completely dark and there are unlocked doors. Three creatures, as in Game 1, attempt to scare you to death.

GAME 3

Game 3 is like Game 2 except that some doors are locked, but you'll find the master key in the first room you enter.

GAME 4

Game 4 is the same as Game 3 except that the master key is in a different location each time the game is played.

GAME 5

In Game 5, everything is the same as in Game 4, but there are two additional tarantulas in the mansion.

GAME6

In Game 6, all five creatures are scurrying about the mansion but only the ghost can pass through a locked door.

GAME 7

In Game 7, any object you are holding will be dropped and moved to another room in the mansion when a bat touches you.

GAME 8

Game 8 is the same as Game 7, but all of the creatures move faster. To make things even tougher, the ghost is not affected by the scepter.

GAME 9

This is the ultimate *Haunted House* challenge. Game 9 has the same gameplay as Game 8, but the floorplan is different and you'll find yourself in a completely different maze of rooms. For an added element of surprise, all the creatures can chase you from room to room, even through locked doors!

GAME DIFFICULTY

LEFT DIFFICULTY

With the left difficulty button in the B position, periodic flashes of lightning will make it easier to see in the mansion as the creatures chase you.

With the left difficulty button set to the A position, you must feel your way around, listening to sounds and bumping into walls.

SCORING

Your score is based on the number of matches used and the number of lives remaining at the end of the game. The game ends when you return to the main entrance of the mansion carrying the urn, or when all nine lives have been lost.

The number of matches used appears in the lower-left corner of the screen. The first number to appear here is 00. The number then increases by one each time you light a match. The lower the number, the better your score.

Each game starts with nine lives, indicated at the bottom-right corner of the screen. You lose one life every time you get "scared to death" (touched by a creature). The more lives remaining at the end of the game, the better your score.

FUN FACTS!

- Atari's *Haunted House* was originally called *Nightmare Manor*.

- An extra object can be revealed when solving the game. Get the urn and go next to the exit wall without ending the game. Push up against the wall and drop the urn. With a match lit, press down and right on the joystick to grab the urn and instantly end the game. Most times the urn will appear, but occasionally a scepter will appear to the right of your position.

- If you stand in one of the left or right stairwells (while using a match), half of the opposite stairwell will start to blink.

- There's a way to get what resembles the initials "DC" to appear where the lives remaining number is located. It seems to involve having less than 0 lives left, so it may require getting hit by two creatures at once.

- According to Todd Rogers, it may be possible to find the staff/wand object during a game.

Tips & Tricks

◆ Try to find the scepter first. Hold it while searching for the urn pieces. It might help to write down the location of each urn piece and then go directly to their locations and pick them up.

◆ It is possible to move through rooms with locked doors without using the key. To do this, you must become familiar with the floorplan and use different stairways as a way to get around locked doors. Remember, there are several stairways on each floor.

REALSPORTS BASEBALL

Join the Atari Aces in the World Series of video baseball — *RealSports Baseball*! It's a hot day in the ballpark—you can see the hot dog and soda pop vendors making their way up and down the bleachers. The crowd roars after each pitch and filling the stadium is the sound of "STEERIKE! YOU'RE OUT!" Down on the field it's a different story—just you and the pitcher facing each other in an enormous diamond of brown and green.

The roar of the spectators fades into the distance as the pitcher winds up. His arm arches back, his leg goes up, and... THUNK! The ball flashes by and hits the catcher's glove at 90 miles per hour. "STEERIKE!" Another windup, another 90 mile per hour fastball and "STEERIKE TWO!" Gripping the bat tightly, you stare back at the pitcher, see him wind up, and watch as the ball seems to float in slow motion down the field toward you. Everything falls into place as you swing with perfect timing, feel the contact, and see the ball sail over the right fielder's outstretched glove and over the wall. HOME RUN!

ABOUT THE GAME

RealSports Baseball was the second baseball title from Atari. A vast improvement from Atari's previous baseball game, *Home Run*, *RealSports Baseball* held its own against Mattel's M-Network title, *Super Challenge Baseball*.

Although the games were similar, *RealSports Baseball* held a bit of an edge against its competitor. To make things more interesting, the computer randomly determined the accuracy of your pitches. This means that you could pitch a perfect fastball on one pitch and completely flub it in the next. This added a new layer to the game and kept things a bit more interesting.

Another advantage *RealSports Baseball* could boast against its competition was the option for single-player games against a computer opponent. This gave *RealSports Baseball* four game variations, adding a more diverse gaming experience for the player.

OBJECT OF THE GAME

You play *RealSports Baseball* just like America's pastime. The object of the game is to score more runs than your opponent.

HOW TO PLAY

To start the first inning, press one of the red controller buttons. The home team will run to the playing field, the catcher will throw the pitcher a new ball, and a batter from the visiting team will step up to the plate.

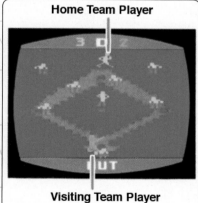

Home Team Player

Visiting Team Player

A team remains at bat until three of its players either strike out, fly out, or are tagged out. A base runner can also be "forced out" when an outfielder with the ball tags the base in front of the runner while another base runner is occupying the base behind him. (Force outs are needed to make those double and triple plays!)

Pitchers can throw either a ball or a strike. Three strikes count as an out and four balls result in a walk. A walked batter automatically advances to first base. If a batter swings at a pitch and misses, it always counts as a strike.

A batter can also hit a foul ball outside the baselines. A foul ball is counted as a strike unless the batter has already made two strikes, in which case it does not affect the count.

CONTROLLING THE BATTER

Make the batter swing by holding down your controller button and flicking the joystick at the same time. The direction you move the joystick determines the direction and trajectory of the ball.

Move the joystick straight up to bunt the ball; to the right to hit a ground ball toward left field; to the left to hit a ground ball toward right field; and straight back to hit fly balls and home runs. Fly balls and home runs are also possible by moving the joystick diagonally to the lower left and lower right. The lower-right position hits the ball to left field and the lower-left position hits to right field.

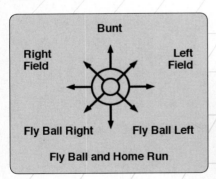

When an outfielder catches a fly ball, the batter is automatically out. If the outfielder misses the ball, however, the ball will sail over the stadium wall, resulting in a home run. After a home run, the ball reappears only after the batter rounds all the bases and touches home plate.

The direction of a hit ball can be affected by the timing of the batter's swing. Just like in regular baseball, swinging early will "pull" the ball to left field.

Swinging late—that is, swinging when the ball is nearly past you—will tend to slice the ball toward right field. By timing your swing carefully, you should be able to hit the ball to any part of the field.

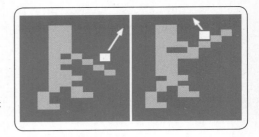

CONTROLLING BASE RUNNERS

To control a base runner, hold the controller button down and push the joystick to either the right of the left (Right: runner advance, Left: runner retreat). After a batter hits the ball, let the joystick return to the neutral (center) position, then push it to the right to make him advance to first base. To continue running, keep holding

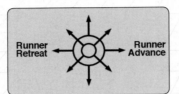

the controller button down and push the joystick to the right. To make a runner retreat—if, for example, he must return to a base to avoid being tagged out—simply hold down the controller button and push the joystick to the left.

STEALING BASES

Stealing a base is a two-step process: First, you transfer control from the batter to a base runner and then make him run. To transfer control, move the joystick in the direction of the base that the runner is on *without* holding down the controller button. Move the joystick right to indicate first base; up to indicate second base; left to indicate third base; and down to indicate home plate. The controlled player will turn slightly brighter in color when doing so.

To make the base runner steal, hold down the controller button and push the joystick to the right. If the pitcher on the opposing team has the ball and is not moving, the base runner will quickly steal the base. If any outfielder with the ball is moving (running or throwing the ball, for example), the runner will move much more slowly toward the base. Therefore, it is best to steal a base when the pitcher is motionless and "isn't looking." After the runner steals a base, transfer control back to the batter by pushing the joystick straight down.

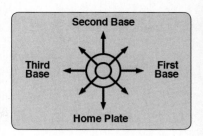

PITCHING THE BALL

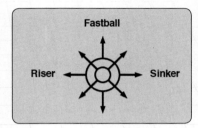

There are two steps involved in pitching the ball: First, select the type of pitch and then you throw the ball. As an ace pitcher, you can select a Fastball, a Riser, or a Sinker. You can also psych out your opponent by throwing an intentional ball. Push straight up to pitch a fastball; directly right to pitch a sinker; directly left pitch a riser; and straight down to pitch an intentional ball. An intentional ball will always be counted as a ball unless the batter swings, in which case it counts as a strike.

Occasionally, a batter can hit an intentional ball (just as a real batter can sometimes hit a ball outside the strike zone), but this happens only rarely. All other pitches deliver more strikes than balls. The computer randomly determines the percentage of strikes to balls; some days your fastball will deliver more strikes than your sinker, other days the reverse will be true. Experiment to discover your best pitch! After selecting a pitch, throw the ball by holding down the controller button and lightly flicking the joystick down.

THROWING THE BALL AROUND THE OUTFIELD

The player with the ball can throw to the pitcher or any of the four basemen. Hold down the controller button and push the joystick in the direction of the base to which you want to throw. Push the joystick to the right to throw to first base, straight up to throw to second base, left to throw to third base, and straight down to throw to the catcher. Leave the joystick in the neutral (center) position to throw the ball back to the pitcher. Remember to release the controller button after the ball is thrown, or you may accidentally throw the ball again after it is caught.

If an intended target misses the ball, it will roll and come to a stop on the field. Pick up the ball by running the controlled player over it. You'll hear the "plop" of the ball hitting the glove when it is picked up.

You can identify a controlled player by color; controlled players are solid yellow or pink. Non-controlled players are two-toned white and blue. If you're in doubt, move the joystick to see which team member is under your control.

RUNNING IN THE OUTFIELD

Use the joystick to move a controlled player in the outfield. The player moves up, down, right, left, and diagonally in the same direction you move the joystick.

GAME OPTIONS

There are four game variations in *RealSports Baseball*: Two two-player games and two one-player games. In the one-player version, the computer automatically controls one team. The computer always knows what pitch you're about to throw, so brush up on your best baseball strategy to beat the computer!

GAME #	# PLAYERS	FEATURES
1	2	SA
2	2	LS
3	1	SA
4	1	LS

FEATURES

SWING AWAY (SA)

The batter can hit every pitch.

LIMITED SWING (LS)

The batter cannot hit pitches that are classified as balls.

SCORING

Each time a batter touches all the bases in a counterclockwise direction and reaches home plate, the team scores one run. Scores are kept on the top of the screen; the home team

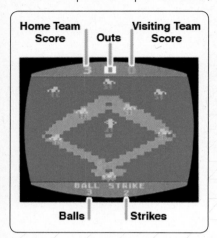

Home Team Score **Outs** **Visiting Team Score**

Balls **Strikes**

on the left and visiting team on the right. The number of outs in the inning also appears on the top of the screen between the two scores.

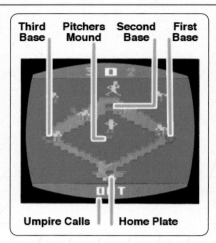

Third Base **Pitchers Mound** **Second Base** **First Base**

Umpire Calls **Home Plate**

The umpire also calls out the inning number each time a team has three outs and runs to the outfield. Look at the bottom of the screen to see the inning number flash onto the screen before the first pitch.

Balls and strikes are recorded behind home plate on the bottom of the screen. The umpire's calls flash after each pitch on the bottom of the screen, too.

FUN FACTS!

RealSports Baseball won a Certificate of Merit for the Best Sports Videogame category in the fifth annual Arcade Awards (Arkies), sponsored by Reese Communications and Electronic Games magazine in 1983. The awards were published in the January 1984 edition of *Electronic Games* magazine.

Tips & Tricks

◆ Hold the controller in your hands so your opponent can't see the direction you move the joystick. If you're pitching, this will prevent your opponent from knowing the pitch type. If you're at bat, this will prevent your opponent from recognizing if you're about to steal a base.

◆ When stealing, try to steal when the pitcher has the ball and is motionless (two-toned). This will allow you to steal the base faster. But watch out! If the pitcher sees you and throws the ball, you'll slow down in mid-run!

◆ Trust the joystick when throwing a ball to a base, even though the direction may not seem right. Pushing the joystick up, for example, will always throw the ball to second base, even if the outfielder is at the top of the screen.

◆ If you can't make the batter swing, he probably isn't a controlled player. Push the joystick down without holding the controller button, then try swinging the bat using both the joystick and the controller button.

◆ If no batter appears at home plate after an out, throw the ball to the catcher and then back to the pitcher. A batter will run out to home plate.

◆ Occasionally, a missed ball will roll near an object on the field making it difficult to see. Simply run the controlled player over the area the ball was last seen to pick it up.

◆ To make sure the pitcher has the ball, press the red controller button once.

◆ If the pitcher has the ball and is being controlled, you must run him back to the pitcher's mound to resume pitching. When he is positioned on the mound, he'll turn back to blue and white and will be ready to pitch once again.

◆ If an outfielder throws a batted ball back to the pitcher before the batter starts running, the batter is counted out.

REALSPORTS VOLLEYBALL

Judge the height of the ball from its shadow in this fast-paced game of volleyball. As the sun sets, the shadow disappears and you're on your own!

ABOUT THE GAME

By 1982, programmers were pushing the limits of the Atari 2600 but the system could not handle the twelve players involved in a typical volleyball game. The good news for Atari was the growth of volleyball played on the beach during the late 1970s and early 1980s.

Beach volleyball games consist of only two players per side, a number the Atari could easily handle. So easily, in fact, that the game's programmer added a timed element (a setting sun) and some whimsy (a shark's fin in the surf) to the background. The end result was a game that so accurately captured the spirit of an emerging sport (one that remains popular to this day) that it has been included in most Atari compilations through the years.

OBJECT OF THE GAME

RealSports Volleyball is patterned after traditional volleyball in which the objective is to win by scoring 15 points first with at least a two-point lead.

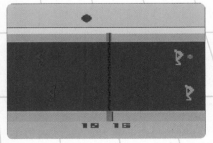

HOW TO PLAY

You control one of the teams (either blue or red) on one side of the court. Both players under your control move in the direction you push on the joystick.

Your players are restricted to half the court, meaning the top player's range is from the black boundary line near the ocean to midcourt, while the other player covers midcourt down to the black boundary line near the bottom of the screen.

To begin play, the team with the ball must serve it over the net. If the ball is on the ground on your side of the net, move the top player over to the ball. The serving player can move up or down (but not closer to the net) before serving. Press the red controller button to serve the ball over the net. Since you have no control over placement, move close to the middle of

the court before serving the ball. It is possible to serve the ball outside the boundary line nearest the ocean.

To return the serve and subsequent hits over the net, move your players toward the ball. Use the shadow of the ball (it appears on the ground) to guide one of your players toward it.

ATARI NEWS
What The Critics Had to Say

"Audio Rating: Excellent

Graphics Rating: Good

Play-Action Rating: Good

Solitaire Rating: Good

Head-to-Head Rating: Good

Overall Rating: 5"

-*1984 Software Encyclopedia, from the publishers of Electronic Games*

"Superb sound and graphic effects make this contest that's between two-man, on-screen teams really come alive."

-*Electronic Games, September 1983*

Tips & Tricks

- To use the ball's shadow as a point of reference, position your player so that the shadow lands on the player's feet.

- In Games 1 and 2, spike the ball whenever you are close enough to the net. There's no advantage to using two set-up shots before spiking and there's always a chance you will hit the ball too far from your other player.

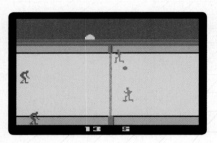

If a player is closer to the net than to the back line, then you can execute a spike. Spiking is a method of returning the ball over the net with a lower trajectory and greater velocity than normal. To spike the ball, press the red controller button just before your player hits the ball.

You receive one point each time your opponent either misses a ball or hits a ball out of bounds that you initially served. If the team that served the ball misses it or hits it out of bounds, the ball goes to the opposite team to serve.

A bell sounds every time a point is scored, while a buzz sounds when the ball goes out of bounds. If a player runs off the court and hits the ball back over the net, the volley is played as if the ball did not go out of bounds.

DIFFICULTY OPTIONS

The difficulty button determines the players' speed. Set in the A position, both players on a team will move slowly. Set in the B position, they move faster.

GAME OPTIONS

GAME #	# PLAYERS	FEATURES
1	1	SU
2	2	SU
3	1	
4	2	

FEATURES

The only feature in *Realsports Volleyball* is setup (SU). Your team will set up the ball by passing it between players before hitting it back over the net. Unless you spike the ball, the third hit always goes back over the net. In games 3 and 4, the ball is returned over the net after the first hit.

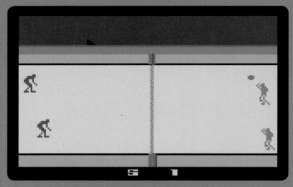

FUN FACTS!

Two background events take place while the game is active. The first impacts how you play the game. If you wait long enough, you can watch the sun set on the ocean. After the sun goes completely below the horizon, the volleyball won't cast a shadow any longer. Additionally, watch the water for the appearance of a shark fin when the sun is about to set.

The manual states that you must win by at least two points, but play will stop when a team reaches 20. That makes service a big deal when the score is tied at 19!

There's a narrow band in the middle of the court that neither of the players under your control can reach. In the image below, the top blue player is as low as it can go and the bottom red player is as high as it can go. The space between the blue player's feet and the red player's head is the unreachable band.

RealSports™ VOLLEYBALL

Atari takes the game to the beach where agile players set and spike under a sun that sets as each game ends. Lifelike players lob serves to unguarded corners, set the ball to teammates, and spike it over the net for a winner! Joystick controls player positions and the red firing button moves their arms for precise ball control. 4 games; 2 skill levels; Play against the computer or with a friend. CX2666.

SUBMARINE COMMANDER

Just imagine that you are the captain of a ship, and it's your job to protect your country. Your modern submarine is equipped with many new features to help you. The control panel includes a radar scope, a sonar depth charge detector, status indicators, a fuel readout, an engine temperature gauge, and of course, torpedoes.

Since you're the commander, you are at the helm. It's up to you to guide the submarine. You'll use your periscope to scan the ocean and detect enemy vessels. When you spot the enemy, launch a torpedo. Destroy their ships before they destroy your submarine. Be on the lookout for dangerous depth charge attacks. A depth charge hit could mean serious damage to your submarine.

Your submarine is equipped with limited supplies, especially fuel. Keep a constant watch on your fuel and energy levels. Every maneuver costs you fuel. When the fuel runs out, your mission is over.

We know you can handle the job, so good luck, Commander!

ABOUT THE GAME

Released in 1982, programmer Matthew Hubbard's *Submarine Commander* was the third and final Sears Tele-Games exclusive as part of Atari's blockbuster contract with the retailer. Unfortunately for *Submarine Commander*'s sales fortunes, Sears shut down their publishing operations later that same year, limiting the game's distribution. As such, it's the hardest among the trio of exclusives for today's collectors to find.

Submarine targeting simulations date all the way back to Sega's 1966 electro-mechanical arcade game, *Periscope*. Perhaps the most popular of this sub-genre of games was Midway's 1976 arcade game, *Sea Wolf*, and its 1978 sequel, *Sea Wolf II*. It's the latter game that *Submarine Commander* draws the most inspiration from and what most other games of this type imitate.

OBJECT OF THE GAME

Your goal is to sink as many enemy ships as possible. In one-player games, try to beat your highest score. In two-player games, each player tries to beat the opponent's score.

HOW TO PLAY

As you sink ships, you score points. Some of the ships drop depth charges, which might damage your submarine.

Depth charges are indicated on the depth charge detector gauge. The gauge alerts you to the closeness and the seriousness of a depth charge. Because your sub is equipped with sonar detection, you can identify the location of enemy ships before they're sighted through the periscope. This allows you to shoot a torpedo before the enemy drops a depth charge.

Your sub also carries 3,000 units of fuel and two torpedo launchers. The fuel level is proportional to the engine temperature. Watch the engine temperature gauge at the top center of the screen. The more maneuvers you make, the hotter the engine gets. Every torpedo launched uses three units of fuel, but every depth charge hit costs 300-377 units of fuel. Some fuel is also used to run the submarine engines. When all the fuel runs out, the temperature gauge turns black, and the game is over.

Use the joystick to view the sea and to move your submarine right and left. What you see on the screen is your view through a periscope. Moving the joystick up and down (forward and backward) allows you to see up close or far away to the horizon.

You can also use the joystick to maneuver the sub right and left. This helps you catch up to an enemy ship or move away from a dangerous depth charge. A broken black line, located just below the temperature gauge, indicates the direction in which your sub is moving. When you move the joystick right, the black lines move right, indicating that the sub is moving right. When you move the joystick left, the black lines move left, and your sub is moving left. When your sub is moving right or left, any torpedoes launched travel with a slight curve in the opposite direction.

To shoot a torpedo, press the red controller button. The torpedoes launch from the side where the torpedo status indicator is green. The torpedo launcher changes sides with every other launch. You will see the green light change sides each time you launch a torpedo.

GAUGES

Each gauge on the control panel serves a specific function. With time and practice, you'll be able to use all of the gauges to your best advantage.

FUEL GAUGE

The fuel gauge at the bottom center of the screen starts with 3,000 units of fuel and counts backward until you run out.

TORPEDO STATUS GAUGE

Torpedo status gauges are located at the bottom of the screen, directly above the fuel gauge. The gauge is green when a torpedo is ready to launch. Press the red controller button, and a torpedo launches from the side with the green light. If a torpedo tube is damaged by a depth charge, it becomes black and doesn't work for the rest of the game.

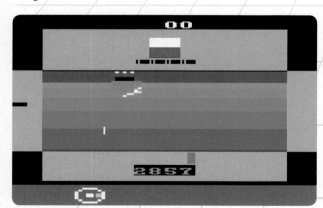

Launching a torpedo.

ENGINE TEMPERATURE GAUGE

Engine temperature is indicated at the top center of the screen. As the engine gets hot, the gauge turns red. The

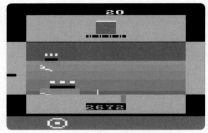

hotter the engine, the more fuel it consumes. If the gauge turns yellow, the engine has been damaged and is running at half speed.

The engine is getting very hot, as indicated by the rising red color.

DIRECTIONAL GAUGE

This is the broken black line located below the engine temperature gauge. When you move the sub right or left, the lines move right or left, as though you're steering the submarine.

SONAR DETECTOR

The sonar detector, located at the bottom-left side of the screen, identifies the location of an enemy ship before it's visible on the screen. When this device turns red, it's indicating the depth and the location of any enemy ship.

DEPTH CHARGE DETECTOR

The depth charge detector is an arrow that appears at the lower-right corner of the screen. It points to where a depth charge is located in the water. If the arrow is white, the depth charge is not dangerously close and you can move your sub in the opposite direction to avoid a hit. If the arrow is red, look out! You're about to be hit unless you quickly move away in the opposite direction.

The red arrow indicates a depth charge is near!

SCORING

You score points when you sink a ship. There are three types of enemy ships in *Submarine Commander*, and each scores a different point value, as shown:

OBJECT	POINT TOTAL
Tanker	20; two hits to go down
Destroyer	15; one hit to go down
PT Boat	35; one hit to go down

If a ship is on the horizon, in which case it appears to be half its normal size, and you can see the blue sky in the background, the scoring is as follows:

OBJECT	POINT TOTAL
Tanker	30
Destroyer	25
PT Boat	45

The game ends when the fuel level reaches zero. After a two-player game is over, the left player's score appears at the top center of the screen; the right player's score appears at the bottom center, where the fuel amount was indicated during gameplay.

DIFFICULTY OPTIONS

Submarine Commander includes two skill levels: A for Expert and B for Novice. The Novice level is for the beginning player. The Expert level is more challenging because every time your sub is hit by a depth charge, you incur damage that could cause the loss of one of your gauges.

For one-player games, use the left difficulty button. For two-player games, the player using the left controller uses the left difficulty button; the player using the right controller uses the right difficulty button. The left player starts the game in two-player games.

GAME OPTIONS

Submarine Commander features eight game variations. All odd-numbered games are for one player; all even numbers are two-player games.

Games 1 and 2 are the easiest. In these two variations, the enemy ships do not shoot depth charges. All you have to do is shoot torpedoes to sink the enemy ships before you run out of fuel.

In Games 3 and 4, only the destroyers attack with depth charges.

ATARI NEWS
What The Critics Had to Say

"Excluding its elaborate graphics, *Submarine Commander* is a very basic shooting-gallery game."

-How to Win at Video Games book, 1982

In Games 5 and 6, you have to avoid the depth charges of both destroyers and PT boats.

Games 7 and 8 are the toughest. You must dodge depth charges from destroyers, PT boats, and tankers.

GAME #	# PLAYERS	FEATURES
1	1	DC0
2	2	DC0
3	1	DC1
4	2	DC1
5	1	DC2
6	2	DC2
7	1	DC3
8	2	DC3

FEATURES

The number after DC indicates how many ships drop depth charges to attack your submarine. Only destroyers use depth charges in DC1 games. Destroyers and PT boats drop depth charges in games marked DC2. DC3 indicates that destroyers, PT boats, and tankers all use depth charges.

Tips & Tricks

◆ Your submarine is equipped with many gauges, each of which is equally important. To learn to scan all of the gauges during gameplay, it's best to master one gauge at a time. Once you learn one, add another gauge. With lots of practice, you will soon be using all of the gauges.

◆ Learn to detect the sounds of the PT boats. If you listen, you can hear them coming just before you see them on the screen.

◆ Try to sink as many PT boats as possible. They're worth the most points, and they only need one hit to go down.

◆ The easiest position to shoot from is the lowest level on the screen. Pull the joystick back (toward you). Once you've mastered all the gauges, use the sonar detector and move up to the horizon (push the joystick forward). Ships on the horizon are worth the most points, but you're more vulnerable to their depth charges.

SWORDQUEST:
THE ULTIMATE SEARCH FOR THE ULTIMATE TREASURE

ABOUT THE SERIES

The cover of the September/October 1982 issue of Atari Age introduced the world to *SwordQuest*. *SwordQuest* began as a sequel to the popular game *Adventure*, then morphed into a planned series of four games. It quickly became much more.

Each game would include a comic book created by an all-star crew from DC Comics. The comics would tell the story of Tarra and Torr, twins whose destiny was to visit four worlds to recover the Sword of Ultimate Sorcery and the Talisman of Truth.

Of course, the biggest revelation was the five prizes that players could win if they were up to the challenge. Using contests to drum up interest in upcoming games was nothing new in the industry, but the value of the prizes caught everyone's attention.

THE CONTESTS

The plan was to hold four contests, one for each game, capped off by a clash of champions. Each game included an entry form that players filled out and returned in order to qualify for a final showdown to win a $25,000 prize. For *Earthworld*, the prize was a gold talisman. *Fireworld*'s prize was a chalice made from gold and platinum. And that's where things ended.

Despite four contests being planned, only the contests for *EarthWorld* and *FireWorld* took place. Players completed the games, found the correct pages in the comic book, then sent in their entries and were selected for a playoff.

The *EarthWorld* contest took place in Sunnyvale, California on May 2, 1983. The eight finalists played a special version of the game and were given up to 90 minutes to complete it. Steven Bell won the contest by being the first person to reach the twelfth level in 46 minutes. In November 1983, 50 finalists arrived in Sunnyvale for *FireWorld*'s contest, which was won by Michael Rideout.

The videogame crash of 1983 and subsequent sale of Atari ended the contests.

WaterWorld was initially sold only through an Atari club, although cartridges appeared in stores after the deadline for contest entries (despite an extension to April 15, 1984) had passed. The game *AirWorld* was never released. The remaining prizes (a crown, philosopher's stone, and a $50,000 sword) were never awarded.

SwordQuest EarthWorld comic book cover.

SwordQuest FireWorld comic book cover.

SwordQuest WaterWorld comic book cover.

ATARI NEWS
What The Critics Had to Say

"The SwordQuest series succeeds in demonstrating how incredibly far video games for the VCS have come."
-Raymond Dimetrosky (*Electronic Fun with Computers and Games*, November 1982)

"[Earthworld]: Graphics: A; Playability: A"
-*Electronic Fun with Computers & Games* (December 1982)

"Five action-packed tests of your skills as a warrior await you in [Fireworld]. You might be required to catch lethal knives, dodge plummeting birds, or kill deadly snakes."
-*Atari Age* (January/February 1983)

"[WaterWorld] is a tricky, absorbing game, filled with magic and mystical challenges, action, and adventure. It will take time and clever reasoning to win, but it's worth it."
-*Atari Age* (September/October 1983)

SWORDQUEST: EARTHWORLD

All you who enter *EarthWorld* will encounter danger, trials, tests, and obstacles. All will have an equal chance to decipher the hidden message.

As you explore *EarthWorld*, you will traverse 12 rooms, each named after a sign of the zodiac. You will encounter danger such as the horns of a charging Taurus bull and you will be called upon to demonstrate your skill and ingenuity.

A variety of magical objects will assist you in the challenging journey ahead. These are strewn about the various zodiac chambers. Carrying certain objects along with you helps with game play. For example, the lamp allows you to see the charging horns in the dark bull pit of Taurus. By leaving the right combination of objects in the right zodiac chamber, you'll discover illuminating clues.

> Come questing with bold siblings twain,
> Prime thieves of ravaged Earth;
> Next journey to the fireworld,
> Land of volcanoe's birth.
> Waves without number—Water's realm—
> But 'ware of evils there;
> Last, ride the Air's winds heaven-high
> To claim a prize most rare.

OBJECT OF THE GAME

As an explorer and clue seeker in the subterranean landscape represented in this game cartridge, your objective is to find the hidden clues and solve the puzzle. Clues must be completed in a specific order. If you meet conditions for a future clue, it will appear immediately after the clue one spot earlier in the list is revealed.

HOW TO PLAY

Use the joystick to move through the maze rooms. Initially, only the top and bottom doorways in each maze room are active. Each maze room is linked to a zodiac chamber that shares the same color. Press the red controller button to enter the zodiac chamber tied to a given maze room. To exit a zodiac chamber, move the cursor over the door symbol and press the red controller button.

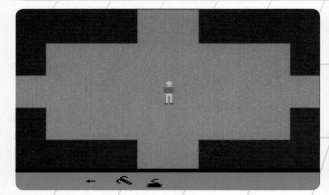

Maze room (Virgo).

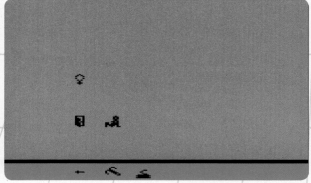

Zodiac chamber (Virgo).

Eight of the 12 zodiac chambers are unguarded. You can freely enter and exit them. To enter the remaining four zodiac chambers (see the following table), you must complete a skill and action challenge. Press the red controller button during a challenge to return to the maze room. Keep in mind that you must complete the challenge (or carry the proper treasure) to reach the zodiac chamber and its contents.

Zodiac chamber color chart.

ZODIAC CHAMBER CHALLENGES

SIGN	CHALLENGE	DESCRIPTION
Aquarius	Rafts in Aquarian Rapids	Push up or down (no lateral movement) to leap to the next line of rafts. Jump through the door at the top of the screen to enter Aquarius's chamber. Falling off a raft returns you to the start point.
Leo	Leo Waterfall	Cross the room by passing through the gaps in the waterfalls. Waterfalls advance slowly to the left with each passage of their gap. Touching a waterfall returns you to the start point. Carry the Talisman of Passage to advance directly to Leo's chamber.
Sagittarius	Sagittarius Spears	Avoid the spears while moving from the bottom of the screen to the top. Touching a spear returns you to the start point. Carry the Leather Armor to pass through the spears unharmed. Carry the Cloak of Invisibility to advance directly to Sagittarius's chamber.
Taurus	Charging Taurus Horns	Avoid the horns while moving from the bottom of the screen to the top. Touching a horn returns you to the start point. Unless you carry the lamp, the horns are invisible. Carry the Leather Armor to pass through the spears unharmed. Carry the Cloak of Invisibility to advance directly to Taurus's chamber.

TREASURES

Most zodiac chambers contain one or more treasures (see the table on the following page). To pick up a treasure, position your cursor over a treasure and press the red controller button. The treasure moves to your inventory at the bottom of the screen. You can carry a maximum of six items in your inventory. You begin the game carrying a dagger, grappling hook, and rope, which all count toward your inventory maximum. To leave a treasure in a room (don't worry, it will be there if you leave and return), go to the bottom of the screen, position your cursor over the object, and press the red controller button.

ZODIAC CHAMBER TREASURES		
SIGN		**INITIAL TREASURES**
Aquarius	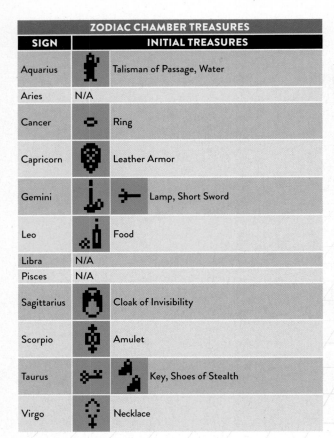	Talisman of Passage, Water
Aries		N/A
Cancer		Ring
Capricorn		Leather Armor
Gemini		Lamp, Short Sword
Leo		Food
Libra		N/A
Pisces		N/A
Sagittarius		Cloak of Invisibility
Scorpio		Amulet
Taurus		Key, Shoes of Stealth
Virgo		Necklace

Most items and treasures are used only for uncovering clues, however, a number of treasures grant additional abilities.

TREASURES AND ABILITIES		
TREASURE	**WHERE FOUND**	**ABILITY IN INVENTORY**
Amulet	Scorpio's Chamber	Maze room exits lead to random maze rooms.
Cloak of Invisibility	Sagittarius's Chamber	Skip Charging Taurus Horns and Sagittarius Spears challenges.
Dagger	Starting Inventory	N/A
Food	Leo's Chamber	N/A
Grappling Hook	Starting Inventory	N/A
Key	Taurus's Chamber	You can now exit maze rooms to the left or right in addition to up or down.
Lamp	Gemini's Chamber	Horns from Charging Taurus Horns challenge are now visible.
Leather Armor	Capricorn's Chamber	Can walk through Charging Taurus Horns and Sagittarius Spears challenges unharmed.
Necklace	Virgo's Chamber	Cancels random room effect of Amulet
Ring	Cancer's Chamber	N/A
Rope	Starting Inventory	N/A
Shoes of Stealth	Taurus's Chamber	Silent footfalls.
Short Sword	Gemini's Chamber	N/A
Talisman of Passage	Aquarius's Chamber	Skip Leo Waterfall challenge.
Warrior's Sword	Complete the game	N/A
Water	Aquarius's Chamber	N/A

OBTAINING CLUES

When you leave the correct treasures in appropriate chambers, the screen flashes a set of numbers upon entering the next maze room. The numbers are clues used in conjunction with the comic book that was packaged with the original game. For example, the first clue (which you see when you enter the maze room outside Aries's chamber) is 16-4. This directed players to the fourth panel of the sixteenth page of the comic. There are eleven clues to uncover, but not all of the clues were valid. An additional clue hidden in the comic book provided guidance on picking out valid clues.

After gathering all the clues, you are returned to the *SwordQuest* screen, which had a final clue in place of the copyright notice. Players could read the clue, then push the red controller button to enter the Warrior's Sword chamber.

These shots show the solution to obtaining the second clue (left) and the second clue itself (right).

- ◆ Play the game with paper and pen. Write down every clue and keep a log of every movement and its result for future reference.
- ◆ Holding certain objects in your inventory helps with gameplay. Some examples of help are making challenges easier, bypassing challenges entirely, and opening new doorways that link to different rooms.
- ◆ Just because you use an object to obtain one clue doesn't mean that same object won't help you in future clues or tasks.
- ◆ To receive a numerical clue, all the objects you leave in a room must be part of a set that is designated for that particular room. If you include any object that does not belong, you cannot trigger a numerical value.
- ◆ The full set of solutions is available after the section for *SwordQuest: WaterWorld*.

SWORDQUEST: FIREWORLD

Welcome to *FireWorld*. You may have already travelled through *EarthWorld* and succeeded in solving the *EarthWorld* puzzle. *FireWorld* is the second in a series of worlds that you must pass through on your quest for the Sword of Ultimate Sorcery.

You enter *FireWorld* as a mighty warrior. Your skill and courage will be tested with dangerous trials and obstacles. The object of the game is to solve the puzzle.

The *FireWorld* puzzle is based on the Tree of Life, with 10 rooms linked together by 10 rooms with doorways. *FireWorld* has ten treasure chest rooms, some containing different magical objects. These objects will help you on your journey through *FireWorld*. Carrying particular objects will help you find clues. Before you can explore these rooms, you'll be called on to demonstrate certain skills, just as Torr and Tarra are tested in the *FireWorld* comic book. As a warrior, your skills are important to conquering *FireWorld*.

You have just leaped into the blazing flames of *FireWorld*—see if you can survive and triumph!

In Earthworl grim, these Twins have fought
Twelve beasts of Zodiac birth,
And mastered thieving as they sought
For Sword of ultimate worth.

Through Fire world's flames they now do rage
While Time its toll does add—
To seven days? A year? An Age?
Who knows in a world gone mad?

OBJECT OF THE GAME

As a warrior, you'll need courage and skill. In addition, you must be a a detective and an explorer to find the hidden clues and solve the *FireWorld* puzzle.

HOW TO PLAY

Use the joystick to move through the 10 connected maze rooms. Each maze room is linked to a treasure chamber that shares the same color. However, you must complete skill and action sequences in order to enter treasure chambers. Moving between maze rooms never requires a skill and action sequence.

Press the red controller button to start the skill and action sequence of a given room. There are six different skill and action sequences, meaning some appear in more than one room. To exit a treasure chamber, move the cursor over the door symbol and press the red controller button.

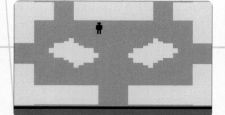

Maze room.

Skill and action sequence.

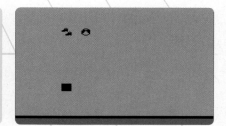

Treasure chamber.

Treasure chambers initially contain anywhere from zero to four treasures. To pick up a treasure, position your cursor over a treasure and press the red controller button. The treasure moves to your inventory at the bottom of the screen. You can carry a maximum of six items in your inventory. To leave a treasure in a room (don't worry, it will be there if you leave and return), go to the bottom of the screen, position your cursor over the object, and press the red button.

BREAKDOWN OF ROOMS		
MAZE ROOM	SKILL & ACTION SEQUENCE	TREASURE CHAMBER CONTENTS (AT START)
Room 1	Flying Fire Goblins	None
Room 2	Deadly Snakes	None
Room 3	Flaming Hot Knives	Shield, Amulet
Room 4	Fire-Breathing Dragons	Shoes of Stealth, Cloak of Invisibility
Room 5	Flaming Firebirds	Rope, Chalice, Leather Armor, Dagger
Room 6	Flying Fire Goblins	Talisman of Passage, Oil Lamp
Room 7	Deadly Snakes	Water, Ring
Room 8	Flaming Hot Knives	Short Sword, Warrior's Sword
Room 9	Fire-Breathing Dragons	Food, Grappling Hook
Room 10	Jawing Salamanders	None

SKILL & ACTION SEQUENCES

Completion of the following sequences grants access to treasure chambers. Holding certain treasures in your inventory makes the challenges (except Deadly Snakes) much easier to accomplish.

FLYING FIRE GOBLINS

You must catch and place these fire goblins into a box. Use the joystick to move the box from side to side. Slide underneath the goblins before they reach the bottom of the screen until you are allowed into the treasure chamber. Eight misses returns you to the maze room. Carry the Amulet to make this sequence easier.

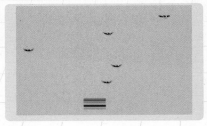

You encounter Flying Fire Goblins in Rooms 1 and 6.

DEADLY SNAKES

A real test of courage. You must pass through this deadly pit of venomous snakes. Use the joystick to guide your avatar around the snake pit. Press the red controller button to fire; you shoot in the direction your avatar travels. Touching a wall causes a new snake to appear, while touching a snake sends you back to the maze room.

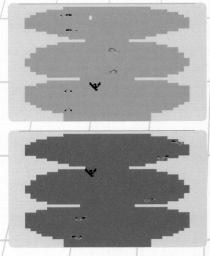

You encounter Deadly Snakes in Rooms 2 and 7.

FLAMING HOT KNIVES

Protect yourself from hot knives that fall from the ceiling by guiding the knives into a stationary pit. Use the joystick to direct the falling knives toward the center of the screen. This one will take some getting used to since you're moving the background, not the pit entrance. Eight misses returns you to the maze room. Don't forget to carry the Shoes of Stealth to make this sequence easier.

You encounter Flaming Hot Knives in Rooms 3 and 8.

FIRE-BREATHING DRAGONS

Use arrows to shoot down fire-breathing dragons and watch out for their hot flames. Press the red controller button to launch a knife at the descending dragons. Move from side to side to line up your shots and avoid incoming dragon attacks; get hit and you're returned to the maze room. Carry the Dagger to make this sequence easier.

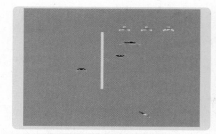

You encounter Fire-Breathing Dragons in Rooms 4 and 9.

FLAMING FIREBIRDS

Dodge the flaming firebirds; if you touch them, they become wild! When tamed, these birds could lead you to a treasure chest of magical objects. The joystick controls a bar at the bottom of the screen. Move the bar to avoid the descending firebirds. If you get hit eight times, you return to the maze room. Carry the Cloak of Invisibility to make this sequence easier.

You encounter Flaming Firebirds in Rooms 5.

JAWING SALAMANDERS

What appear to be innocent snakes could turn out to be huge salamanders. You must dodge the salamanders to stay alive. The joystick controls a bar at the bottom of the screen. Move the bar to avoid the salamanders, which come in various sizes and spin as they descend. If you get hit eight times, you return to the maze room. Carry the Leather Armor to make this sequence easier.

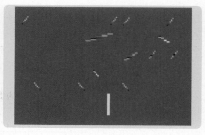

You encounter Jawing Salamanders in Room 10.

TREASURES

Most items and treasures are used only for uncovering clues, however, a number of treasures grant additional abilities.

- ◆ Play the game with paper and pen. Write down every clue and keep a log of every movement and its result for your future reference.

- ◆ Holding certain objects in your inventory helps with gameplay. Some examples of help are making challenges easier and opening new doorways that link to different rooms.

- ◆ Just because you use an object to obtain one clue doesn't mean that same object won't help you in future clues or tasks.

- ◆ It is possible to warp to different maze rooms by standing in the corner of a room and rotating the joystick. The most important location where this works is the top-right corner of Room 9, which allows you to reach Room 10 without the Chalice.

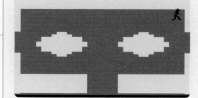

- ◆ The full set of solutions is available after the chapter for SwordQuest: WaterWorld.

TREASURES		
TREASURE	WHERE FOUND	ABILITY IN YOUR INVENTORY
Amulet	Room 3	Easier Flying Fire Goblins.
Chalice	Room 5	Reveals extra exits in maze rooms.
Cloak of Invisibility	Room 4	Easier Flaming Firebirds.
Dagger	Room 5	Easier Fire-Breathing Dragons.
Food	Room 9	N/A
Grappling Hook	Room 9	N/A
Leather Armor	Room 5	Easier Jawing Salamanders.
Oil Lamp	Room 6	N/A
Ring	Room 7	N/A
Rope	Room 5	N/A
Shield	Room 3	N/A
Shoes of Stealth	Room 4	Easier Flaming Hot Knives.
Short Sword	Room 8	N/A
Talisman of Passage	Room 6	N/A
Warrior's Sword	Room 8	N/A
Water	Room 7	N/A

ROOMS CHANGED BY THE CHALICE

Carrying the Chalice reveals a number of new exits in three rooms. Without the Chalice, there's only one way to enter Room 10 (see "Tips and Tricks" for more information). With the Chalice, each of the following rooms now has a path to Room 10.

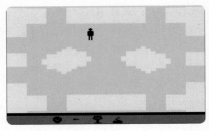

Room 5 (with Chalice).

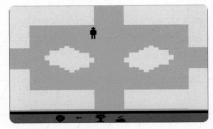

Room 8 (with Chalice).

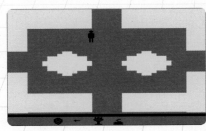

Room 9 (with Chalice).

ADVANCING THE GAME

When you leave the correct treasures in appropriate chambers, the screen immediately displays a number. (Please note that chambers—plural—is correct.) You must place correct treasure (or treasures) in two separate rooms. Not only that, but the rooms must be completed in order.

For example, to obtain the first number (00), place the Chalice in Room 1's treasure chamber, then place the Food, Oil Lamp, Ring, and Shoes of Stealth in Room 10 (check "Tips and Tricks" for help with this). Once all four treasures are in Room 10, you'll see the number. If your inventory is full, you can place all the items in the second room before placing the object in the first room. Just return to the second chamber, pick up one of the objects, then replace it.

Unlike *EarthWorld*, the numbers in *FireWorld* are a countdown to indicate how many chambers you've cleared. To complete the game, you must get to 09, starting from 00.

SWORDQUEST: WATERWORLD

Powers of Prime

WaterWorld is the third in a series of individual contests comprising the Atari SwordQuest Challenge. The ultimate objective is to pass certain tests of dexterity and cleverness.

OBJECT OF THE GAME

Your goal is to travel successfully from room to room, discover the relationships of the treasures to each other and to the rooms, and place a correct combination of treasures in the appropriate room to receive a numerical clue.

HOW TO PLAY

Use the joystick to move through seven numbered and connected rooms. There are 16 treasures scattered throughout these rooms. These treasures are related to each other and the seven rooms. Isolating the rooms from each other are three skill and action sequences that you must master in order to successfully enter a room and manipulate the treasures in that room.

Pressing the red controller button while you are in the midst of a skill and action sequence is a sign of surrender. You are transported directly to the desired room, but without the power to see or successfully manipulate all the treasures in that room.

Room V (fail), no Crown.

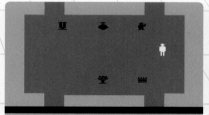
Room V (success), the Crown appears.

Skill and action sequence (Sea of Sharks).

To pick up a treasure, move on top of it and press the red controller button. To transfer treasures back into the room, you must first enter the carrying pouch. To do this, move over the carrying pouch symbol at the top of the screen and press the red controller button. To emerge from the pouch, simply push up on the joystick.

You can carry a total of six treasures in your inventory. You gain information about the treasures and their relationships by transferring them back and forth from the room to the carrying pouch in each of the seven rooms.

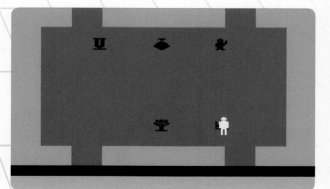

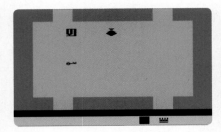

Each room needs a unique set of seven treasures to trigger a clue. If you correctly place at least four of the seven treasures designated for a specific room, a numerical clue is revealed at the bottom of the screen.

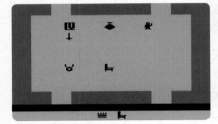

A relationship demonstrated.

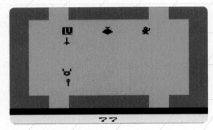

A clue revealed.

BREAKDOWN OF ROOMS		
ROOM	ALWAYS VISIBLE	SUCCESS REQUIRED TO SEE
Room I	Shoes of Stealth	Shield
Room II	Royal Seal	Amulet, Scepter
Room III	Money Purse, Peasant's Ring	King's Ring
Room IV	Medallion	Throne, Warrior's Sword
Room V	Chalice, Talisman of Passage	Crown
Room VI	Lamp	Key
Room 0	N/A	N/A

SKILL & ACTION SEQUENCES

When you move between rooms, you must complete a skill and action sequence within a short timeframe. Completing a sequence grants access to all treasures in a room. Holding certain treasures in your inventory allows you to bypass some or all sequences.

SCHOOL OF OCTOPI

Swim to the opening at the bottom of the screen while avoiding the octopi. If you touch an octopus, it carries you in the direction it's swimming, but does not return you to the start point. The School of Octopi appears when you travel between Room I & Room II and between Room IV & Room V.

SEA OF SHARKS

Swim across the screen and touch the right edge of the screen. Touching a shark returns you to the start point. You must cross the Sea of Sharks to reach Room I (yes, every time you start over), when moving between Room III & Room IV and Room VI & Room 0.

TREASURES

TREASURE	WHERE FOUND	ABILITY IN YOUR INVENTORY
Amulet	Room II (success)	N/A
Chalice	Room V	N/A
Crown	Room V (success)	Skip all skill and action sequences.
Key	Room VI (success)	N/A
King's Ring	Room III (success)	N/A
Lamp	Room VI	N/A
Medallion	Room IV	Skip Slippery Ice Floes skill and action sequences (between Rooms II & III and Rooms V & VI).
Money Purse	Room III	Skip Sea of Sharks skill and action sequences (between Rooms III & IV and Rooms VI & 0).
Peasant's Ring	Room III	N/A
Royal Seal	Room II	Skip School of Octopi skill and action sequences (between Rooms I & II and Rooms IV & V).
Scepter	Room II (success)	N/A
Shield	Room I	N/A
Shoes of Stealth	Room I (success)	N/A
Talisman of Passage	Room V	N/A
Throne	Room IV (success)	N/A
Warrior's Sword	Room IV (success)	N/A

SLIPPERY ICE FLOES

Move side to side (or up and down) the rows of ice floes. You can continue to move left and right while standing on an ice floe. Get to the gap at the top of the screen to complete the challenge.

Touching the water returns you to the start point. Don't worry about fading ice chunks, as they never completely submerge.

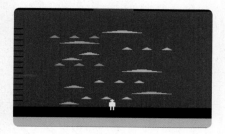

Ice floes appear between Room II & Room III and between Room V & Room VI.

TREASURES

Most items and treasures are used only for uncovering clues, however, a number of treasures grant additional abilities.

ADVANCING THE GAME

Each time you uncover a clue, the game resets. All treasures return to their original rooms and you must swim through sharks to return to Room I. Unlike *EarthWorld* and *FireWorld*, there's no set order to the clues. It's worth your while to note the clues you've already uncovered so you can skip placing treasures in certain rooms.

Tips & Tricks

- ◆ To get a numerical clue, all the treasures you leave in a room must be part of a set that is designated for that particular room. If you include anything that does not belong, you cannot trigger a numerical clue.

- ◆ For each skill and action sequence, there is a different treasure that will allow you to pass directly into the next room without having to undergo that specific test. There is also one overarching treasure that will allow you to travel successfully from room to room without having to undergo any of the sequences.

- ◆ *WaterWorld* demands logical thinking along with trial-and-error methods. You will try several types of combinations before you discover a set that will work.

- ◆ All the hints are true. Some hints may not appear to be perfectly clear, though, as they can be interpreted in more than one way. Don't get lost. Make notes. Keep a journal.

- ◆ The full set of solutions is available on the following pages.

SWORDQUEST SOLUTIONS

Use the following information to complete each game in the *SwordQuest* series.

SWORDQUEST: EARTHWORLD

Place the items from the Treasure column into the zodiac chambers listed in the Chamber column to reveal the clues, which are also provided. The Clue indicates a page and panel number from the comic. The clue from the poem (Prime Numbers) tells you the clues that are valid (page 13, 5, 17, 37, and 47). The final solution was "Quest in Tower Talisman Found."

CLUE #	TREASURE	CHAMBER	CLUE	WORD ON PAGE
1	N/A (enter maze room)	Aries	16-4	spire
2	Dagger	Gemini	8-4	search
3	Grappling Hook	Cancer	25-6	the
	Rope	Leo		
4	Ring	Aquarius	13-3	quest
	Key	Scorpio		
	Necklace	Gemini		
5	Short Sword	Virgo	5-3	in
	Food	Scorpio		
	Grappling Hook	Libra		
6	Dagger	Taurus	27-2	espied
	Shoes of Stealth, Water	Aries		
7	Amulet	Gemini	FireWorld	N/A
	Food	Taurus		
	Leather Armor	Aquarius		
	Water	Pisces		
8	Cloak of Invisibility	Capricorn	17-3	tower
	Lamp	Libra		
	Ring	Virgo		
	Short Sword	Leo		
	Talisman of Passage	Cancer		
9	Lamp	Cancer	37-5	talisman
	Leather Armor	Aquarius		
	Necklace	Libra		
	Rope, Shoes of Stealth	Virgo		
	Talisman of Passage	Sagittarius		
10	Amulet, Grappling Hook	Scorpio	15-4	gold
	Cloak of Invisibility	Aquarius		
	Food	Virgo		
	Key	Aries		
	Ring	Taurus		
	Short Sword	Gemini		
11	Amulet, Lamp	Cancer	47-5	found
	Cloak of Invisibility	Aries		
	Dagger, Key	Taurus		
	Food, Rope	Scorpio		
	Leather Armor, Ring, Grappling Hook	Libra		
	Necklace, Water	Gemini		
	Shoes of Stealth	Aquarius		
	Short Sword	Capricorn		
	Talisman of Passage	Sagittarius		

SWORDQUEST: FIREWORLD

The numbers in *FireWorld* are a countdown to let you know how many chambers you've cleared. They do not relate to comic book pages. The clue from the poem (add to Seven) tells you the clues that are valid come from page numbers that total seven when added together (7, 16, 25, 34, 43). Other pages have words, but you can ignore them. The final solution was "Leads to Chalice Power Abounds."

Before you can reach the screen to input the solution, you must reveal the numbers (from 00-09). Place the treasures listed in the Treasures column into the chamber listed in the Chamber # column. The rooms must be completed in order, but you can place all the items in the second room before placing the object in the first room. Just return to the second chamber, pick up one of the objects, and then replace it.

NUMBER	CHAMBER #	TREASURES
00	1	Chalice
	10	Food, Oil Lamp, Ring, Shoes of Stealth
01	2	Rope
	9	Cloak of Invisibility, Grappling Hook, Talisman, Water
02	3	Amulet
	8	Chalice, Grappling Hook, Leather Armor, Talisman
03	4	Cloak of Invisibility
	6	Oil Lamp, Ring, Shield, Short Sword
04	5	Shield
	6	Food, Oil Lamp, Ring, Rope
05	4	Cloak of Invisibility
	5	Amulet, Leather Armor, Talisman, Warrior's Sword
06	10	Food
	4	Dagger, Oil Lamp, Shield, Short Sword
07	2	Grappling Hook
	3	Dagger, Food, Oil Lamp, Rope
08	9	Water
	2	Dagger, Leather Armor, Oil Lamp, Talisman
09	2	Warrior's Sword
	1	Amulet, Chalice, Leather Armor, Talisman

SWORDQUEST: WATERWORLD

Each room needs a unique set of seven treasures to trigger a clue. Place at least four of the seven treasures designated for a specific room to reveal the clue.

ROOM	TREASURES (PLACE 4/7 LISTED)	CLUE
I	Chalice, Crown, King's Ring, Medallion, Royal Seal, Scepter, Throne	26
II	Crown, Key, King's Ring, Lamp, Money Purse, Shield, Shoes of Stealth	93
III	Amulet, Crown, Lamp, Medallion, Money Purse, Peasant's Ring, Talisman	85
IV	Amulet, Crown, Medallion, Scepter, Shoes of Stealth, Talisman, Warrior's Sword	77
V	Amulet, Chalice, Key, Peasant's Ring, Royal Seal, Throne, Warrior's Sword	16
VI	Key, King's Ring, Lamp, Peasant's Ring, Scepter, Throne, Warrior's Sword	64
0	Amulet, Chalice, Key, Royal Seal, Scepter, Talisman, Warrior's Sword	32

The comic book pages with the solution are 8, 21, 22, 19. The complete solution is "Hasten Toward Revealed Crown."

YARS' REVENGE

Journey to the Razak Solar System, where an evil Qotile is swatting the Yars—mutant houseflies. This relentless enemy, hidden behind a protective shield, fires deadly missiles at the Yars. Help the Yars avenge their community! Send a Yar scout out to break a path through the shield by eating the bricks or exploding them with missiles. Then bring out the Zorlon Cannon and destroy the Qotile with a well-placed blast.

ABOUT THE GAME

What began as Howard Scott Warshaw's failed attempt to recreate the vector-based Cinematronics *Star Castle* arcade game from 1980 ended up becoming one of the Atari 2600's most beloved original titles.

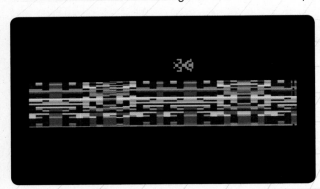

From its chunky graphics and use of color to its sound effects, *Yars' Revenge* is perhaps the one game that makes the best overall use of the Atari 2600 hardware's distinctive feature-set. The fact that this technology was married to fantastic just-one-more-try gameplay is one of many reasons the regard for this game has grown considerably since it was first released.

The Qotile is destroyed, so it's time for a victory dance!

OBJECT OF THE GAME

The primary objective of the game is to break a path through the shield and destroy the Qotile with a blast from the Zorlon Cannon. The secondary objective is to score as many points as possible.

TERMINOLOGY

TERM	DESCRIPTION
Yar	Fly simulator under direct user control.
Energy Missile	Missile shot by Yar, removes cells.
Qotile	Laser-base-like object on the right side of the screen, behind the shield.
Shield	Energy shield protecting the Qotile, composed of cells.
Cells	Elements of which the shield is composed.
Destroyer Missile	Guided missiles put out by the Qotile to destroy Yars.
Zorlon Cannon	Pulsing, scintillating fireball, appears on the left side of the screen and traverses the screen horizontally.
Swirl	Whirling pinwheel fired by the Qotile to destroy Yars.
Neutral Zone	Colorful and glittering path down the center of the playfield. When in the zone, a Yar cannot operate fire commands and cannot be harmed by Destroyer Missiles. However, the Yar can be destroyed by a Swirl in the zone.

HOW TO PLAY

The shield is the red area in front of the Qotile base. It appears in one of two shapes: as an arch, or a shifting rectangle. The shield is made up of cells. The Yar scout can destroy these cells by firing at them with Energy Missiles from any location on the playfield, or by devouring them on direct contact. The Zorlon Cannon can also be used to destroy the cells, but this is a waste of a powerful weapon.

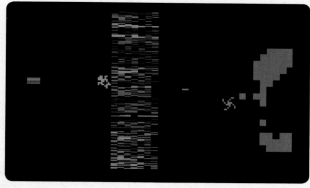

A Swirl attack.

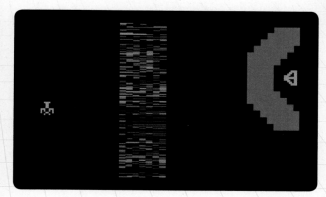

Once a path has been cleared through the shield, the Zorlon Cannon must be used to destroy the Qotile. To call up the cannon, the Yar can either eat a cell or run over the Qotile.

The Zorlon Cannon appears on the left side of the playfield and moves in a direct line with the Yar. This means the Yar is in its line of fire. It's important, therefore, to aim the cannon at the Qotile, fire it, and fly out of the way fast!

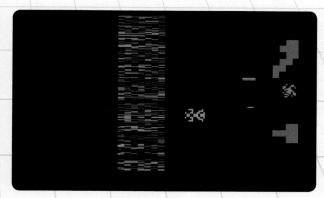

Firing the Zorlon Cannon (green bar).

The Qotile shoots off two weapons: Destroyer Missiles and Swirls. The Destroyer Missiles come in a more or less constant stream, one at a time. The Yar must do his best to dodge them. Periodically, the Qotile transforms into a Swirl. This Swirl winds up and rushes off after the Yar. A Swirl can be destroyed with the Zorlon Cannon by hitting it either at its base location or in mid-air. As a player's score increases, the Swirl becomes increasingly dangerous.

The glittering path down the center of the screen is the Neutral Zone. This area protects a Yar from Destroyer Missiles but not from Swirls. While in the Neutral Zone, a Yar cannot fire any Energy Missiles of his own.

When a Yar is hit by a Destroyer Missile, a Swirl, or his own Zorlon Cannon, he dies. Each player has four Yars (turns) to play in a game. Additional Yars can be earned.

CONTROLLING THE YAR

The Yar moves in whatever direction the joystick is pushed. The screen "wraps" from top to bottom, bottom to top. This means that if you fly the Yar off the top of the screen, it will appear at the bottom, and vice versa.

The red controller button has two separate firing functions: it fires an Energy Missile in the direction the Yar is pointed, or operates the Zorlon Cannon when it's on the screen.

The red controller button is also used to restart turns and games. Press it after each turn to start a new life, or continue a successful one. Press it at the end of the game to play that same game version again.

ATARI NEWS
What The Critics Had to Say

"A combination of familiar play elements and somewhat revolutionary packaging concepts combine to make Yars' Revenge a potential blockbuster that misses greatness by an eyelash."

-*Electronic Games magazine, October 1982*

The front cover of **The Qotile Ultimatum!** comic book.

The fourth page from **The Qotile Ultimatum!** comic book details the form and function of the Yar fly simulator.

SCORING

SCORE CHART

ACTIVITY	POINTS	BONUS
Cell, hit by missile	69	—
Cell, devoured by Yar	69	100 points
Qotile, destroyed	1000	—
Swirl, destroyed in place	2000	—
Swirl, destroyed in mid-air	6000	Additional life

HIGH-SCORE GAME FEATURES

POINTS	ACTIVITY
70,000	Swirl triples in frequency and sometimes fires instantly. Shield turns blue.
150,000	Swirl returns to normal frequency but remains in mid-air to hit you. Shield turns gray.
230,000	Swirl triples in frequency and sometimes fires instantly. Shield turns pink.

The game ends when the fuel level reaches zero. In one-player games, try to beat your highest score. In two-player games, each player tries to beat the opponent's score. After a two-player game is over, the left player's score appears at the top center of the screen; the right player's score appears at the bottom center, where the fuel amount was indicated during gameplay.

DIFFICULTY OPTIONS

Yars' Revenge includes two difficulty levels: A and B. Level B is for normal gameplay. Level A is for the skilled player. When the difficulty button set to the A position, the Swirl is propelled faster, making it harder for the Yar to dodge. Also, if the Zorlon Cannon and the Destroyer Missile touch, they destroy each other.

In a one-player game, use the left difficulty button. For two-player games, the left player uses the left difficulty button and the right player uses the right difficulty button.

GAME OPTIONS

Use Select to choose the game number you wish to play, from 0 to 7. The game number appears in the center of the screen.

Once you select the game number you wish to play, press Reset to start the game. To start the same game over again, press either Reset or the red button on your joystick. Reset can also be used to start a new game at any time.

GAME #	DESCRIPTION
0	This is the simplest version, a good choice for young children to play. It features a slow Destroyer Missile.
1	This is the two-player version of Game 0.
2	This is the "normal" game, with two alternating shield configurations, plus a Destroyer Missile and a Swirl traveling at normal speeds.
3	This is the two-player version of Game 2.
4	This game features a Zorlon Cannon that bounces off the shield. (Watch out! It can destroy you on its return flight.) There are two alternating shield configurations, plus a Destroyer Missile and a Swirl traveling at normal speeds.
5	This is the two-player version of Game 4.
6	Ultimate Yars one-player version. Ultimate Yars features a bouncing Zorlon Cannon, plus some unusual twists that distinguish it from the other Yar games. First, you must bounce the Yar against the left side of the screen to make the Zorlon Cannon appear. Also, to make the cannon appear, you need five Trons. Trons are units of energy you can collect at the following rate: 1. Eat a cell from the shield: 1 Tron 2. Touch the Qotile: 2 Trons 3. Catch a Zorlon Cannon shot after it bounces off the shield: 4 Trons If a Yar bounces of the left side with fewer than 5 Trons, it will not get a shot, but it won't lose the Trons it has either (each time a Yar is destroyed, it loses its Trons). Each Yar has a capacity of 255 Trons. If a Yar tries to take on more than that, it shorts out and the Yar loses all its Trons. The count of Trons is not displayed on the screen. Yar scouts understand the count instinctively.
7	Ultimate Yars two-player version.

FUN FACTS!

○ A small comic book, *The Qotile Ultimatum!*, was included in the game package to better illustrate the story behind the game.

○ Atari released a record album containing a theme song and dramatization of the story in the comic book.

○ "Yar" is the first name of then-Atari CEO Ray Kassar spelled backward. In the comic book, the "revenge" in the game's title refers to the Yars avenging destruction of their world, Razak IV, a play on "Kassar."

○ In 2005, a remixed sequel to *Yars' Return*, called *Yars' Return*, was released. This game is also found on the Atari Flashback systems.

○ Although programmer Howard Scott Warshaw gave up on the idea of recreating the *Star Castle* arcade game on the Atari 2600, two different homebrew ports have since been released. D. Scott Williamson's port was released in 2012 and made use of a 4K ROM to prove that a workable version could have been made back in the day. Chris Walton and Thomas Jentzsch's port was released in 2013 and made use of a 32K ROM to create a more arcade-accurate version.

Tips & Tricks

◆ The Qotile continually changes colors. The color sequence is your cue to the appearance of a Swirl, and gives you warning to plan your attack and defense.

◆ If you fly over the Qotile as it changes to a Swirl, it will destroy you, so be careful.

◆ To rack up more points, shoot the Swirl in mid-flight. Do this by summoning the Zorlon Cannon, laying back in the Neutral Zone, and waiting for the Swirl to appear. When the Swirl appears, duck out of the Neutral Zone and shoot just as the Swirl takes off.

◆ When you destroy the Qotile, or a Swirl, there's an explosion, during which the Yar stays on the screen. Use this opportunity to make up your own victory dance. And watch out for the Ghost of Yars! You'll see his mean streak, so stay off it! (But if you really want to see the "Ghost of Yars," see below.)

◆ After you hit a Swirl in mid-air three times in succession and the colorful explosion subsides, a thin, vertical black line can be seen branching off from the spot the Swirl occupied (the "Ghost of Yars"). If you're able to position your Yar fighter through this line for long enough, it causes the game to end and programmer Howard Scott Warshaw's initials to appear ("HSWWSH," which, like Ray and Yars, is written forward and backward).

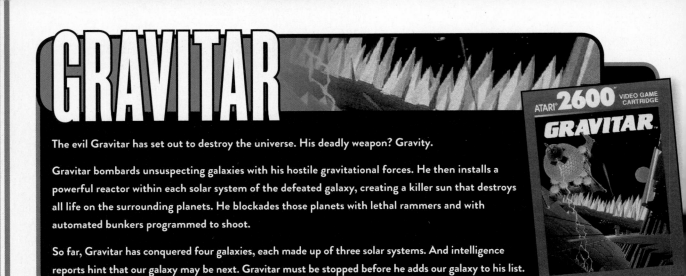

GRAVITAR

The evil Gravitar has set out to destroy the universe. His deadly weapon? Gravity.

Gravitar bombards unsuspecting galaxies with his hostile gravitational forces. He then installs a powerful reactor within each solar system of the defeated galaxy, creating a killer sun that destroys all life on the surrounding planets. He blockades those planets with lethal rammers and with automated bunkers programmed to shoot.

So far, Gravitar has conquered four galaxies, each made up of three solar systems. And intelligence reports hint that our galaxy may be next. Gravitar must be stopped before he adds our galaxy to his list.

ABOUT THE GAME

While the developers of *Gravitar* used a few play mechanics made popular by other arcade games like *Asteroids* and *Space Invaders*, they were inspired to create a game far more complex and adventurous. *Gravitar* is a thrust and exploration game that includes both flying enemies and stationary ground targets. The best part? The vector-based arcade game's depth was retained for its Atari 2600 port.

While the graphics in *Gravitar* seem simple, quite a few different images and indicators are included in the game. The amount of work and space these images must have taken as a whole makes the grand scheme rather impressive. Most of what is seen on the screen is space; however, given the context of the game, this makes sense. Also noteworthy is that when your ship enters different realms, the entire screen changes as you go from outer space to the surface of a planet or bunker.

The purpose of the creation of *Gravitar* was not to be groundbreaking in the sense of introducing new concepts or controls, but it did introduce a new scope of gaming. The capacity of the cartridge was pushed to its limit because of the different screens involved in *Gravitar*. This not only took everything that existed in gaming before and pushed the concepts further, but it also proved that you don't have to incorporate new mechanics to be able to develop a unique and entertaining piece of software.

OBJECT OF THE GAME

Your task is to break Gravitar's hold on the 12 solar systems under his power. You can do this by destroying all bunkers on every planet or by setting off the reactor in the alien reactor base.

HOW TO PLAY

Each solar system consists of a killer sun, an alien reactor base, and three or four blockaded planets—each housing fuel deposits and enemy bunkers.

To move from one solar system to the next, you must either visit all the planets and destroy every enemy bunker, or activate the reactor at the core of the alien reactor base and escape before it explodes.

When you complete your mission in the three solar systems of one galaxy, you are automatically transported to another galaxy, where your rescue mission continues.

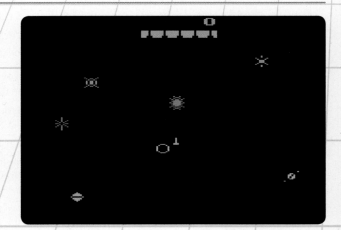

You start the game with six to 100 starships, depending on the game level, and with 10,000 fuel units.

Your ship consumes fuel every time you use your thrust engines, activate your shields, or extend your tractor beam. A warning beep sounds when your fuel level goes below 2,000 units.

The game ends when you run out of fuel or lose all your spaceships. When you complete your mission, the game resets and your points continue to accumulate.

SOLAR SYSTEMS

As the ship leaves its entry port in the solar system, you must steer out of the gravitational field of the killer sun and head for a planet. If your ship is drawn into the killer sun, you will crash.

The alien reactor base of each solar system sends out enemy saucers to shoot at you, except in Game Level 3. If you fly near a saucer, you will both be thrown out into deep space, where you must duel until your ship or the saucer is destroyed.

PLANETS

One way to complete your mission in a solar system is to visit every planet and destroy all bunkers. You enter a planet's atmosphere by flying near it. You cannot leave a planet until you have blown up every bunker.

Each planet has its own craggy landscape, and, except in Game 5, each has a strong gravitational force that makes

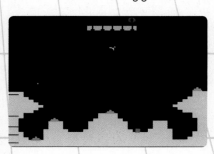

your flight around the planet treacherous. If you fly too close to a planet, your starship will be crushed by its gravity.

Watch out for the rammers that hover above most planets. If one of these enemy ships rams you, you lose a starship.

Shoot your missiles to blow up the bunkers and the rammers. You can also destroy a bunker by crashing into it, but you'll lose a spaceship. Use your tractor beam to pick up fuel capsules as needed.

After destroying all the bunkers, fly your ship to the top of the screen to leave the planet and return to the solar system screen. The planet you have just left will then explode.

ALIEN REACTOR BASE

The other way to complete your mission in a solar system is to destroy the alien reactor base. The alien reactor base is a port into the next solar system. It consists of a winding tunnel that leads to a reactor at the core of the planet.

A clock at the top of the screen counts down the seconds you have to reach the reactor. Activate it by firing into its center, and escape before it explodes.

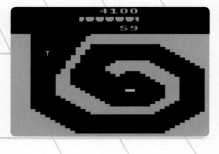

As you move through the first two galaxies, your countdown time on the alien reactor base decreases, from 60 seconds in the first solar system to a harrowing 25 seconds in the sixth. When you reach the third galaxy, the countdown cycle starts over.

You can leave the alien reactor base without setting off the reactor. If your ship is destroyed on the base, you will be returned to your entry port in the solar system. If you blow up the alien reactor base, the explosion will catapult you into the next solar system.

GALAXIES

When you make it through all three solar systems in one galaxy, you automatically go on to the next galaxy.

The four galaxies are similar, except for factors of light and gravity. In the second and fourth galaxies, each planet exerts a reverse gravitational force that repels your ship. In the third and fourth galaxies, the landscape of each planet, including that alien reactor base, is completely dark; only the bunkers, rammers, and fuel deposits are visible.

GAME OPTIONS

Press Select to choose one of the five game levels. (The game level number appears at the bottom of the title screen.)

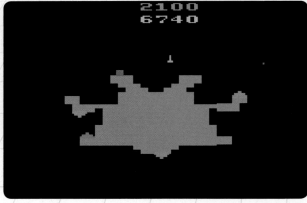

FUN FACTS!

The original name for the arcade version of *Gravitar* was *Lunar Battle*; a prototype PCB exists labeled as such, as does a wiring harness.

Depending on the highest score, one of eight list names appears above the table of initials: Flunky (0-20,000), Gunner (20,001-40,000), Co-Pilot (40,001-80,000), Pilot (80,001-100,000), Ace Pilot (100,001-200,000), Pontius Pilate (400,001-800,000), Gotta-Be-Lucky (above 800,000).

The maximum fuel units you can have is 25,000.

If your reserve ships reach 128, the game will reset.

It's possible to touch and hover inside a bunker without being destroyed. According to programmer Mike Hally, there wasn't enough processing time to check for collision detection between the two.

It's possible to shoot (and even fly) through areas where two connecting lines meet. The game has some difficulty with certain adjoining angles and the collision detection with the ship and its shots. By exploiting this, you can get inside a planet and destroy enemy objects from within, although getting back out may not be possible. Performing this trick on negative-gravity planets may also be impossible.

LEVEL 1

Level 1 is the most challenging, with only six spaceships at your disposal.

LEVEL 2

At Level 2, you have 15 ships in your fleet.

LEVEL 3

At Level 3, you have six spaceships, but the planetary bunkers and enemy saucers cannot fire at you.

LEVEL 4

Level 4 offers a good practice game. You have 100 spaceships in your fleet, but watch out for shooting saucers and enemy bunkers.

LEVEL 5

At Level 5, you have 25 spaceships and no gravity to fight; this level is a good place for beginners to start.

NUMBER OF PLAYERS

Gravitar is for one player only.

SCORING

ITEM	POINT TOTAL
Saucer	100 points
Rammer	100 points
Bunker	250 points
Fuel Depot	5,000 fuel units
Bonus Ship	Every 10,000 points

You score points for destroying enemy saucers, rammers, and bunkers. Each time you enter a new solar system, you can receive 7,000 fuel units, two bonus ships, and 4,000 extra points. You can earn a total of 999,950 points before the score resets. At the end of the game, your final score appears below the game level number.

- Be careful when using your shields. Although they protect your ship from enemy fire, your shields can't withstand a crash or collision with an enemy ship.

- When leaving the entry port, rotate the ship to the left or right, then thrust forward to move away from the sun.

- Use a light touch on the joystick when thrusting. If your ship hits the side of the screen, it will be repelled by a force field and may be hard to control.

- Since the force of gravity gets stronger as you near a planet's surface, aim the nose of your ship away from the planet when picking up fuel. You can then thrust away from the surface as soon as you have the fuel.

- To pick up the fuel, steer your ship over the fuel depot and activate the tractor beam by pulling the joystick handle toward you. You can pick up fuel with your ship aimed in any direction.

- When picking up fuel, pull back on your joystick and quickly release it. You use a minimum amount of energy this way, and your chances of crashing are reduced.

- Consider waiting until you've destroyed every bunker on a planet before you beam up the fuel. Don't fly near the top of the screen, or you'll enter the solar system before you get all the fuel.

- When traveling through the dark galaxies, find a planet's surface by firing missiles. Each time your missile hits, the explosion briefly illuminates the landscape. This technique works in the alien reactor base as well.

REALSPORTS SOCCER

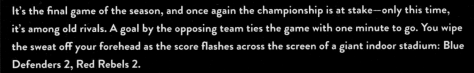

It's the final game of the season, and once again the championship is at stake—only this time, it's among old rivals. A goal by the opposing team ties the game with one minute to go. You wipe the sweat off your forehead as the score flashes across the screen of a giant indoor stadium: Blue Defenders 2, Red Rebels 2.

With precious seconds ticking away, the crowd is growing restless in the stands. The team lines up for the final kick-off. You hear the screech of the referee's whistle and the ball shoots toward your center position with the velocity of a bullet. You dart forward and kick the ball to a wing player, but a Rebel skillfully steals it away, leaving you off balance. Crashing to the side, you hear the ball whizzing past your left ear.

Don't worry! A player on your team intercepts the ball and kicks it to a teammate. But in the tension of the moment, he misses. You close in from the wing. Too late! A Rebel gets control of the ball and dribbles it toward your goal. Like a shadow, you follow close behind. Only you can steal the ball and prevent him from scoring a winning goal. In a split second, your foot snaps the ball from beneath his feet and brilliantly kicks the ball high across the field. What a pass! The crowd rises to their feet and cheers, anticipating a possible victory.

With 20 seconds to go, you sprint toward the center of the action. A star player for the Rebels tries deflecting the ball to the sideline, but under pressure from your team, the ball spins toward you.

You rush to meet the ball before your opponents close in. With a tremendous low kick, the ball barely leaves the ground as it shoots into the goal. A Rebel makes a quick dive and...misses.

The crowd erupts into a frenzy. Your team has won the game—and the championship! Proud fans jump up and down in the stands. In the resounding roar, you hear the loud, clear chant of victory.

ABOUT THE GAME

Programmer Michael Sierchio's *RealSports Soccer* was the second and last Atari-produced soccer game for the Atari 2600 after *Championship Soccer/Pele's Soccer* (1980/1981), and third overall after M Network's *International Soccer* (1982), which only supported two-player games. Only *RealSports Soccer* features a side-scrolling perspective of the action and is arguably the smoothest-playing and most accessible of the bunch. All three soccer games are found on the Atari Flashback products.

OBJECT OF THE GAME

Soccer players, get ready! With three players on your team, your objective is to bluff, pass, and outmaneuver your opponents to score the most points before the clock runs out. You score one point for each goal. Play against the computer, or play against a friend.

HOW TO PLAY

At the start of the game, the ball is placed at the center of the halfway line. Blue fielders are on the left side of the line, reds on the right.

Either team can take possession of the ball. Players are assigned to one of three lanes in the playing field and must dribble the ball within their lane or pass to another fielder.

Each player controls one player at a time, while the computer controls the rest of the team. As the offense, you control the player with the ball. As the defense, you can switch control from one player to another by pressing the button on your joystick controller.

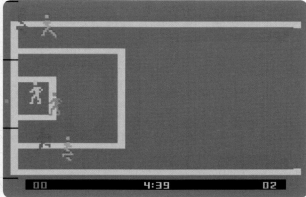

Use the wraparound feature in *RealSports Soccer* to run your player off one side of the screen and have him reappear on the screen's other side. When using this feature, the controlled player must not be in possession of the ball. A controlled player can run off either side of the screen, but cannot run off the end of the field.

Only your controlled player can score a goal. But watch out! If the ball doesn't go all the way into the goal, a defensive player can still block the goal and take control of the ball. If the ball does go in, you'll hear the shriek of the referee's whistle. You score one point, the clock stops, and the ball is turned over to the other team for the kick-off.

The referee's whistle sounds off at three different times throughout the game: at kick-off, after goals, and at the end of the game. Gameplay lasts for five minutes or nine minutes, depending on the game you choose.

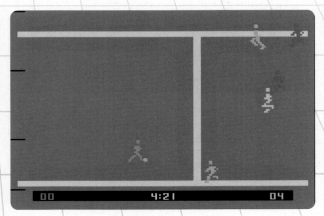

A controlled player appears brighter than his teammates.

USING THE JOYSTICK

Use the joystick to move your controlled player in the direction you want the player to run or to dribble the ball. Notice that controlled players appear brighter than their teammates. To kick or pass, point the joystick in the direction you want the ball to go, and press the red controller button. Fielders must touch the ball with their legs to have control; the ball cannot be passed or blocked with any other part of the body.

ATARI NEWS

What The Critics Had to Say

"Another *RealSports* game, *Soccer*, was a big disappointment to us, especially after playing *Tennis*. The difference between the two games is vast. *Soccer's* action is slow and predictable. Playing the game involves nothing more than simple joystick maneuvering, which you can master in minutes."

-*BLIP magazine, July 1983*

DEFENSE

When playing defense, you can switch control from one player to another. Press the red controller button until the desired player appears brighter. Notice that the control switches from player to player in sequence. When you're ready to steal the ball, run your controlled player into the ball.

OFFENSE

When playing offense, your controlled player moves more slowly than the defensive controlled player. Pass the ball to a teammate to avoid a steal or to move the ball into another lane. The receiving fielder automatically becomes a controlled player.

DIFFICULTY OPTIONS

The left difficulty button in the A position has no function. In the B position it creates a wraparound feature.

GAME OPTIONS

Use Select to choose the skill level, duration of the game, and number of players among 12 variations.

In one-player games, the computer controls the red team.

Each game has three skill levels and playing option of five minutes or nine minutes.

As you progress through each level of difficulty, gameplay speeds up, and in one-player games the computer's teamwork becomes quicker and more skillful.

Press Reset to start and restart the game.

DIFFICULTY LEVEL	PLAYING TIME	NUMBER OF PLAYERS
01	5:00	02
01	9:00	02
02	5:00	02
02	9:00	02
03	5:00	02
03	9:00	02
03	5:00	02
03	9:00	02
01	5:00	01
01	9:00	01
02	5:00	01
02	9:00	01
03	5:00	01
03	9:00	01

The 01 difficulty level is considered Easy. The 02 difficulty level is considered Intermediate. The 03 difficulty level is considered Advanced.

The back of the box for the European version of RealSports Soccer.

FUN FACTS!

○ The 1988 European release of *RealSports Soccer* was called *Football: RealSports Soccer*.

○ Oddly enough, the 1988 re-release and European versions of *RealSports Soccer* omit certain sound effects and disable the wraparound feature from the original version of the game.

Tips & Tricks

◆ Try moving the ball from foot to foot, or reversing your direction unexpectedly. Bluffing your opponent is a good way to distract him while you pass the ball to another teammate.

◆ Passing is essential since a defensive fielder can always outrun the player with the ball. The easiest way to improve your passing is to practice in two-player games without another player. This way, you don't have to worry about losing the ball to a defender.

◆ Defend your goal! Remember that your controlled player's feet must touch the ball in order to block a goal.

◆ In defensive play, you can usually outrun your opponent. Just stay in front, and you're sure to win! And don't forget to practice intercepting and stealing the ball—then pass it to a teammate!

CRYSTAL CASTLES

Once upon a time, Bentley Bear was rambling through the woods, daydreaming about poached salmon. He stopped to take a nap in his favorite hollow tree trunk. But when he awoke, he found himself inside a huge castle glittering with diamonds, emeralds, and pearls.

Though Bentley didn't know it at the time, he was trapped in Crystal Castles, home of Berthilda the Witch and her evil cronies. To escape their spell, he must harvest the gems in the castles before Berthilda and her malicious gang send him into permanent hibernation.

ABOUT THE GAME

In the early 1980s, Atari struck gold by recreating a string of popular arcade games as cartridges, such as mega-hits *Space Invaders*, *Asteroids*, and *Missile Command*. Atari tagged *Crystal Castles* as the next conversion after the game burst onto the arcade scene in 1983. How big was it? In order to meet consumer demand for *Crystal Castles*, Atari produced a combined 5,000 cabinets and cocktail table units over the game's lifetime.

The coin-op crowd lauded *Crystal Castles'* graphics, controls, and even the design of its cabinet. The game's appeal led to it appearing as one of the games contestants could play on the arcade-themed game show, *Starcade*.

While the conversion from coin-op cabinet to home console cartridge required scaling back certain features, such as warp points, the overall gaming experience remained the same.

The Atari team managed to keep isometric (meaning appearing as three-dimensional on a two-dimensional screen) level maps, something that hadn't been done before on a game for the 2600.

The appeal of *Crystal Castles* persisted after Atari discontinued the 2600. It's commonly included in Atari game collections for home computers and consoles. Even modern reviewers rate it as one of the best games released for the 2600. If you haven't played it yet, you're in for a treat!

OBJECT OF THE GAME

Rack up a high score by guiding Bentley Bear through a series of castles. Avoid the deadly touch of the castles' evil inhabitants by jumping over them. Collect magic gems, pick up special items, and defeat certain enemies to score points.

HOW TO PLAY

You begin at the first castle of the level you selected (1-8). Each level features four castles, and each castle contains up to seven enemies that try to thwart Bentley's efforts to collect gems. Completing a level's fourth castle advances you to the next level's first castle.

Use the joystick to guide Bentley Bear through the castle interiors.

Press the red controller button to make Bentley jump. Run over the gems to collect them. Jump over enemies to avoid them in tight spaces.

There are two beneficial items found on some levels: a Magic Hat and a Pot of Honey. Collect the Pot of Honey as quickly as enemies allow, otherwise a Swarm of Bees (see "Enemies") appears to protect the pot.

The Magic Hat grants temporary invincibility to Bentley when he runs into it, or jumps over it. For the first three levels, the hat stays in one spot. For Levels 4-8, the Magic Hat bounces around the level until Bentley collects it. In Levels 9 and above, the Magic Hat turns into a Crystal Ball if Bentley doesn't get to it quickly.

FUN FACTS!

• Bentley Bear is a playable character in *Atari Carts*, a racing game for the Atari Jaguar.

ENEMIES

 Berthilda the Witch occupies the fourth (final) castle of each level. Her only predictable aspect is her favorite snack—large furry mammals, served with a bear-naise sauce. Avoid her as much as possible, unless Bentley is wearing the Magic Hat. Run into Berthilda while wearing the Magic Hat to change her from threat into bonus points.

You begin with five lives, and earn additional lives at intervals of 20,000 points. The primary way to score points is by collecting gems. The first gem you collect on each level is worth a single point. Subsequent gems are worth one additional point each (the second gem is worth 2, the third gem is worth 3, etc.), up to 99 points per gem. Harvesting the final gem in a castle is initially worth 1,000 points, increasing by 100 points for every castle you clear. The enemies in some levels consume gems, so you are not guaranteed this bonus amount.

 Crystal Balls eat gems. They chase Bentley with a rolling motion. They're small and easy to avoid with jumps.

 Gem Eaters compete with Bentley for gems. As long as Bentley isn't wearing the hat, he can turn Gem Eaters into dust by running over them just as they swallow their lunch. Look for a red segment in a Gem Eater's otherwise green body.

 Ghosts don't pop up often. They're more scenery than threat. They don't chase Bentley, preferring to stay in a limited area.

 Nasty Trees beeline for Bentley and gobble up gems. Avoid these woody monsters by trapping them behind a wall or in a corner. Jumping over a Nasty Tree causes it to shrink down briefly.

The other ways to score points include picking up the Magic Hat (500 points), consuming the Pot of Honey (1,000 points), running into a Gem Eater enemy while it's consuming a gem (500 points), and hitting Berthilda the Witch while wearing the Magic Hat (3,000 points).

 Skeletons are rarely encountered and don't actively chase Bentley. They move slowly and stick to a small area in a castle.

 The **Swarm of Bees** appears for one of two reasons. First, they protect Pots of Honey; they come and go as long as the Pot of Honey remains on the level. Second, if you take too long to collect the gems in a castle, the Swarm of Bees acts as a reminder to get you going.

 The final opponent is more hazardous item than mobile enemy. The **Witch's Cauldron** turns Bentley into bear stew if he touches it. Avoid this deadly pot by jumping over it.

- ◆ Line up Bentley's feet with the gems you want to collect.
- ◆ Harvesting the last gem in the castles earns extra points.
- ◆ Elevators make perfect escape routes. However, they only operate one at a time.
- ◆ Bentley is invincible while he's jumping.
- ◆ Bentley can temporarily stun Nasty Trees and Gem Eaters by jumping over them. But this maneuver doesn't work if he's wearing the Magic Hat, or while the Gem Eaters are swallowing gems.
- ◆ When floating scores appear on the scene, creatures can't move through them, nor can the creatures move through each other.

MILLIPEDE

Rid your garden of those bothersome bugs! An army of menacing millipedes—cousins to the famed Centipede—have invaded your garden patch, and you must shoot arrows at them to rid your plot of these pesky pests. But wait! The millipedes aren't the only insidious insects you have to destroy. Jumping spiders, buzzing bees, bouncing beetles, mosquitoes, dragonflies, inchworms, and earwigs all have unique and deadly powers of their own!

ABOUT THE GAME

Considering it's in the top 10 best-selling arcade games of all time, creating a sequel to *Centipede* seemed inevitable. While some sequels chose to completely redefine their predecessor's gameplay, others played it safe by making a handful of key tweaks and additions to the original's beloved formula. *Millipede* falls into this latter category, holding true for both the arcade original and the Atari 2600 port.

Unlike many Atari 2600 games, *Millipede* had a fairly large team assigned to it. Dave Staugas programmed the game, Jerome Domurat created the graphics, and Robert Vieira and Andrew Fuchs worked on the sound.

OBJECT OF THE GAME

Wipe out the multi-segmented millipede (and anything else that gets in your way) as it winds its way through the mushroom forest toward the bottom of the screen. When all millipede segments have been destroyed, you move on to the next, more difficult level.

HOW TO PLAY

Move your bug blaster with the player-one (left) joystick and shoot with the red controller button. Your movement zone is limited to the gray area at the bottom of the screen.

SCORING

You begin the game with three lives. For every 15,000 points you earn, you're awarded another life.

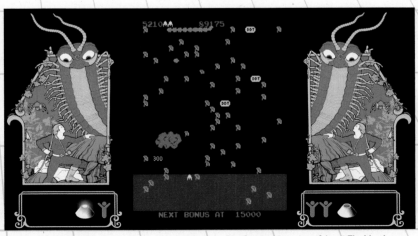

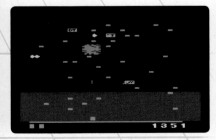

The original **Millipede** arcade game as emulated on the PlayStation 4 version of **Atari Flashback Classics Volume 1** (2016).

OBJECT	POINT VALUE(S)	DESCRIPTION
Mushroom	1	Mushrooms are all right, but they're slowly choking you out of your garden.
Millipede head	100	The millipedes attack from the top of your garden. They march back and forth across your patch until they get to the bottom. When a millipede bumps into a mushroom, it reverses direction. If any part of the millipede touches you, you're finished!
Millipede segment	10	
Spider	300/600/ 900/1,200	Jumping spiders enter from either side of the screen. How many points you get for ridding the garden of a spider depends on how close it is when you shoot it.
Beetle	300	Beetles crawl in when you least expect them. They also have a particular pattern they follow, so pay attention!
Mosquito	400	Swat mosquitoes for big points. But you'd better be quick with your arrows—mosquitoes also swarm!
Bee	200	Bees buzz randomly through the magic patch. They have a distinct sound, so they're easy to recognize. But watch out when they swarm at you, or you're sure to get stung!
Inchworm	100	The inchworm can't move too quickly, but it's tricky just the same. When you shoot this little critter, the movement of all the insects on the screen is slowed down for about four seconds.
DDT Bomb	800	Thank goodness for pesticides! Pierce one of the DDT Bombs in your garden to earn an automatic 800 points. Explode the DDT at the right time, and the vapor wipes out any bug it touches! For each bug destroyed by DDT, you earn triple the points you'd normally get for it.
Dragonfly	500	Be careful! These flying beasts like to swarm, too.
Earwig	1000	Earwigs are hard to hit, but if you're on target, they're worth a lot. Earwigs also poison mushrooms on contact, changing their color if you don't get them before they cross the width of the screen. Get the earwigs before they cause more damage.

Every time you lose a bug blaster, you receive five points for every flower and every three mushrooms left on the screen.

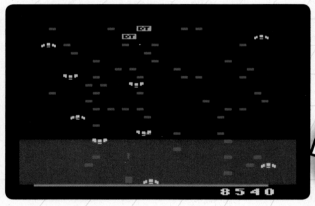

ATARI NEWS
What The Critics Had to Say

"One cool new feature is the presence of DDT boxes scattered among the mushrooms. When shot, these emit poisonous clouds which engulf approaching insects. It's a brilliant concept and it really does add additional strategy."

-The Video Game Critic, 2001/9/23

FUN FACTS!

One of the names considered for the arcade game was *Centipede Deluxe*. It's likely that the lukewarm commercial reception for *Asteroids Deluxe* played a role in the change to the final name.

GAME OPTIONS

After the *Millipede* title screen appears, press Select or the red controller button to select the number of points you want to begin a game with. In the first game of any playing session, you can start with 0, 15,000, or 30,000 points. Move your controller forward to increase your score, and back to decrease your score. After the first game, you can start at up to 15,000 points below your previous high score, in 15,000-point increments up to 300,000. If you just played a game and scored 107,000 points, for example, you can start your next game at 90,000.

Tips & Tricks

- Make sure you keep your eye on the millipede while you're getting rid of the other pests. The millipede can sneak up on you if you're not careful, so keep it under control.

- If a millipede touches a poisonous mushroom—poisonous mushrooms are different colors from most—watch out! The millipede will charge directly at you!

- When the insects swarm, you're in for big trouble if you're not alert. Only a spider can enter the garden while the mosquitoes, bees, or dragonflies are swarming. You get 100 extra points (above the normal point value) for the second swarming bug you destroy, 200 for the third, and so forth—up to 1,000 extra points per bug. But beware! Swarming bugs fly fast and furious!

- Each insect has its own unique sound, so keep your ears open and you can anticipate what's coming next.

SOLARIS

The Zylons are back—those spaceway sneaks, villains of Venus, Saturnian scoundrels! They're swarming through the galaxy in huge forces, attempting another takeover. They've got to go! And we need YOU to go get 'em.

But it's a hush-hush mission. If the Zylons guess you're onto them, you're a goner. So the official report says you're out to find the lost planet Solaris and rescue the Atarian Federation Pioneers stranded there. But if the Zylons reach Solaris before you do, they'll destroy it.

You've got to hyperwarp from quadrant to quadrant, facing vicious attackers such as Kogalon Star Pirates, Planet Destroyers, and Cobra Fleets. But don't worry—your fighter, the StarCruiser, is specially outfitted with a Galactic Scanner and plenty of photon torpedoes. Just don't let the Zylons destroy a Federation Planet, or your quadrant mutates into a terrifying Red Zone.

Ready? Then hop into the StarCruiser, rev the engine, and go! And remember—if anything flies your way, blast it!

ABOUT THE GAME

Doug Neubauer, who had previously created *Star Raiders* for multiple Atari systems, created *Solaris*. The purpose of *Star Raiders* was to take tactical and action elements from contemporary space-themed television shows and movies, and translate them to interactive entertainment format. *Star Raiders* was first released in 1979.

Solaris, meanwhile, was released in 1986. Some terms and entities such as the Zylons carry over from *Star Raiders* to *Solaris*, but with different names and forms. The philosophy of players using star charts to plan their next missions carries over as well. *Solaris* is most known today for boasting some of the best graphics to ever come out of the Atari 2600, as well as some of the most involved gameplay.

OBJECT OF THE GAME

Your mission is to destroy Zylons as you battle your way through galactic mazes trying to reach Solaris.

HOW TO PLAY

You start the game with three fighters. You score points by blasting the enemy with your photon torpedoes. When you lose a ship, it's replaced until all your StarCruisers are gone. When a reserve ship appears, press the red controller button to restart game action. Push the joystick handle to the right or left to fly your StarCruiser in that direction.

Push the handle forward to dive, or speed up when flying over a planet; pull backward to climb, or slow down over a planet. Press the red controller button to fire your photon torpedoes during battle.

To attack a Zylon force or defend a Federation Planet, move to its sector and press the red controller button. You immediately hyperwarp to that sector. Watch your Targeting Computer during hyperwarp. It shows your StarCruiser hyperwarping in and out of focus, while the number on the right of the Computer displays your hyperwarp focus value (0 is a perfect warp, 3 is terrible). Move the joystick handle left or right to keep your fighter in focus.

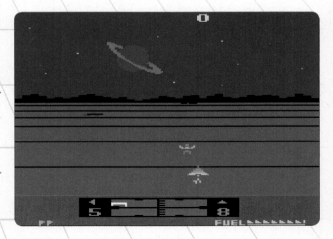

Once you land in an enemy sector, start blasting. Watch your Targeting Computer to find unseen Zylon ships. The number on the left of the Computer tells their left/right distance from you; the number on the right tells their up/down distance. Zero means they're straight ahead.

When your Targeting Computer is damaged, it flashes bright white. Use the left/right, up/down numbers to track the enemy until you can dock at a Federation Planet for repairs.

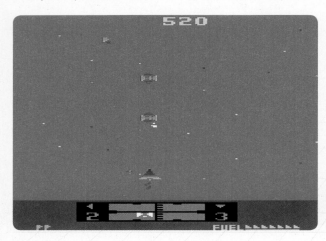

When you've destroyed all Zylons in a sector, the Galactic Scanner reappears. (If you're using a second joystick, press its red controller button to redisplay your Scanner at will, even during battle.) To hyperwarp to another quadrant, move the

StarCruiser to a sector with an Exit and press the red controller button. Choose an enemy sector from that quadrant and get going!

An alarm rings when Zylons are attacking a Federation Planet in your quadrant; you can also spot the attack on your Galactic Scanner—the planet flashes. You've got 40 seconds to save the planet. If you fail, the whole quadrant regresses into a Red Zone, and joystick control is reversed. Watch it!

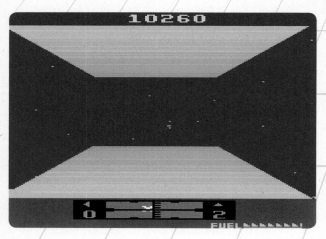

When your fuel gets critically low, another alarm buzzes. Hyperwarp to a Federation Planet as soon as you can for refueling. Dock into a Docking Bay (fly into it) to refuel and repair any damage to your StarCruiser. If you run out of fuel, your StarCruiser explodes.

Battle gets increasingly fast and furious as the game progresses. You must continue to search for Solaris while destroying all enemy ships. You'll know Solaris when you find it—it's the only blinking planet in the galaxy.

The game ends when all your ships are destroyed or you reach Solaris. Press Reset, then the red controller button, to play again.

THE GALACTIC SCANNER

A few moments after you launch your StarCruiser, the Galactic Scanner appears, detailing one of the 16 quadrants in the galaxy. The quadrant's 48 sectors can be occupied by Zylons, Zylon Planets, Corridors, Wormholes, Star Clusters, or Federation Planets. The quadrant has four Exits, one on each side, leading to other quadrants. A flashing X shows your sector position.

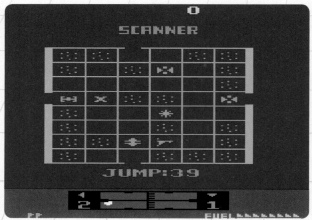

Move the joystick handle left, right, forward, or back to move the StarCruiser to an occupied sector in the quadrant. Sectors with Star Clusters are blockades; you cannot enter them. Zylons often occupy sectors blocking an Exit or threatening a Federation Planet.

Watch the Jump Value at the bottom of the Scanner. When it reaches 0, Zylons may change their sector positions. A Federation Planet starts flashing when Zylons enter its sector. You must defend the planet immediately or it will be destroyed.

SCANNER

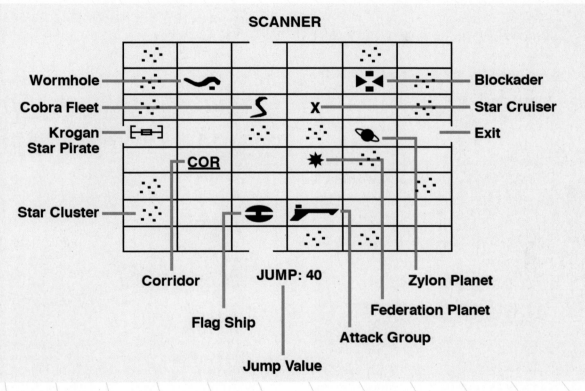

Wormhole

Cobra Fleet

Krogan Star Pirate

Star Cluster

Corridor

Flag Ship

JUMP: 40

Jump Value

Blockader

Star Cruiser

Exit

Zylon Planet

Federation Planet

Attack Group

COR

GOOD GUYS

 Solaris is the only blinking Federation Planet in the galaxy. Watch your Scanner to find it.

 Federation Planets can't defend themselves from Zylons. When the enemy destroys one, the whole quadrant turns into a Red Zone. To rescue your planet, blast all Zylons off it. If you don't, a whole new fleet attacks.

 Space Cadets are stranded on Zylon Planets. Fly over them to pick them up. Rescuing all Cadets on a Zylon Planet earns you 8,000 points, an extra fighter, and blows up the planet. (Ignore Space Cadets on Federation Planets—they're just waving at you.)

 Docking Bays are where you refuel and repair damage to the StarCruiser. Find them on Federation Planets.

 Hyperwarp through a **Wormhole** to jump over a wall of Star Clusters in the Galactic Scanner.

BAD GUYS

 Hyperwarp to **Zylon Planets**. Rescuing all Space Cadets stranded there blows up the planet and earns you a bonus fighter and points.

<u>COR</u>

 Corridors are tricky. **Guardians** protect the entrance and don't shoot unless you shoot first. Once inside a Corridor, you must fly over the **Key** (and blast some Guardians) to gain safe passage through the Ion Doors. If you make it through, another Zylon Planet blows up and you earn 8,000 points!

 Blockaders are space minefields. Dodge 'em or shoot 'em.

 Attack Groups contain Mechnoids, FlagShips, and a smattering of Kogalon Star Pirates.

 Kogalon Star Pirates attack Federation and Zylon ships alike. They hang back, then take potshots. They also make sweeping runs to ram your ship. Look out!

 Vicious **Cobra Ships** are sent out to persuade you to vacate a sector.

 Big, clumsy **FlagShips** send out Distractors as defenders. They also shoot Federation Ships. A FlagShip's direct hit will destroy your StarCruiser.

 Distractors are fast but carry little firepower. You lose fuel when hit by one.

 Mechnoids are easy targets at first, then get nastier. These mechanical ash cans like to move up close or just off to one side, then pow!

 Gliders employ a slippery, sliding-gliding motion.

 Raiders attack Federation Planets.

Targeters come right at you.

SCORING

ITEM	POINT TOTAL
Making it through a Corridor	8,000
Rescuing all Cadets on a Zylon Planet	8,000
Flagship	500
Raider	400
Kogalon Star Pirate	320
Targeter	320
Glider	320
Mechnoid	300
Blockader	260
Cobra Ship	80
Guardian	60
Distractor	20

When you rescue all Space Cadets on a Zylon Planet, you earn an extra StarCruiser and blow up the planet. You blow up another Zylon Planet when you make it safely through a Corridor.

At one point *Solaris* was planned to be a tie-in game for the movie *The Last Starfighter*. These plans fell through when Atari itself was purchased in 1984.

- Map your progress! It will help you find Solaris more quickly.

- Try to keep your StarCruiser in focus during hyperwarp. The better job you do at focusing, the less fuel you waste. When you arrive in the enemy sector, you'll also be closer to the Zylon fleet.

- Destroy the enemies closest to Federation Planets first.

- Save fuel in an enemy sector by blasting at neutral planets only to avoid colliding with them.

- Don't shoot your Docking Bays or you'll turn the quadrant into a Red Zone.

- Most Zylons can be beaten by being aggressive, but FlagShips require flanking tactics, as the Distractors they launch can soak up your shots. Go around the Distractors (dipping low is your best bet), then come back to hit the FlagShip.

- You can only have up to four ships in reserve; any ships earned beyond that aren't counted.

- If you have the second joystick plugged in, press the red controller button to access the Galactic Scanner anytime you want!

DESERT FALCON

All around you are long stretches of sand, ancient pyramids baking in the hot dead air, and constant danger.

The legends that brought you here are 30 centuries old. The tales tell of thieves who plundered the Pharaoh's tomb, loading bags of gold, silver, and precious gems onto their camels, then making off into the desert. But in the night, horrible desert beasts pursued the robbers, and the priceless treasure was scattered and lost. Not even a camel was ever seen again.

Now you search for the lost treasure, daring the beaks and claws of the desert guardians. As you scan the endless sand for the glitter of jewels, your eye catches sight of gliding shadows. Something's coming!

You could turn back now and be safe. Or you could go on, and dare to steal the Pharaoh's jewels.

ABOUT THE GAME

Desert Falcon was originally developed for the Atari 7800, but was also released for the Atari 2600. Many people referenced similarities to *Zaxxon*, and *Desert Falcon* did indeed share a similar diagonal, isometric view and "shoot 'em up" style gameplay with the classic arcade game.

With the release delay of the 7800, *Desert Falcon* came out at a time when Atari had to compete against other systems such as the Nintendo Entertainment System and the Sega Master System. Unfortunately, Atari's 2600 couldn't match the hardware of the new systems, and the 2600 version of *Desert Falcon* suffered from limited graphics and sluggish controls.

HOW TO PLAY

The Pharaoh's lost treasures—enormous gems, big golden eggs, and silver ingots—are scattered among the ancient pyramids and obelisks. Fly toward the treasures, then hover or hop over them to pick them up and earn points. Use your joystick to maneuver.

The treasures are guarded by flying and crawling beasts. Burrowing Uwes crawl out of the sand to charge at you, and Vultures, Warrior Phleas, Scarabs, Flying Fish, and Phantom Gliders attack from the air. Darts fly at you, spit out by the Howling Sphinx waiting at the end of the trail. All these enemies will destroy you if they hit you.

Protect yourself by firing darts. A direct hit destroys enemy creatures and results in points. You can also maneuver around enemies. At higher levels, watch out for flame-throwing Fire Pots and dart-shooting Mini-Sphinxes.

You begin the game with five lives. Each time you're hit or you crash into an object you lose a life, but you will recover as long as you have lives left.

The end of each desert trek brings you to the Howling Sphinx. You must shoot this Sphinx in the middle of its face to get past it, all the while dodging the darts and nasty creatures it spits at you.

ACTION	JOYSTICK OPERATION
Fire darts	Press red controller button once.
Activate super powers	Double-press red controller button in quick succession.
Fly; gain altitude	Pull joystick backward.
Land, hop, or swim	Push joystick forward.
Maintain altitude in the air; stop on land	Release joystick.
Move left	Push joystick left.
Move right	Push joystick right.

SUPER POWERS

Hop over any three hieroglyphs scattered in the sand to gain super powers. Super powers give you great advantages, such as letting you destroy all enemies on-screen at once or paralyze the Howling Sphinx.

Check the Gaming Box at the bottom of the screen to find out which power you've gained. Some powers are used up when you double-press the red controller button; other powers last for about 20 seconds. A new power is awarded when you pick up three more hieroglyphs, whether or not the previous power was used.

There are many super powers for you to discover. But beware: in the higher levels of play, you also have a chance of earning super problems, such as Shackles.

GAMING BOX

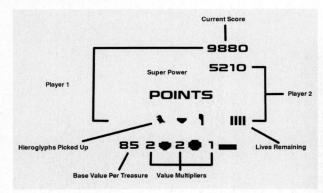

HIEROGLYPHS

SUPER POWERS	EFFECT
Air Bomb	All airborne enemies and enemy darts in sight are destroyed.
Decoy	Enemies are tricked into flying toward a decoy spot.
Hold Sphinx	The Howling Sphinx is unable to spit creatures or darts at you.
Invincible	Nothing can destroy you.
Omnicide	All enemies on-screen are destroyed.
Points	You are given free points.
Polywater	You can fly and hop, but not swim.
Roulette	You are given two random hieroglyphs. The next hieroglyph you pick up determines your next super power.
Shackles	You can fly and swim, but not hop.
Warp	You fly at lightning speed to the Howling Sphinx.

SCORING

SHOOTING DESERT BEASTS

Each enemy you destroy earns you points. Destroying a flying enemy increases the base value of treasures. You cannot shoot the Howling Sphinx's darts.

DESERT BEASTS	POINTS SCORED	POINTS ADDED TO BASE VALUE OF TREASURES
Mini-Sphinx	1000	0
Warrior Phlea	500	5
Scarab	300	3
Flying Fish	200	2
Vulture	200	2
Burrowing Uwe	150	0
Phantom Glider	100	1

DESTROYING THE HOWLING SPHINX

The first Howling Sphinx destroyed is worth 5,000 points. Each additional destroyed Sphinx is worth your previous Sphinx score plus an extra 1,000 points. The maximum value for destroying a Howling Sphinx is 10,000 points.

STEALING TREASURES

During regular gameplay, each treasure you pick up earns you the base value, and increases that treasure's value multiplier by 1. In the bonus round, each treasure is worth the base value times its value multiplier.

BONUS LIVES

You earn a bonus life at every 10,000 points scored. You can have a maximum of four lives remaining.

BONUS ROUND

Destroying the Howling Sphinx gains you entrance to the bonus round. Here your goal is to pick up as many treasures as you can in the time allowed.

During the bonus round, your time allowed is counted down in seconds in the Gaming Box. The bonus score is tallied next to the time. When the round ends, the bonus score is added to your current score. The last hieroglyphs or super power you gained reappears, along with your remaining lives.

You are not attacked in the bonus round, and colliding with objects doesn't cost you a life; only time is lost.

GAMING BOX

24233

17205

TIME   **SCORE**

Time Allowed —— **25**   **544** —— Bonus Score

136   **4**   **1**   **1**

Gem Value Multiplier

Silver Ingot Value Multiplier

Base Value per Treasure

Golden Egg Value Multiplier

EmuMovies

Gaming Box: On the bottom line, from left to right, are: Base Value per Treasure, Gem Value Multiplier, Golden Egg Value Multiplier, and Silver Ingot Value Multiplier. The line above the bottom line contains, from left to right: Time Allowed and Bonus Score.

DESERT GUARDIANS

MINI-SPHINX

WARRIOR PHLEA

SCARAB

FLYING FISH

FIRE POT

VULTURE

HOWLING SPHINX

BURROWING UWE

PHANTOM GLIDER

GOLDEN EGG

GEM

SILVER INGOT

- *Desert Falcon* was originally called *Nile Flier*.

- While under the effects of a super power, hop around in a lake and the initials "BP" may appear over your character's head. The "BP" stands for "Bob Polaro," the game's programmer.

- Gauge the altitude of flying beasts by watching their shadows.

- Figure out what combination of hieroglyphs awards you which power. For instance, the combination "Bird, Cane, Bowl" gives you Warp (except at Novice level), while the combination "Cane, Bird, Bowl" (the same hieroglyphs in a different order) gives you Air Bomb. Pick up the appropriate combination when its power do you the most good.

- In the bonus round, go for the treasures that have the highest-value multiplier.

SPRINT MASTER

Ready, set, go!

Speed into the *Sprint Master* hall of fame! Choose your track, from practice-caliber squares to the curvaceous championship courses. Rev up at the starting line, and take off!

Keep a good grip on the controls. You'll need a delicate touch and a cool head to avoid sliding into the wall on those arcing curves.

Watch your time. Take advantage of the bonus speed and traction boxes at the necessary moments. Grab the lead on the first lap, or let your challenger outpace you and then make him eat dust in the final laps.

Outrace an opponent, or go at it again to beat your own time. Sprint to the finish and win!

ABOUT THE GAME

Sprint Master was based on the 1986 arcade game *Super Sprint* by Atari Games. *Super Sprint* supported up to three players, each with a racing wheel to control the corresponding car. The arcade game made 59th place in *Next Generation* magazine's *Top 100 Games of All Time* in 1996.

Sprint Master, however, was limited to two players and didn't support the driving controller for the 2600. Given the hardware limitations of the 2600 when compared with the arcade, *Sprint Master*'s graphics were much simpler than those of its arcade inspiration. These limitations didn't seem to detract from the gameplay, which established *Sprint Master* as a solid racing game for the Atari 2600.

OBJECT OF THE GAME

The object of *Sprint Master* is to beat your opponent to the finish line. You encounter hazards and power-ups, so strategy is key as you race toward the goal. Avoid hitting the walls and other hazards that slow you down. Utilize speed boosts and traction power-ups to keep an edge on the other car.

HOW TO PLAY

Both cars are positioned at the starting line. Then it's ready, set, go! Accelerate with the red controller button and steer with your joystick. Push the joystick left or right to turn in that direction. Pull the joystick back for an emergency brake. Release the controller button to slow down.

Laps and times appear at the top of the screen.

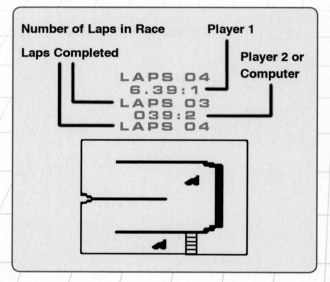

Drive over the blue box on the track to gain traction. Drive over the red box for a burst of speed. Hitting an unpredictable tar slick makes you speed up or slow down. Smacking into a wall costs you time, so move back into position and get going! The race car that completes the required laps in the fastest time wins!

After a game, press the Reset button or the first player's controller button to run the same race again. Press the Game Select button or move the first player's joystick in any direction to return to the title screen.

DIFFICULTY OPTIONS

Use the left difficulty button on the console to change your steering. In the A setting, steering becomes more difficult, as you have less traction. In the B setting, more traction makes steering easier.

GAME OPTIONS

Use the joystick to select a one-player or two-player game. (In a one-player game, you race against the computer.) When the option you want flashes, press the controller button. Then do the same to choose whether the cars will bounce or crash when they collide with something, and how many laps (up to 50) the cars will run.

Press the controller button to get to the raceway. The current selected track appears, with a grid of all track selections above it.

Use the joystick to see each track selection. When the track you want is on-screen, press the controller button.

Finally, use the joystick to change the selected type of track—blacktop, dirt, or ice. Once that's selected, press the controller button to begin.

FUN FACTS!

Start the game in one-player mode, with the bounce option, the first track layout, and a dirt or ice track. When the race starts, grab the speed boost (upper-right red power-up) and head back past the starting line to the blue oil slick. If you bounce off the top barrier and into the slick before the five-second mark (0.05:0), your car turns into the letters "BP" for a split second. The letters "BP" stand for Bob Polaro, the game's programmer.

Tips & Tricks

- Pick up momentum in the straightaways. Keep to the inside of the track on curves.

- On blacktop, head for the red boxes to gain as much speed as you can.

- On ice, go for the blue boxes for extra traction.

- Stay on the track. You can take shortcuts across the grass, but you may bump into invisible barriers and lose valuable time.

- Watch the track. Some tracks have barriers that appear and disappear and could cost you time. You can also use these gates for shortcuts, but you need to make sure you get through before the gate closes.

SUPER BASEBALL

Batter up!

The late-summer sun sits high above the ballpark. The centerfield flags are barely moving. You can feel the sun's heat reflecting off home plate. The crowd behind you murmurs, afraid to break the spell. It's the bottom of the ninth, the score is tied, and the pennant is on the line.

You have a runner on base and only one out. The pitcher tries to stare you down. But you know he's getting tired, and his sinker ball is starting to creep up into the strike zone.

Finally, he makes the throw. Your whole body moves into the swing. With the crack of the bat still ringing in your ears, you head for first. As you round the bag at first, you look up in time to see a fan in the centerfield bleachers make the catch. You head for home, and the crowd goes wild!

You've just won the pennant with a two-run homer. Now on to the championship!

ABOUT THE GAME

Super Baseball is similar to Atari's *RealSports Baseball*, with minor improvements. A title screen was introduced, allowing an easier and clearer selection of the game mode. Programming changes allowed for more accurate throws to bases and a tougher computer opponent.

Graphically, the game has sharper colors and more defined, easier-to-see player characters complete with baseball caps. Atari ditched the three-toned player uniforms of *RealSports Baseball* in favor of a single color. The monotone uniforms were generally seen as a step backward in graphical changes to Atari's previous title.

OBJECT OF THE GAME

Super Baseball follows the same rules as real baseball. Two teams of nine players take turns playing the field and batting. The game is played for nine innings, with one inning consisting of both teams having a turn to bat.

The batting team tries to score as many runs as possible. A run is scored when a player has completed a run around the bases and returned to home plate. The team in the field tries to prevent the batting team from scoring runs by getting three outs. Outs are accumulated in three ways: catching a hit ball, throwing a hit ball to a destination base before a runner reaches the base, or striking out a batter.

HOW TO PLAY

The home team takes the field, and the first batter enters the batter's box.

UP AT BAT

To hit the ball, press and hold the red controller button while moving the joystick. The direction in which the joystick is moved determines the type of swing.

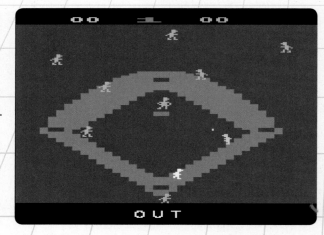

SWING TYPE	JOYSTICK DIRECTION
Bunt	Up
Right field	Up and left
Left field	Up and right
Fly to right field	Down and left
Fly to left field	Down and right

If the swing results in a hit and no one is on base, the runner automatically moves to first base. If the batter gets a hit and one or more runners are on the bases, press the red controller button and use the joystick to move the runner(s) along the baseline.

If the batter hits a solo home run, the runner automatically runs the bases. If one or more runners are on the bases when a home run is hit, press the red controller button to run the bases.

To have a runner steal a base, push the joystick toward the base the runner is on. To return the action to the batter, pull the joystick toward you.

Strikes and balls are displayed on the bottom of the screen, and outs are displayed at the top of the screen between the teams' scores. After three outs, the team at bat takes to the field.

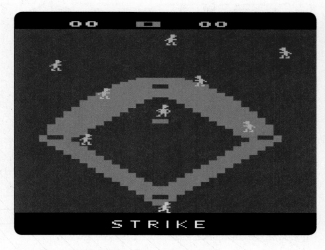

IN THE FIELD

When your team is in the field, first select your pitch by moving the joystick. The direction of the joystick determines the type of pitch.

PITCH	JOYSTICK DIRECTION
Fastball	Up
Intentional ball	Down
Riser	Left
Sinker	Right
Curve left	Up and left
Curve right	Up and right

Once you've selected the pitch, hold the red controller button down and move the joystick handle down quickly to release the pitch.

To throw the ball from one player to another, move the joystick handle to select the direction of the throw, then press the red controller button to release the ball.

THROW DESTINATION	JOYSTICK DIRECTION
Home plate	Down
Pitcher	Center position
1st base	Right
2nd base	Up
3rd base	Left

GAME OPTIONS

There are three game modes in *Super Baseball*, selectable on the menu screen when you start up the game. You can choose between two single-player games (first up to bat or second up to bat) and a two-player game.

- The fielder closest to the ball automatically makes the play. Begin moving the fielder into position, using the joystick, as soon as the ball is hit.

- If the ball is thrown away, the runners don't advance. Play is delayed until the appropriate fielder picks up the ball and throws it back to the pitcher.

- When throwing the ball to an infielder, picture the joystick as sitting in the middle of the baseball diamond. When the handle is in the center position, pushing the red controller button throws the ball to the pitcher. Home plate is down from the pitcher, first base is to the right of the pitcher, second is up from the pitcher, and third base is to the left of the pitcher.

- Remember to select a pitch before you release the red controller. If you release it without having selected a pitch, it's counted as an intentional ball.

- As in a real baseball game, the team with the highest number of runs after nine innings wins the game. However, if the game is tied at the end of the ninth, it could be a long day at the old ballpark.

Atari's gameplay improvements may have overcorrected some of *RealSports Baseball*'s shortcomings. Players move much faster in *Super Baseball*—so much so that it's difficult to hit a home run against the computer. Bunting almost always results in an instant "out," as the catcher moves rapidly to grab the ball and tag your player before you have a chance to get to first base.

SUPER FOOTBALL

Super Football offers 3-D football action. On-screen, you get a full view of the field from above and behind the offensive team. And you control the action as the players line up, kick, run, pass, and score.

With Super Football, it's nonstop gridiron action until the final whistle!

ABOUT THE GAME

Atari may seem like they had a little bit of hubris in the naming of Super Football, but the game is really pretty super. It's a huge improvement over many of the sports-centric games released on the Atari 2600. The unfortunate part is that the game was released near the end of the 2600's cycle, thus there were no further advancements on this version. This doesn't mean that it didn't influence future sports games, or more specifically football games. If you pay attention, you might note some of the same strategies you'd use in the Madden NFL franchise.

Super Football is the result of a promise Atari made several years before its release. During an effort to push sales of Atari 2600 units, Atari released a press article claiming to have a big package of new software coming from their company. When Super Football was released, it was clear that this was part of that promise, so needless to say it was welcomed with open arms, as it was highly anticipated.

Overall, Super Football made great leaps and bounds for the Atari 2600, even though the ideas and technology had to be passed on to the next console to be recognized. However, that doesn't detract from the power that Super Football had on the world of gaming during its release. The game was well-received and liked by gamers all around.

OBJECT OF THE GAME

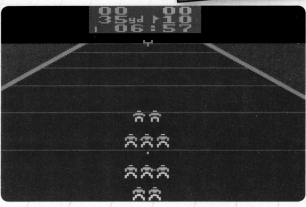

Use your skills and knowledge to be the best football player in the world. Your goal is to get the ball from one side of the field to the other by picking the right plays and moving forward as best as you can, all while scoring more points than your opponent. You will also have a chance to play defense against the opposing team and prevent them from scoring against you.

HOW TO PLAY

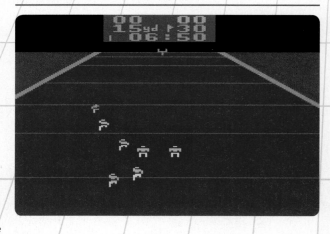

BUCKLE DOWN AND SCORE

The game begins with both teams running onto the field and taking their positions on the scrimmage line. Player 1's team (left joystick control) wears red jerseys, and the computer's or Player 2's team (right joystick control) wears green jerseys. Once the action starts, the player currently under joystick control on each team has a slightly different-colored jersey.

The defensive (red) team faces you. The green team kicks off to the red team, and the red team's receiver catches the ball.

The red receiver is now under Player 1's joystick control. Move your joystick in any direction to maneuver him up the field toward the end zone, while avoiding the green team's players. When the receiver is tackled, the two teams take their positions at the line of scrimmage, with the offensive team at the bottom of the screen.

With both teams at the scrimmage line, you have an opportunity to choose your plays. Then the action continues.

THE SCOREBOARD

The scoreboard at the top of the screen shows both teams' scores on the top line. On the second line, the number on the left shows which yard line the ball is currently on. The number on the right shows how many yards the ball must be moved in order to get a first down. The down that's underway is indicated by one to four flags in the center of the scoreboard. The quarter indicator in the lower-left corner shows which quarter the game is in by displaying one to four vertical bars. The clock on the bottom line keeps track of time remaining in the quarter.

The scoreboard is red when the ball is in the defensive half of the field and blue when the ball is in the offensive half. The game begins with the green team kicking off to the red team. Play stops at the end of the second quarter (halftime), and then the red team kicks off to the green team.

The game ends when the clock reaches 00:00 in the fourth quarter.

At the end of a game, press Reset to play again with the same number of players at the same level, or press Select to make a different game selection.

RUNNING THE PLAY

With both teams at the scrimmage line and the plays selected, the offense can press the red controller button to hike the ball. If the button is not pressed after about four seconds, the ball is automatically hiked.

Once the ball is hiked to the quarterback, both teams carry out their plays. The defensive player rushes the quarterback, the offensive receiver runs the selected pattern, the halfback (or tight end) tries to block the rusher, the linemen blocks, and the cornerback and safety try to cover the receiver. When the quarterback has the ball, he's under your control. The quarterback can either run with the ball or pass to the receiver, depending on the play selected.

PASSING

Wait until the receiver is "open" before throwing the ball to him, then press the red controller button to initiate a pass. You can move your joystick handle left or right to make the quarterback "lead" the receiver and throw the ball in that direction. Release the button to pass the ball.

ILLEGAL FORWARD PASS
The quarterback cannot pass the ball once he crosses the scrimmage line.

RUNNING

You can decide either to make the quarterback run with the ball or pass to a receiver, depending on the play selected. Once the ball is thrown, joystick control switches to the receiver. Move the joystick handle to get the receiver in a good position to make the catch.

Maneuver your ball carrier up the field. Move your joystick to make him avoid defensive players, and use your blockers as shields.

When the ball carrier is tackled, the teams go to the scrimmage line for another play selection.

The offensive team has four downs to advance the ball 10 yards. If it's fourth down, you can punt the ball, or try for a field goal if you're within 50 yards of the goal line. If the offense misses a field goal, the defense takes the ball. If a punt is kicked into the end zone, the defense takes over at the 20-yard line.

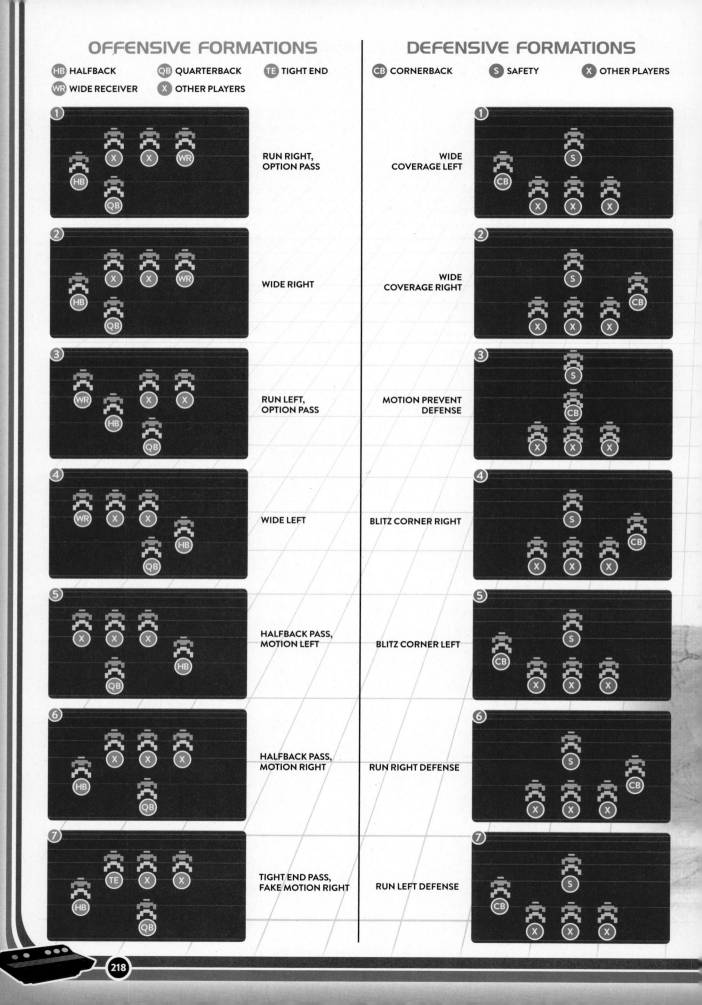

OFFENSIVE FORMATIONS

HB HALFBACK **QB** QUARTERBACK **TE** TIGHT END
WR WIDE RECEIVER **X** OTHER PLAYERS

1. RUN RIGHT, OPTION PASS
2. WIDE RIGHT
3. RUN LEFT, OPTION PASS
4. WIDE LEFT
5. HALFBACK PASS, MOTION LEFT
6. HALFBACK PASS, MOTION RIGHT
7. TIGHT END PASS, FAKE MOTION RIGHT

DEFENSIVE FORMATIONS

CB CORNERBACK **S** SAFETY **X** OTHER PLAYERS

1. WIDE COVERAGE LEFT
2. WIDE COVERAGE RIGHT
3. MOTION PREVENT DEFENSE
4. BLITZ CORNER RIGHT
5. BLITZ CORNER LEFT
6. RUN RIGHT DEFENSE
7. RUN LEFT DEFENSE

A touchdown is scored when the ball carrier crosses the goal line in the end zone. The teams then run onto the field to try for the extra point. After the extra point try, the offense kicks off to the defense.

TOUCHDOWN!
The ball carrier cannot be tackled between the five-yard line and the goal line.

If the defensive team intercepts a pass thrown by the offensive quarterback, the defensive team becomes the offense and attempts to move the ball up the field toward the goal at the top of the screen. No runback is allowed on an interception.

SELECTING PLAYS

When the teams go to the scrimmage line, you select a play by moving the joystick. Once you've made your selection, lock it in by pressing the Fire button.

PLAY SELECTION
At Game Level 1 (Novice), plays are automatically selected.

On fourth down, either a punt or a field goal takes place. The offense has about 25 seconds to select its play and lock it in. If no play is locked in, the previous play is used. After the offense selects its play, the defense has two to four seconds (depending on the game level) to select its play. Again, if no play is locked in, the previous play is used.

The plays you select appear on the scoreboard, in place of your score. When both teams' plays are locked in, the scores reappear and play resumes.

SUPER FOOTBALL PLAYBOOK

OFFENSIVE PLAYS

The offense can select both a formation and a pattern (the route the receiver will run). The formation number appears as the left digit of your score and the pattern number as the right digit. Move the joystick handle left or right to choose a formation (from 1 to 9). Move the joystick handle forward or back to choose a pattern (from 1 to 4).

Once the play is underway, use the joystick to control the quarterback or the receiver, depending on which man has the ball.

On motion plays, the halfback goes into motion before the ball has been hiked. When the ball is hiked, the halfback begins the pattern from that point if he's the receiver. On run plays, the quarterback still has the option to pass.

OFFENSIVE FORMATIONS

1	Run right option pass
2	Wide right
3	Run left option pass
4	Halfback pass motion left
5	Halfback pass motion right
6	Tight end pass fake motion right
7	Punt formation
8	Field goal formation

ATARI NEWS
What The Critics Had to Say

"An average at best football game for the Atari 2600. The game is pretty fun to play, even today, and is definitely worth buying just to see the origins of today's football games."
-Psycho Penguin (2000)

"What a difference six years made. This game is light-years ahead of any other football game made for this system, especially with reference to the computer opponent."
-MMyers (2002)

"It's a shame this cartridge was released near the very end of the Atari 2600's life cycle, because it really knocked my socks off. *Super Football* is the missing link between the early 'flat' football games and the Genesis *Madden* titles."
-David Mrozek (2006)

PLAY FORMATIONS

When the offense selects either formation 8 or 9, the defense automatically selects the same formation.

OFFENSIVE PATTERNS

The receiver (wide receiver tight end or halfback) starts the play by running up the field. At that point the receiver runs to points on the field depending on the pattern you selected.

DEFENSIVE PLAYS

The offense selects a formation, and the formation number appears as the left digit of your score. Move the joystick left or right to choose a formation (from 1 to 9).

Once the play is underway, use the joystick to control the cornerback.

On a blitz, the defense rushes two players. The safety plays a deep zone and tracks either the wide receiver or the quarterback.

DEFENSE FORMATIONS

1	Wide coverage left
2	Wide coverage right
3	Motion prevent defense
4	Blitz corner right
5	Blitz corner left
6	Run right defense
7	Run left defense
8	Punt formation
9	Field goal formation

GAME DIFFICULTY

LEVEL	TIME
1 (Novice)	3 minutes per quarter
2 (Standard)	7 minutes per quarter
3 (Advanced)	10 minutes per quarter
4 (Expert)	15 minutes per quarter

NUMBER OF PLAYERS

Super Football is a game available for play with one or two players.

SCORING

Touchdown	6 points
Field goal	3 points
Extra point	1 point

If the losing team kicks a field goal or extra point with time expiring and the winning team has rolled the score (but their score "appears" lower), both teams wave their hands.

- Tracking the ball during a pass is difficult. Remember to have the wide receiver leading the pass, and get ready to keep running to avoid being tackled.

- Don't wait too long before passing the ball, as the quarterback doesn't have a "cannon," meaning he doesn't pass the ball more than about half the width of the field.

- When on defense, always have your player in the immediate area in front of the receiver with the ball, as it's rather difficult to tackle the ball carrier once the ball is caught.

DOUBLE DUNK

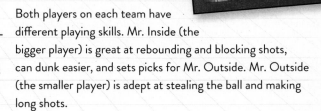

You've spent the day playing some friendly two-on-two basketball. You and our buddy are psyched. You've aced the last three games, and the other guys are getting desperate.

Your inside man dribbles deftly toward the basket. But their man moves in quickly. If he gets the ball, you may get bounced!

Your man passes. You get the ball and line up your shot. The last few seconds of the game tick away. Sink this shot quickly and the game is yours!

ABOUT THE GAME

Programmer Matthew Hubbard's *Double Dunk* was the third and final basketball game created for the Atari 2600. Following *Basketball* (1978) and the unreleased *RealSports Basketball* (1983), *Double Dunk* distinguishes itself from this group by featuring two-on-two, top-down, half court gameplay that's far flashier than its predecessors. All three basketball games are available on the Atari Flashback products.

OBJECT OF THE GAME

Test your skills as you lead your team to victory. On offense, use the joystick and the red controller button to choose your plays, set picks, pass, jump, and shoot. On defense, use the red controller button to block shots and grab rebounds.

HOW TO PLAY

Two teams with two players (Mr. Inside and Mr. Outside) on each team compete in this basketball game. You control your players with the joystick controller. If your team has the ball, your controller moves the player who has the ball. If the other team has the ball, your controller moves the player who is guarding the man with the ball (the player with his hands raised).

Both players on each team have different playing skills. Mr. Inside (the bigger player) is great at rebounding and blocking shots, can dunk easier, and sets picks for Mr. Outside. Mr. Outside (the smaller player) is adept at stealing the ball and making long shots.

One of the most effective plays is the pick play. The purpose of a pick play is to get both defensive players hung up on the offensive Mr. Inside, allowing the offensive Mr. Outside to get an open shot.

The defensive team can anticipate a pick play by selecting the lower-left or lower-right position on the joystick controller during play selection. This allows the defensive Mr. Inside to pick up coverage on the offensive Mr. Outside because the defensive Mr. Outside is hung up on the offensive Mr. Inside.

Choose your offensive or defensive play before the ball is put into play. After a score or a turnover, select your offensive or defensive play (you don't get to select a play after a defensive foul, rebound, or a steal).

OFF and DEF flash at the bottom of the screen until you choose an offensive or defensive play. To select your play, move the joystick controller into the appropriate position and press the red controller button.

Once the ball is in play, use the controller to move your players. When your team is on the offense, press the red controller button once to start the next part of your selected play.

If you pull the joystick back and press the button while the ball is in play, the player with the ball will ignore the play and perform a jump shot. When the player jumps, press the button a second time to make the player shoot the ball.

If a player is close to the basket when he shoots, he will dunk the ball. After an opponent misses a shot and you get the rebound, you must clear the ball by moving your player until both feet are behind the 3-point line before you can shoot again.

If your team is on defense, you can either attempt to steal the ball or jump to block a shot. To attempt a steal, press the red controller button while your defensive player is close to the ball handler. Make sure the ball handler is dribbling when the attempt is made.

To block a shot, wait until the shooter jumps for the shot. Time your own jump to block the shot.

The score appears at the top of the screen, along with the number of points needed to win the game (or the game clock) and the 10-second shot clock.

SCORING

You score 2 points for each successful shot. If you shoot a 3-pointer, you score 3 points for a successful shot. Shots from the foul line after a defensive foul are worth 1 point each.

OFFENSIVE PLAYS

Match the offensive play descriptions below to the controller positions indicated. After moving the controller in the direction indicated for a play, press the red controller button. Depending upon the number of times you press the button, a different action occurs when play begins.

PLAY	CONTROLLER POSITION	NUMBER OF BUTTON PRESSES
Pick and Roll Left or Right	Upper left or upper right	1. Mr. Inside moves to post to set up quick. 2. Pass to Mr. Inside. 3. Jump 4. Shoot
Give and Go Left or Right	Left or right	1. Mr. Inside moves to post to set up quick. 2. Pass to Mr. Inside. 3. Pass to Mr. Outside. 4. Jump 5. Shoot
Pick Left or Right	Lower left or lower right	1. Mr. Inside moves to post to set up pick. 2. Jump 3. Shoot
Mr. Inside Shoots	Top	1. Pass to Mr. Inside. 2. Jump 3. Shoot
Mr. Outside Shoots	Bottom	1. Bottom 2. Jump 3. Shoot

DEFENSIVE PLAYS

Select the defensive play by moving the controller in one of the directions indicated. The defensive play you select matches the corresponding offensive play for the same controller position.

PLAY	CONTROLLER POSITION	DESCRIPTION
Lane Defense	Top	Inside defender guards against pass.
Tight Defense Right	Upper right	Defenders guard close.
Pass Defense Right	Right	Defenders guard against passes.
Pick Defense Right	Lower right	Inside defender switches off if pick is successful.
Rebound Position Defense	Bottom	Inside defender stays close to basket.
Pick Defense Left	Lower left	Inside defender switches off if pick is successful.
Pass Defense Left	Left	Defenders guard against passes.
Tight Defense Left	Upper left	Defenders guard close.

GAME OPTIONS

After the *Double Dunk* title screen appears on-screen, press Select to display the game options screen. Move the joystick controller up or down to select from the seven options. Then, move the controller left or right to change (yes or no, 1 or 2 players, and so on) that game option.

Press Reset or the left controller button to begin the game. During play, press Select to return to the options screen. Press Reset to restart the game.

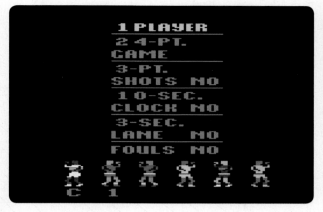

OPTION	DESCRIPTION
One or two players	Play against the computer or an opponent. Select a 1-player or 2-player game.
Game length	The game lasts a set amount of time (2, 5, 10, or 15 minutes) or until one of the teams reaches a certain score (10, 24, 36, or 48 points). Select the time or score you want to use.
3-point shots	Award 3 points for shots made from the area outside the curved line. Select either yes or no.
10-second clock	If the offensive team does not shoot within 10 seconds, the other team gets the ball. Select either yes or no.
3-second lane violation	If an offensive player stays in the lane longer than 3 seconds at a time, the other team gets the ball. Select either yes or no.
Foul detection	Penalizes players for fouls. Select either yes or no.
Team color selection	Select from six team colors. A C (computer), 1 (first player), or 2 (second player) appears under a team's selected color. To select a team's color, move the joystick controller right or left to identify a color. Press Select. Choose a different color for each player or the computer.

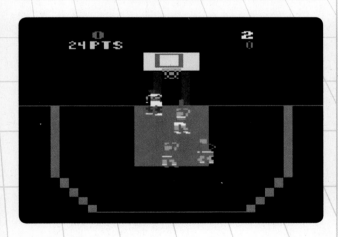

Tips & Tricks

- Keep your opponent off guard by varying your selection of plays.
- If the defense has your play covered, remember that you can make the player with the ball shoot at any time.
- Shoot at the basket when your player is jumping up. Don't shoot as your player is coming down from a jump. If you wait to shoot, chances are you won't make the basket.
- Be careful to stay inbounds when rebounding.
- Time your jumps for successful blocks.
- When rebounding, there's no foul called for goal tending.

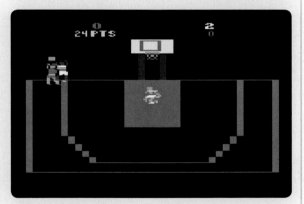

Go here for the best chance to make a 3-pointer.

- Try to shoot 3-pointers from the upper-left, bottom-center, and upper-right parts of the court.
- During the last few seconds of a game, take a cue from the real game. If you have the lead and time is running out, run the clock down by running around the 3-point line. If you are playing until a specific score is reached, foul your opponent to give away a maximum of 1 point rather than 3. And if you're behind, go for 3-point shots.

FUN FACTS!

You can display programmer Matthew Hubbard's initials by scoring 199 points against the computer opponent. When the game ends, "Design by MLH" appears on-screen.

OFF THE WALL

Far away in the Mysterious East on the other side of the world, there lived an adventurous lad named Kung Fu Lu. Lu's grand longing was to crush the ancient, evil wall that plagued his friendly neighbors.

Guarding the wall was a mystical dragon and a cunning blackbird. The dragon would cast balls at brave Lu. If Lu successfully deflected them with his staff, he gained good fortune and special powers. If he missed a ball, it cost him one of his five lives he was granted as a child. The frightful blackbird tried to prevent Kung Fu Lu from destroying the wall, but Lu remained undaunted and continued on until he smashed the last remaining brick.

ABOUT THE GAME

Off the Wall was the first of a handful of games developed for the Atari 2600 by Axlon, a company started by Nolan Bushnell. Bushnell had returned to Atari in 1988 after being absent from the company since his exit in 1978. He promised—and delivered—new releases for the 2600 in a home gaming market that had recovered from the disastrous mid-1980s.

Despite more than a decade passing since the Atari 2600 was first released, *Off the Wall* demonstrated there was a bit more life left in the system. The inclusion of random power-ups, including one with a random effect, added an additional layer to the traditional *Breakout*-style game experience.

OBJECT OF THE GAME

The objective in *Off The Wall* is to score the highest number of points. Play against another player or try to beat your best score.

HOW TO PLAY

Position Lu in the path of the falling ball; use his staff to deflect the ball back to the brick wall to break out bricks. If Lu misses a ball, he loses a life.

Score points by using the ball to knock bricks out of the wall, hitting the dragon beyond the bricks or catching the Mystery Token. Some Mystery Token effects do not involve points.

In each game, you start with five lives. The number of lives remaining appears in the upper-left corner of the screen, with one square for each remaining life. If you break out all the bricks, or hit the dragon six times, the wave finishes and you receive another life.

Each time you hit the dragon, the background behind the bricks becomes lighter. Clearing four waves automatically advances you to the next skill level: Peasant to Student, or Student to Master.

DIFFICULTY OPTIONS

Change the difficulty button to increase (position A) or decrease (position B) Kung Fu Lu's speed.

GAME OPTIONS

There are three different skill levels to select at the start of a game: Peasant, Student, and Master. Each of these levels has four different waves of playing action. Each skill level and each wave is more difficult than its predecessor.

TWO-PLAYER GAME

In a two-player game, each player takes a turn. Player one breaks bricks until he or she misses the ball and loses a life. The second player continues with the same brick field. The game continues, moving into higher skill levels, until each player runs out of lives.

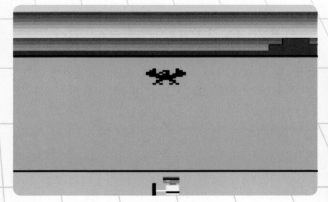

GAME FEATURE: BLACKBIRD

A Blackbird appears after the first wave on the Peasant level. It appears immediately on the Student and Master levels. The bird tries to fly between the bricks and the ball. If the ball hits the bird, the bird deflects the ball back in the direction from which it came.

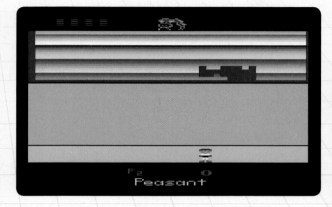

GAME FEATURE: SPECIAL POWER TOKENS

After you hit the ball the first time, different tokens begin dropping at random. Catch a token to receive special powers. Each token has its own special power. You keep these special powers until you miss a ball or the token timer (a bar graph in the upper-right corner) runs out.

ZIG ZAG

This token makes the ball travel in a zigzag pattern after being hit by Lu. On the way down, the ball travels in a normal, straight path.

MYSTERY TOKEN

This token has one of four effects; three are helpful, while one is a disadvantage. The token's positive effects are granting an additional life, adding bonus points (based on the current skill level), or stopping the Blackbird. The token may also speed up the ball, making it harder to hit.

MAGNETIC PADDLE

With this token, Lu's staff becomes a magnet that draws the ball to Lu's location. After hitting the ball, moving Lu to the left moves the ball in the same direction. Because this token is so powerful, its timer runs down at twice the normal speed.

NUKE BALL

This token causes the ball to break out a much larger chunk of bricks when it hits the wall.

MEGA PADDLE

This token enlarges Lu's staff. The larger staff makes it easier to hit the ball.

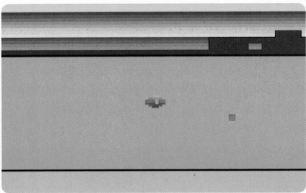

SCORING

EVENT	POINT VALUE
Knock out bricks	1 - 5
Catch Mystery token (Peasant)	50
Catch Mystery token (Student)	75
Catch Mystery token (Master)	100
Hit the dragon	100

Tips & Tricks

◆ If you hit the ball at an angle into the bricks, it bounces off the inside bricks and knocks out far more bricks compared to a direct hit.

◆ Don't move too fast or you could overshoot the ball.

◆ Use your tokens strategically.

◆ Try to use the Blackbird to your advantage.

○ While the gameplay for *Off the Wall* resembles *Breakout*, it was designed to work with the joystick and not the paddle controller, which was the standard for other *Breakout*-style games.

○ Despite sharing a name, the *Off the Wall* coin-op arcade game that released in 1991 was not related to this Atari 2600 game.

RADAR LOCK

You're locked in fight-to-the-death air combat with the enemy! You may be outnumbered—somehow you've been separated from your buddies—but this is far from your first mission. You've been flying your trusty little delta-wing fighter for more months than you care to remember.

Suddenly you sight an enemy Interceptor at 12 o'clock! These babies are a piece of cake. You sneak up from behind and zap it with a few rounds from your machine gun.

Just when you're feeling a little cocky from your last successful hit, an enemy Bomber appears out of nowhere. This one's not so easy. Not only is its tail gunner an expert shot, but the Bomber is surrounded by a fleet of Escorters, and you can't even get at it with your guided missiles.

It's going to take all of your expertise, along with your arsenal of ammunition, proximity missiles, and guided missiles, just to stay alive. Any minute you could be sabotaged by a cagey patroller or become the unsuspecting victim of a sneaky Stealth Fighter.

Prepare for the dogfight of your life. It's going to be a killer!

ABOUT THE GAME

As stunning and unique as *Radar Lock* is, it was also a game that flew far under the radar, so to speak. *Radar Lock* was a difficult game, and understanding the controls took time and practice, but that didn't keep it from being interesting and groundbreaking. The game was released at a strangely late time in the Atari 2600's life cycle, and that could be a real reason why it was accepted the way it was.

Radar Lock wasn't the first flight simulator that came to the 2600—it arrived the year after *Tomcat F14 Fighter Simulator*—but it was a major improvement on the genre. Primary differences included missions that featured a surrounding context, and extremely unique controls.

The way the controllers work in *Radar Lock* is one of the most interesting facets of this game. The fact that you're required to use both controllers in order to fly your jet effectively is what makes it a realistic flight simulator. The two-player mode allows the second player to work the second controller, relieving the first player of a little pressure.

Overall, *Radar Lock* provided a unique experience for Atari 2600 gamers, combining simulation with high-speed arcade action. It may not have been seen by many, but it definitely set a high standard on the platform.

OBJECT OF THE GAME

The object of the game is to use your state-of-the-art delta-wing fighter to defeat the enemy fleet in air combat. Your fighter plane is equipped with guided missiles, proximity missiles, and rapid-fire machine guns. The game consists of five missions of increasing difficulty.

When the game begins, your jet starts up, increases speed, and takes off from the airfield. The scene then switches to the combat screen.

At the end of each mission, you must refuel in flight. Use the left controller's red button to control your speed during the in-flight refueling sequence.

HOW TO PLAY

Hold down red controller button to accelerate, and release the button to return to normal flying speed. Using the long-range radar and missile lock, fly to the fuel tanker. When you're close to it, the tanker lowers its fuel hose. Once the nose of your jet is locked into the fuel hose, your mission is complete. You receive bonus points for your remaining fuel and weapons and then advance to your next mission.

CONTROLLING YOUR FIGHTER

Use the controllers to operate your delta-wing fighter. Move the left controller to maneuver your jet in flight. Move the right controller to select the weapons you wish to use.

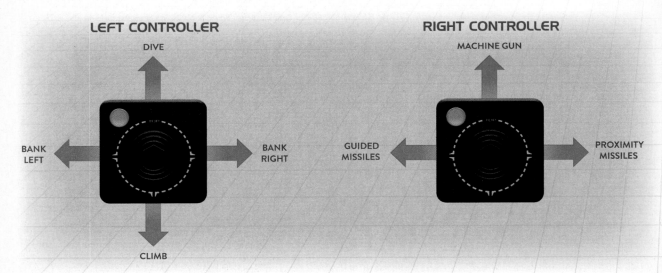

LEFT CONTROLLER
- DIVE
- BANK LEFT
- BANK RIGHT
- CLIMB

RIGHT CONTROLLER
- MACHINE GUN
- GUIDED MISSILES
- PROXIMITY MISSILES

THE INSTRUMENT PANEL

The instrument panel is located at the bottom of the screen. The missile-lock radar is located in the center of the instrument panel, and the long-range radar is to the right.

Use the long-range radar to locate enemy jets and the refueling tanker when they're not visible on the screen. The small dot in the middle of the radar screen marks the location of the jet. Enemy jets appear in front of or behind your jet.

The fuel gauge is shown to the left of the missile-lock radar. When you're low on fuel, the gauge flashes and you hear a warning tone. You must reach the tanker and refuel before your fuel runs out completely.

The number of lives you have left is shown in the lower-left corner of the instrument panel. The number of rounds you have left in your machine gun is shown on the right.

The weapon you have selected is shown at the top of the screen, just below the score.

WEAPONS

Your jet starts out equipped with five guided missiles and about 2550 rounds of machine gun ammunition. In Missions 3, 4, and 5, your jet also carries three proximity missiles.

GUIDED MISSILES

If you wish to fire guided missiles, you must change your weapon selection. Move the right controller to the left. Your missiles remaining display across the top of the screen.

The primary function of guided missiles is to destroy enemy Bombers. When an enemy jet is within range, the missile-lock radar turns bright blue and you hear a beeping tone. Steer your jet until the locked-on enemy jet is in the crosshairs. The missile-lock radar then turns deep red, and you hear a steady tone. Fire your missile immediately to destroy the enemy jet.

MISSILE-LOCK RADAR

When an enemy jet is not within range, the missile-lock radar is light blue if the jet is in front of you and violet if the jet is behind you.

MACHINE GUNS

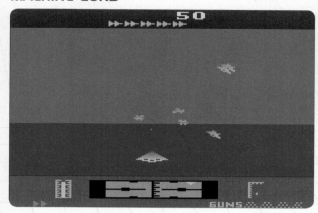

In addition to the guided missiles, your jet is equipped with rapid-fire machine guns. You begin your missions with this weapon ready to fire. The number of rounds remaining is displayed in the bottom-right corner of the screen. Use the machine guns to destroy all enemy jets except for Bombers; it takes 25 hits from a machine gun to destroy a Bomber.

PROXIMITY MISSILES

In Missions 3, 4, and 5, your jet is equipped with proximity missiles. Press the red controller button to launch a missile; release the button to detonate it. Detonating a missile destroys all visible enemy jets except Bombers.

WARNING:
Do not release the red controller button too soon, or you risk detonating the missile too close to your own jet and destroying it.

THE ENEMY FLEET

As you fly missions against the enemy, you encounter different enemy aircraft. Similar in appearance, these aircraft differ in their basic color and capabilities.

◆ **Drones** appear only in Mission 1. They are red and look like Interceptors, only they can't shoot. Drones are easy to hit and make good target practice for higher missions.

◆ **Interceptors** first appear in Mission 2 and are the basic enemy jet. They're also red and are the easiest of the fighter jets to destroy. They aren't equipped with tail gunners, so they can't hit you when you're behind them.

◆ **Patrollers** first appear in the second wave of Mission 2 and are yellow. In Mission 2, they follow assigned patrol routes. In higher missions, Patrollers can sneak up from behind and shoot you.

◆ **Escorters** first appear in Mission 3 and are blue. Their primary purpose is to protect enemy Bombers, and they tend to fire quickly.

◆ **Stealth Fighters** first appear in Mission 4 and are black. Stealth Fighters can jam your long-range radar so you don't know exactly where they are. They can sneak up behind you and fire on you, although they aren't as aggressive as Patrollers.

◆ **Bombers** are large, white delta-wing jets that are very difficult to destroy. They first appear in Mission 3. The Bomber has a tail gunner so that it can fire behind itself. Proximity missiles can't harm a Bomber, and it takes 25 machine-gun hits to destroy one, so guided missiles are your best bet with these. Bombers usually follow assigned routes.

◆ **Super Bombers** are the most dangerous enemy jets. They appear only in Mission 5. They're blue and red delta-wing jets, and guided missiles are the most effective weapons for destroying them. Super Bombers fire a barrage of missiles at once, making them especially lethal.

BEHIND YOU!

Some of the enemy jets fire at you from behind. When they have you in their sights, expect to hear a warning tone and see the message "BEHIND YOU" displayed at the top of the screen.

THE MISSIONS

There are five missions in this game.

Mission 1: Drones

Mission 1 is the easiest of the missions and offers good target practice against the Drones, which can't shoot. Start with this mission to practice maneuvering your jet, shooting your weapons, and refueling.

Mission 2: Interceptors and Patrollers

Wave 1: Interceptors are the primary enemy attack jet. They can shoot only what is in front of them.

Wave 2: Patroller jets follow assigned routes. Use your long-range radar to locate the Patroller squadron. After you've identified them, use thrusters (or afterburners) and quick maneuvering to bring them into your sights. Use your thrusters when you want quick acceleration. When you complete Mission 2, you earn an extra life.

Mission 3: Bombers

Wave 1: In Mission 3, Bombers follow assigned patrol routes. They shoot from either the front or the back and are difficult to destroy. They're also protected by Escorters.

Wave 2: The Patrollers try to sneak up and shoot you from behind. When you complete Mission 3, you earn an extra life.

Mission 4: Stealth Fighters

Wave 1: In Mission 4, your ship gains the ability to roll. This makes it much easier to maneuver, and the game moves much more quickly at this point.

Wave 2: Enemy Stealth Fighters appear. They can jam your long-range radar and sneak up behind you, so move quickly to avoid being hit. When you complete Mission 4, you earn an extra life.

Mission 5: Super Bombers

Wave 1: You get one last warm-up round of Interceptors before the Super Bombers appear.

Wave 2: Your final mission is to destroy five Super Bombers, which are escorted by Patrollers, Stealth Fighters, and Escorters.

NUMBER OF PLAYERS

ONE-PLAYER GAMES

In one-player games, the pilot controls both the firing of weapons and the jet's flight. Press the red controller button on the left controller to fire the selected weapon. To increase your jet's speed, hold down the button on the right controller.

OUT OF AMMO!

When the currently selected weapon runs out of ammo, it automatically changes to the next available weapon. Move the right directional control if you wish to select a different weapon.

TWO-PLAYER GAMES

In two-player games, the flight officer uses the left controller to fly the ship. The weapons officer uses the right directional control to select weapons and the right red controller button to fire them.

SCORING

Drone	50 points
Interceptor	100 points
Escorter	250 points
Stealth Fighter	400 points
Patroller	500 points
Bomber	950 points
Super Bomber	2,000 points

At the end of each mission, you score bonus points as follows:

Each gallon of fuel remaining	1 point
Each bullet remaining	1 point
Each missile remaining	350 points
Completing the mission	801 points

You earn a bonus jet after completing Mission 2, Mission 3, and Mission 4.

Tips & Tricks

◆ You have only five guided missiles. Use them wisely.

◆ Proximity missiles are especially effective for destroying the Escorter fleet that protects an enemy Bomber.

SECRET QUEST

Save the human race!

First there was one alien space station, then there were three. Now there are eight. If left unchecked, laser gates, dragons, and other evil creatures will wipe out the human race.

To destroy each station, you must confront the aliens in face-to-face combat and discover the secret destruct code. Once you have the code, use it to activate the station's self-destruction mechanism. Then the race begins. Can you get to the teleport room before the station explodes into the vacuum of space?

Are you ready? Remember, you'll need precision battle skills, a keen sense of direction, speed, and pure guts to save the human race.

ABOUT THE GAME

In the late 1980s, Atari founder Nolan Bushnell signed an agreement to design and develop video games on an exclusive basis for the Atari 2600 and 7800 consoles through his company, Axlon, which most famously made talking plush toy AG Bear (1985). This was actually the second time Bushnell signed an agreement with Atari since leaving the company in 1978. The first was in 1983 when Bushnell offered Atari the consumer rights to arcade games from Sente, a company he had purchased.

Since Bushnell had no ability to program Atari 2600 games himself, the task fell to programmer Steve DeFrisco. Under Bushnell's design guidance, DeFrisco advanced the state of action adventure gaming on the Atari 2600 with *Secret Quest* roughly eight years after *Adventure*. Although nowhere near as beloved as Warren Robinnet's early masterpiece, *Secret Quest* is perhaps the best example of how well understood programming the Atari 2600 had become by that time and how much of a difference additional memory (256 bytes of extra RAM thanks to the SARA Superchip in the cartridge) and ROM space (in this case, 16K versus *Adventure*'s 4K) could make in a game's overall feature-set.

Secret Quest proved to be the last game Atari released for the Atari 2600 in the US. It's been said that *Secret Quest*'s development and release was part of a last-ditch effort by Atari to demonstrate that the software library on their modest system from 1977 could still compete with more sophisticated 1980s consoles like the Nintendo Entertainment System and games like *The Legend of Zelda* (1987). Whatever the cause for its creation, the end result proved to be a great send-off for the venerable console.

OBJECT OF THE GAME

Destroy all eight alien space stations. The secret orders you received list basics on how to destroy a station. The rest is up to you.

1. **Search through the rooms and find the secret destruct code on each level.**

2. **Find the self-destruction mechanism and activate it by entering the secret destruct code(s).**

3. **Race to the teleporter room and escape the alien station before it explodes. The teleporter automatically sends you to the next station.**

Along the way you pick up weapons and other objects and fight alien creatures such as Spinner and Dragon. Fighting aliens takes precious oxygen and energy, which you can replenish each time you destroy all aliens in a room.

The game ends when you destroy all eight stations, run out of oxygen, or don't make it to the teleporter room in time after activating the self-destruct mechanism. When the game ends, the title screen appears with your total score.

HOW TO PLAY

WEAPON	STRENGTH VALUE	ENERGY USED
Energy Sword	2	1
Sonic Blaster	4	2
Particle Beam	8	4

Once the title screen appears, enter your initials by moving your controller up or down until the letter you want appears and left or right to move between the two entry positions. You must enter both initials to start the game.

Press Reset or the red controller button to start play. During play, you can press Reset to return to the title screen.

MOVING AROUND THE STATIONS

Use the directional control to move around the stations. Each time you pass through a door the screen changes to show the next room.

FINDING AND USING OBJECTS

If you're good, you will find weapons, oxygen bottles, energy pods, and sonic keys. To pick up an object, walk over to it and touch it. You will be able to pick up all objects you find, but you can have only one active weapon or sonic key. You can change the active weapon/sonic key from the status screen. To use an active object, press the red controller button.

WEAPONS

You will need weapons to fight the aliens. There are three weapons to find: the energy sword, sonic blaster, and the particle beam. When you touch your first weapon, it appears in your hand as the active weapon.

Finding the Energy Sword.

Press the fire button to use the active weapon. You may have to zap an alien a number of times to destroy it.

Each weapon has a strength and energy value. Stronger weapons do more damage to the aliens. When you use a weapon, you lose energy units.

The following chart shows the strength and energy depletion value of each weapon type.

OXYGEN BOTTLES & ENERGY PODS

Each time you destroy a room full of aliens, an oxygen bottle or energy pod appears. Touch these objects to replenish lost oxygen and energy. Fighting aliens depletes energy and/or oxygen. Exploring depletes oxygen at the rate of one oxygen bottle every minute. The game ends if you run out of oxygen. If you run out of energy, the game continues, but you will not be able to use any weapons until you find more energy.

Indicator bars at the bottom of the screen show how much energy and oxygen you have. Each mark on the indicator equals 16 units of energy or one bottle of oxygen.

SONIC KEYS

Sonic doors appear throughout the space stations. In order to open a sonic door, you must have a sonic key. These keys are scattered around the stations. When you find a sonic door, make sure the sonic key is active, then press the red controller button to open the door and reveal a secret stairway. Activate a sonic key from the status screen as explained under Active Object in the Status Screen section. Each sonic key can only be used once.

STATUS SCREEN

The status screen shows the following:

◆ **Current Station: When you destroy a station, it disappears from the status screen. The current station flashes.**

◆ **Current Level: A stack of bars indicates how many levels the current station contains. The current level flashes.**

◆ **Active Object: The active object is either a weapon or a sonic key. To change active objects, press the red controller button until the object you want appears.**

◆ **Re-entry Code: If you want to exit the game so you can return later at the same station, write down this code so you can restart at the status screen.**

DESTROYING A STATION

Your secret orders specify the following procedure for destroying a station. The procedure is dangerous and risky, but it's the only known way to destroy these evil space stations.

1. On each level of a station, look for a code symbol (station 1 has only 1 level; all others have multiple levels). To move to different levels within a station, use the stairs and sonic doors. You might want to write down the code(s).

2. When you find the codes on all levels of a station, search for a room with a flashing horizontal bar. This room contains the self-destruct mechanism. When you arrive at this room, move the directional control forward to display codes and left or right to move between the entry positions. Be sure to enter the codes in the correct sequence.

3. When you enter all codes, press the fire button, and race to the teleporter room. A number countdown appears to show you how many seconds you have to make it.

4. When you arrive at the teleporter room, touch the teleporter to escape the station before it explodes into smithereens. Once you touch the teleporter, you are transported to the next station.

SAVING A GAME

You can leave a game in progress and start again later at the same station with the points you've already earned.

Any number of games can be left and resumed, as long as each game is started with a different set of initials.

SAVE

To leave a game you wish to restart later, follow these steps:

1. Note the initials you entered when you started the game.

2. Push TV Type to display the status screen.

3. Write down the re-entry code sequence that appears at the bottom of the screen.

4. Continue playing or switch off your system.

RESTART

Follow these steps to restart a game:

1. Start a new game.

2. Enter your initials. You must enter the initials you used when you started the game you want to resume.

3. When the game screen appears (the first room of station 1), push TV Type to display the status screen. You can only restart the game from the first room of station 1.

4. Push Select to begin changing codes. The first code will flash.

5. Move the directional control forward or backwards to change codes and left or right to move between the codes. Be sure to enter the codes in the correct sequence.

6. Push Select to return to the game screen at the previous level.

SCORING

The following table shows the number of points you earn each time you destroy an alien.

ALIEN	POINTS
Dragon	750
Snake	700
Firecracker	650
Ghost	600
Stomper	550
Squid	500
Medusa	400
Spinner	350
Floater	250
Machine	200
Chopper	150
Potato Man	100
Bear Trap	50

• Learn your way around the stations by drawing a map as you go.

• If you are in a multi-level station, write down the code you find on each level so you will be able to remember the entire code when you enter the room containing the self-destruct mechanism.

• Avoid losing all of your energy. If you lose all of your energy, you can't use a weapon. If you can't use a weapon to destroy aliens, you will not be able to get oxygen. If you can't get oxygen, you will not live long. Neither will the human race.

FATAL RUN

The year is 2089. A collision with a comet has left the Earth reeling from radiation poisoning. There's little hope for humanity's survival. It's up to you to help the few remaining people.

You must leave the protective fortress Albagon and deliver the newly developed radiation vaccine to the survivors. Your journey will not be an easy one. Nefarious henchmen are waiting to knock you off and steal the vaccine to ensure that they will survive to rule the planet. Every driver on the road is out to get you. Your only hope is to get them first.

You must find the rocket poised to launch a satellite that can nullify the effects of this cosmic accident that turned the world upside down. If you're sharp enough to learn the secret code words and tough enough to live to use them, you can launch the rocket and save the world!

Good luck! Humanity is in your hands.

ABOUT THE GAME

Fatal Run was officially released only in PAL territories. An enhanced version was released for the Atari 7800, featuring beefed-up graphics. Observant gamers may notice its graphic similarity to *Pole Position*, even on the Atari 2600/VCS version!

OBJECT OF THE GAME

The object of the game is to drive through all 32 levels and release the life-saving satellite. Along the way you must distribute the radiation vaccine throughout the major cities, while collecting the pieces of the launch code. If you complete the code and all levels, the satellite launches and you win the game.

HOW TO PLAY

Use the controller to maneuver your vehicle. Move the directional control forward to accelerate and back to brake. Move the directional control left or right to move the car in the corresponding direction. When the directional control is in the center position, the car coasts.

Your car is equipped with a machine gun. Press the red controller button to fire at the enemy.

The Status Display at the bottom of the screen gives the information you need to plan your strategy and complete your run. The Status Display shows your current score and the speed at which your car is traveling.

In addition, you can see the status of your car's engine, tires, and armor; the number of shots you have left; and the amount of fuel remaining in your car.

You receive a 10-point reward for each road segment you pass over. There are 180 segments in each level, so completing a level results in 1,800 bonus points. The Status Display shows the percentage of points you have not yet received.

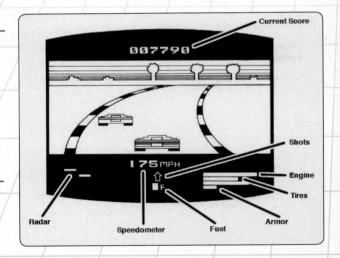

At 32 kilobytes, *Fatal Run* stands as one of the largest, original Atari VCS/2600 carts ever programmed!

As you move from city to city, you encounter various obstacles. The black patches on the screen are oil slicks, which can damage your tires. Yellow-and-white-striped roadblocks should be avoided at all costs; if you hit one of these, it can damage your car severely. Roadside obstacles include houses, trees, and other hazards. Hitting obstacles damages your car and slows you down.

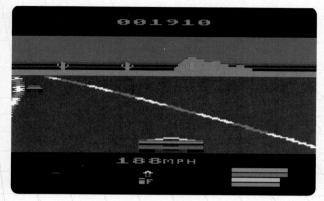

You must also be on the lookout for henchmen. They try to run you off the road, often banding together to stop your progress. Press the red controller button to destroy the enemy vehicles with machine-gun fire.

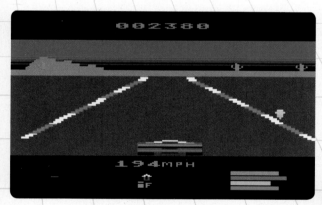

If you run out of ammo, destroy the car in front of you with a power surge. To power-surge, hold down the controller button and move the directional control forward. If you fail to power-surge the car in front, you may crash, damaging your vehicle.

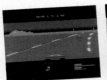

Drive for Your Life!

If an enemy car comes up behind you, destroy it by pulling back quickly on the directional control to brake. To survive a side attack, smash into the vehicle and destroy it. If the enemy car gets you first, you receive damage.

You receive 20 bonus points for permanently passing an enemy car. To do this, stay ahead of him until he disappears off the bottom of the radar. If he comes up from behind and passes you again, you receive no bonus points.

Look for yellow diamonds alongside the road. You'll see the diamonds after you destroy enemy vehicles. Grab one of these to restore your car's engine and armor. In addition, you can replace your fuel and ammunition by running over dots along the way. Green dots replace bullets and blue dots replace fuel. If you still have fuel remaining when you run over a blue dot, you receive 20 bonus points. If you've run out of fuel by then, you receive no bonus points.

When you reach a city, the screen displays the city's status. If you reach the city in time to save any of its inhabitants, the survivors appear on the screen. You receive bonus points for each person you save. Use your bonus points to upgrade the condition of your vehicle or purchase fuel.

If you arrive too late to save the city, fewer survivors appear and you receive fewer bonus points. After you receive your bonus points, press the controller button.

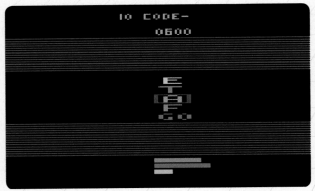

A message from headquarters appears on your screen. Read the message, then press the button again. The Vehicle Upgrade screen appears. To upgrade your vehicle or purchase fuel, move the controller up or down until your selection is highlighted. Then move your controller right to purchase the highlighted item. After purchasing upgrades, highlight the word GO and press the controller button.

If you arrive safely at the rocket base, the rocket launches the world-saving satellite and you win the game.

◆ **Learn which store items you need to purchase at the cities. If you're really good at acquiring the off-road yellow diamonds, you may only need to purchase better tires and fuel at most stops.**

◆ **Watch out for cars behind you! Quick braking can destroy them without damage to your car.**

◆ **Learn to power-surge. Head-on collisions hurt more than just your car's expensive paint job.**

◆ **After you've finished each level, you will have accumulated 1,800 points for the road segments completed within that level.**

GAME OPTIONS

You may either start a new game at the beginning or resume play at a specific location, as follows:

NEW GAME

Move the controller forward or backward to highlight NEW. Press the controller button. The instruction screen appears, showing a city with information running across the screen's bottom. Press the controller button again to begin play.

RESUME GAME

To begin the game at a specific level, move the controller to highlight RESUME. Press the controller button. The Code Selection screen appears. To identify the level code (shown after every fourth run during the game), position the square Character Selector next to the number or letter you want to choose (up to seven characters), then press the controller button. Select the asterisk (*) character and press the controller button to start the game.

When you complete the game, press Reset to return to the Title and Options Selection screen. During play, press Reset if you wish to restart the game.

SCORING

ACTION	POINT TOTAL
Ramming enemy car	10 points
Shooting enemy car	10 points
Completing road segment	10 points
Running over blue fuel dot with fuel remaining	20 points
Permanently passing enemy car	20 points
Destroying enemy car	200 points
Picking up yellow diamond	500 points

MOTORODEO

You're second in the grueling competition of an all-day MotoRodeo. Your customized truck, a cherry little number, speeds through the dangerous obstacle course. You quickly break through a brick wall, rumble through a muddy ditch, and jump high into the air. You grin widely as you land on a Plymouth, crushing it beneath the weight of your monster truck.

Up until now, you and your opponent—Trucker Tom—have been neck and neck throughout the competition, but you've just pulled ahead. Your truck paid its dues during the early part of the competition, but you're confident that you've got the skills needed to outmaneuver Tom as you race for the finish line.

Your adrenalin pounds. You psych yourself up for the few remaining obstacles. You're only slightly ahead of Tom, but there are still a few more walls and cars to crush. Good thing you learned qui ckly to jump the mud, which is slowing Tom down.

You rev your engine, add a burst of acceleration, and jump the last mud hole as you race for the finish line. Trucker Tom has finally met his match!

ABOUT THE GAME

MotoRodeo was released over a decade after the launch of the Atari 2600. Over that time, programmers picked up ways to push the aged system to its limits and it seems each of those tricks went into making this game.

MotoRodeo included options that allow you to practice individual skills outside of a race. Players drove simultaneously and on a split-screen, which meant head-to-head racing was no longer limited to time trials or a track that could fit on a single screen. *MotoRodeo* even allowed you to customize the conditions for winning a race.

OBJECT OF THE GAME

There are two objectives in MotoRodeo, but only one is active at a time. The first objective is to complete the course faster than your opponent, while the second is to complete the course with more points than your opponent.

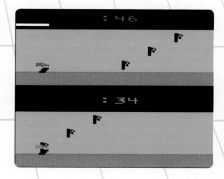

HOW TO PLAY

MotoRodeo is a multi-obstacle, split-screen trucking extravaganza. When playing against an opponent (human or computer), each obstacle you encounter requires speed, timing, and maneuvering skill to overcome. Consider skipping ahead to the "Game Options" section first, since the game hits you with a slew of choices even before the first race begins.

Once in control of your vehicle, press the red controller button to accelerate and push the joystick down to perform a wheelie on flat ground. If you pick up a nitro unit (), tap the joystick up for a quick burst of acceleration and a small jump.

Pushing left and right on the joystick results in different effects, depending on where your vehicle is located. In muddy bogs, alternate pushing right and left to advance through the mud faster. To control spin during a jump, push the joystick left (clockwise) or right (counterclockwise).

DIFFICULTY OPTIONS

The difficulty button does not alter the difficulty of the game. Instead, it is used to determine the objective of a race. Change the left difficulty button to A for point scoring. The goal is to finish the race with the most points, keeping in mind that 100 points are awarded to the first vehicle to cross the finish line. Position B is used for timed races; the first player to cross the finish line wins.

GAME OPTIONS

Choosing game options takes place on the title screen. Push up or down on the joystick to cycle through vehicle and control options. You choose driver (player or computer), body type (blazer or truck), and wheel type (tires or trax). When you're satisfied with the initial set up, press the red controller button to advance to another selection screen.

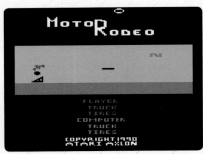

FEATURES: COMPETITION

When playing for the first time, skip past the Competition options and choose one of the skills under Practice. Use the practice sessions to gain experience with the obstacles that appear during the competition runs.

Choosing Hard, Medium, or Easy changes how many obstacles are located along the course. Easy contains the fewest obstacles, while Hard has the most.

FEATURES: PRACTICE

Select from the following to gain experience with each obstacle encountered during competition runs. Depending on the difficulty button setting, the game either tallies points earned during your run, or tracks your time in completing these shortened courses.

All practice courses include many types of obstacles, not just its namesake. For example, the jump course includes mud, nitro, and 50-point bonuses.

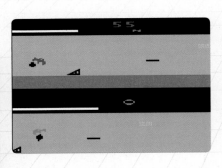

JUMP

Learn to jump and control your truck or blazer while it's in the air. You can practice driving up a short triangular ramp while learning to jump and land.

PLATFORM

Platforms, which are suspended in mid-air, are the same length as your vehicle. Use platforms to extend your jump, or earn extra points by bouncing on the platform.

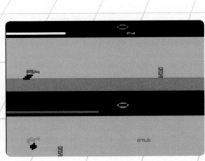

CAR CRUSH

Crush the white cars. After landing on top of a car, wriggle the joystick left and right to continue to crush the car. Perform a wheelie when starting to crush a car to jump over the car instead of continuing to crush it.

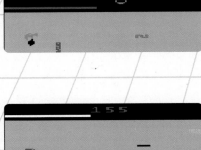

WALL

Crash into the wall to knock it down. You may need to hit the wall a few times to finish the job. The faster you drive, the quicker you'll knock down the wall. Perform a wheelie after building up enough speed to knock down the wall and hop over it.

SPRING

Pink platforms on the ground throw your vehicle into the air when all four wheels are on top of it.

RAMP

Orange ramps shift between three positions: vertical, jump position, and flat. Vertical ramps serve as barriers. Ramps in jump position work the same as black jump ramps. When an orange ramp is flat on the ground, you can't use it to jump.

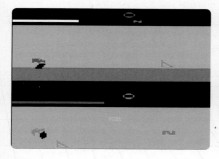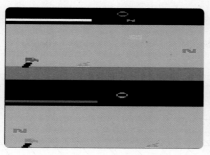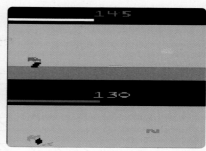

MUD

Jump over mud bogs when possible. If your vehicle becomes mired in a mud bog, wriggle the joystick left and right.

SPIN

Curved ramps launch your vehicle into the air and put a spin on it. Wriggle your joystick left or right to spin.

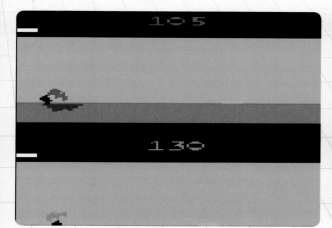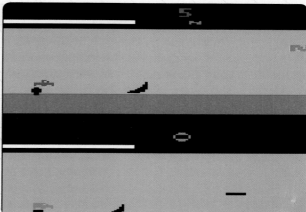

SCORING

EVENT	POINT VALUE
Land upright and flat from a jump	5
Hit a wall	10
Crush a car	20
Bounce on truck's tires while on a platform	25
Jump to a collapsing ramp	25
Touch '50'	50
Cross finish line first	100

ATARI NEWS
What The Critics Had to Say

"Turbo power-ups let you catch big air, which is terrific fun, but plowing through mud by moving the joystick back and forth is just arduous. *MotoRodeo* lets you race for time or points, and the computer opponent is definitely a worthy competitor."

- The Video Game Critic (June 2000)

FUN FACTS!

○ *MotoRodeo* was one of the final games released for the Atari. It arrived in stores 13 years after the first Atari VCS consoles.

○ This game was one of two commercially released games developed by Axlon, a company started by Atari founder Nolan Bushnell.

Tips & Tricks

◆ Perform a wheelie when you hit an obstacle to fly a little higher and farther.

◆ Only use Nitro when your vehicle is on the ground and in an upright position.

◆ Wriggle the joystick left and right to escape from mud bogs faster.

ATARI® FLASHBACK
THE ESSENTIAL COMPANION

Written by Bill Loguidice, Ken Schmidt, Dan Herrera, Geson Hatchett, and Mitchell Lucas

ISBN: 9780744018868

Printing Code: The rightmost double-digit number is the year of the book's printing; the rightmost single-digit number is the number of the book's printing. For example, 17-1 shows that the first printing of the book occurred in 2017.

20 19 18 17   4 3 2 1

001-309993-Oct/2017

Printed in the USA.

PRIMA GAMES STAFF

VP & Publisher
Mike Degler

Editorial Manager
Tim Fitzpatrick

Design and Layout Manager
Tracy Wehmeyer

Licensing
Paul Giacomotto

Marketing
Jeff Barton

Digital Publishing
Julie Asbury
Shaida Boroumand

Operations Manager
Stacey Ginther

CREDITS

Book Designer
Tim Amrhein

Production Designer
Tim Amrhein

Production
Liz Stenberg

3930000b016330